'*The Slavic Myths* combines analysis with celebration, context with storytelling, academic debate with new versions of some of the great folktales that emerged long, long ago from the crucible of the Carpathian Mountains. Vampires and werewolves are centrally featured – of course – and so are lesser-known figures, such as Queen Libuše and the city she founded; Mokoš, the powerful goddess who totters on chicken legs; the *bannik*, a water-demon who shares your hot bath; and a host of other gods and monsters and warring women. The book provides a welcome entrée into the intricate world of Slavic mythology, with plenty of esoteric facts to get your teeth into, stories to be read aloud at the witching hour, and memorable black-and-white woodcut-style illustrations.'
Sir Christopher Frayling, author of *Vampyres*

'Delightfully dark and whimsical, this collection of folk tales from Slavic mythology unearths the bones of the original stories, boldly forcing us to question what we know about a mostly oral tradition that has been silenced for far too long.'
Olesya Salnikova Gilmore, author of *The Witch and the Tsar*

'A delectable tasting menu of the rich myth and folklore that flowered for centuries among the Slavic peoples inhabiting the vast swath of Europe from the Adriatic to the Baltic and the Danube to the Urals. Synthesizing a great deal of solid scholarship, but wearing their erudition lightly, the authors include a curated array of original texts from Serbia, Czechoslovakia, Russia and other lands – wonderful tales of vampires, werewolves, witches, heroic maidens and warriors – that illustrate the different traditions and show how the ancient tales continue to resonate to this day.'
Vladimir Alexandrov, B. E. Bensinger Professor Emeritus of Slavic Languages and Literatures, Yale University

THE
SLAVIC MYTHS

NOAH CHARNEY · SVETLANA SLAPŠAK

WITH 38 ILLUSTRATIONS

To Urška from her Waterman & to Božidar
from his Baba Yaga

First published in the United Kingdom in 2023 by
Thames & Hudson Ltd, 181A High Holborn, London WC1V 7QX

First published in the United States of America in 2023 by
Thames & Hudson Inc., 500 Fifth Avenue, New York, New York 10110

The Slavic Myths © 2023 Thames & Hudson Ltd, London
Text © 2023 Noah Charney and Svetlana Slapšak
Cover and interior illustrations by Joe McLaren

Cover and interior layout designed by Fred Birdsall and Stephen Hickson, Fred Birdsall studio

All Rights Reserved. No part of this publication may be reproduced or transmitted in any form or by any means, electronic or mechanical, including photocopy, recording or any other information storage and retrieval system, without prior permission in writing from the publisher.

British Library Cataloguing-in-Publication Data
A catalogue record for this book is available from the British Library

Library of Congress Control Number 2023937425

ISBN 978-0-500-02501-7

Printed in China by Shanghai Offset Printing Products Limited

Be the first to know about our new releases,
exclusive content and author events by visiting
thamesandhudson.com
thamesandhudsonusa.com
thamesandhudson.com.au

CONTENTS

Introduction 7
The Slav Epic 21

1 Black Butterfly 33
  Vampires 61

2 At Stake 85
  Werewolves 103

3 Threshold 121
  Libuše and Women 129

4 Do Not Weep 135
  Three Versions of the Great Goddess 155

5 Ilya Muromets 167
  Perun, Supreme God 175

6 The Waterman 187
  Creatures of the Deep 193

7 Firebird 203
  Slavic Magic 213

Last Words 225

Map 228
Acknowledgments 230
Notes 231
Bibliography 233
Index 236

INTRODUCTION

You can probably name a few Egyptian gods: Osiris? Isis? Norse gods, surely: Thor (now more familiar than ever thanks to Marvel comics and films), Loki, Odin. And you likely know the Greco-Roman gods best of all, as they've been familiar throughout European culture since ancient times. After a brief retreat into the shadows following the collapse of the Roman Empire they were rediscovered by scholars of the Renaissance, who decided that the glories, beliefs and thoughts of ancient Rome and, above all, Athens represented the zenith of human civilization – and so you can spot Zeus/Jupiter, Athena/Minerva, Neptune/Poseidon, Venus/Aphrodite, Ares/Mars and their ilk, running like vivid threads through the fabric of what has been called Western culture. And it's not only the gods. We still know the stories of many Greco-Roman heroes and their adventures: Jason and the golden fleece, Theseus and the Minotaur, the twelve labours of Hercules.

But what of Slavic gods, monsters and heroes? While the Slavic pantheon, including the likes of Vuk, Veles and Perun, may not be household names, there are some other figures born of Slavic legend who certainly are – though perhaps you're not aware of their origins. What, for instance, could be more ubiquitous in popular culture than vampires and werewolves? It might come as a surprise to learn that these denizens of darkness emerged from the shallow graves of Slavic belief long before they stepped out onto the global stage.

Considering the tens of millions of people in the world who are ethnically Slavic – including millions in anglophone countries who are of Slavic ancestry – there have been remarkably few books in English about Slavic mythology, legends and gods. This applies just as much to editions of the myths themselves, the evocative tales of adventure,

INTRODUCTION

magic and lore, as it does to academic or anthropological texts about them. There are countless books for all ages about Aesop's fables, the Grimms' fairy tales, the ancient myths of Greece and Rome, of Egypt, of the Maya, of the Norse north; so the dearth of similar resources for the Slavic tradition seems like a surprising oversight for a corner of world history that is so wonderfully rich, and a touchstone for such an enormous potential readership.

This book offers a step towards correcting that imbalance by introducing some of the monsters, legends, gods and heroes of the Slavic world. It aims to explore what the original, pre-Christian Slavs believed before their pagan traditions were either overwritten by or, as was more often the case, interlaced with Catholicism (among western Slavs) or Orthodox Christianity (among eastern).

Together we'll encounter vampires and werewolves, Baba Yaga and her witch's home on its chicken legs, petulant gods and ethereal goddesses, warring women, devil-defeating damsels and a river-dwelling merman. But first, let's meet the Slavs themselves and get to know the basics of their belief system.

MEET THE SLAVS

One surprising aspect of Slavic mythology is that most of the ideas we associate with it today are relatively modern.

The Slavs themselves are not, of course. They were an immense and heterogeneous group of tribes who began to move out of the region of the Carpathian Mountains (present-day Romania and Moldova) over the course of the 5th and 6th centuries CE. They spread in all directions, moving west towards Central Europe (as far as the modern Czech Republic), north-east towards what is now Russia and the Eurasian regions, north to the Baltic states, south into the Balkans as far as Crete, and even east, with some archaeological evidence showing up in China. But precious few literary or artistic sources survive from this earliest period of Slavic migration. Without written records or artwork there are few clues for historians and archaeologists to follow, a paucity of puzzle pieces from which to imagine how the complete picture might have looked. Archaeological data has been significantly enriched in the 20th and 21st centuries, with many previously unknown ritual sites and settlements uncovered. But the extent of material residue that helps us understand the Slavic past remains far more meagre than it is for some other ethnic groups, many of which shine more brightly in the popular imagination by virtue of having left a more extensive and vivid archaeological or written record.

The oldest record of someone writing about Slavs comes from two 6th-century CE Byzantine writers: Procopius, writing in Greek of the Sklaboi, and Jordanes, writing in Latin of the Sclaveni. Both were historiographers working under the Byzantine emperor Justinian I. Jordanes describes a tribe called the Veneti (after which the Veneto region of Italy, including the city of Venice, would be named), their metropolis Aquileia, their territory reaching 'the bridge on Isontio', and many other cities. He also notes that by the time they became known as the Veneti, they were already descendants of even more ancient tribes called the Antae and the Sclaveni. Just to confuse things, Procopius writes that 'the Sclaveni and the Antae actually had a single name in the remote past, for they were both called Sporoi in olden times'.[1] It's fun to think of what 'olden times' meant to a historian writing in 545 CE. But Procopius goes on to tell us some useful things about this tribe:

> For these nations, the Sclaveni and the Antae, are not ruled by one man, but they have lived from of old under a democracy, and consequently everything which involves their welfare, whether for good or for ill, is referred to the people. It is also true that in all other matters, practically speaking, these two barbarian peoples have had from ancient times the same institutions and customs. For they believe that one god, the maker of lightning, is alone lord of all things, and they sacrifice to him cattle and all other victims; but as for fate, they neither know it nor do they in

INTRODUCTION

any wise admit that it has any power among men, but whenever death stands close before them, either stricken with sickness or beginning a war, they make a promise that, if they escape, they will straightaway make a sacrifice to the god in return for their life; and if they escape, they sacrifice just what they have promised, and consider that their safety has been bought with this same sacrifice. They revere, however, both rivers and nymphs and some other spirits, and they sacrifice to all these also, and they make their divinations in connection with these sacrifices.[2]

'Barbarians' in this context was a term for any people who spoke neither Greek nor Latin, the only two 'civilized' languages. The Slavs lived under a democracy, as Procopius described it – a surprise, since most tribes were ruled by kings – and believed in one god, Perun, whom Procopius called 'the maker of lightning' and to whom they made sacrifices. This information must be taken with a pinch of salt, as a 6th-century historian would have been working on field reports many steps removed from personal experience, and in fact we know that there were Slavic kings as well as multiple gods. Procopius goes on to describe these people as living in scattered houses while regularly changing their settlement locations. Jordanes, meanwhile, says that they have 'swamps and forests for their cities',[3] which suggests they were semi-nomadic – not in terms of moving every day with herds, but of setting up short-term, mobile villages using the safety of dense forests and wetlands.

Slavs apparently went into battle either lightly clothed or in their birthday suits with only their genitals covered, wielding shields and spears and fighting on foot. Procopius called them 'neither very fair or blonde, nor indeed do they incline entirely to the dark type, but they are all slightly ruddy in colour. And they live a hard life, giving no heed to bodily comforts.'[4] Apparently there were a lot of them: a Byzantine record claims that there were so many Slavs, the grass would not regrow where they had marched.

INTRODUCTION

The early 7th-century historian Theophylact Simocatta wrote that Slavs were big and muscular but that they preferred music, singing and dancing to war activities. A 10th-century Byzantine text describes a group of Slavs travelling down a river in monoxyls: boats carved out of a single tree trunk, akin to the dugout canoes used by Amazonian tribes. A 10th-century Arab diplomat, Ahmad ibn Fadlan, described a ritual undertaken by Slav merchants living beside the Volga River: they would enter a circular sanctuary and kneel before a pillar painted with a god's head. Other deities were painted on wood inside the circle. He also described a funerary ritual in which the deceased was placed on a boat in a sitting position and his wife, seated alongside him, was stabbed to death as a sacrifice. Then they were both pushed into the water while the boat was set alight. The 11th-century writer Thietmar of Merseburg described a temple made of timber situated on a fortified hill, its exterior adorned with sculptures fitted with animal horns. Inside were various sculpted idols dressed in helmets and armour, each dedicated to a different god, with the most important (according to this record) being Zuarasici (Svarožič, the son of Svarog – the suffix -ič, often found in southern Slavic surnames, denoting 'son of'). Alas, no record of these temples or idols survives.

As well as Slavic kings, there were Slavic empires. In the 7th century, a Frankish merchant called Samo offered financial support to the Slavs in their war with another tribe, the Avars. When the Slavs won, they made Samo their king. He proved a good one, building the first Slavic state in Europe, which was referred to as Samo's Empire and sprawled across most of Central Europe from 631 to 658 CE. Other settled territories followed in later centuries, including the 7th-century Duchy of Carantania (encompassing southern Austria and northern Slovenia), Great Moravia (833–907, throughout most of Central Europe) and the principalities of Nitra (in the 9th century in present-day Slovakia) and Balaton (a part of modern Hungary).

The oldest documents written by Slavs are in a language called Old Church Slavonic and date to around the 9th century. They refer

INTRODUCTION

to the people as *Slověne* (related to, but not to be confused with, Slovenes from modern Slovenia, where both authors of this book live). The term derives from *slovo*, a word that means 'word', and refers to a group of people who speak the same language. This contrasts interestingly with the old Slavic word for Germans, *nemets*, which approximately meant 'mute or mumbling' – essentially, 'people the Slavs couldn't understand'.

Originally, Old Church Slavonic was written in a lost alphabet called Glagolitic. This alphabet is believed to have been designed by one man – Saint Cyril, a 9th-century monk from Thessaloniki – to offer the Slavs a way of writing that would be distinct from the Latin alphabet used by the Frankish bishops and rulers who were encroaching on their territories. Cyril and his brother, Saint Methodius, were sent on a mission by the Byzantine emperor Michael III in 863 to introduce Christianity to the pagans of the western Slavic empire of Great Moravia. In order to bring religion closer to their target audience, they translated liturgy into the contemporary Slavic language spoken by most living in Great Moravia. This was what came to be known as Old Church Slavonic, though it was the language that the pagan Slavs spoke among themselves (it was dubbed 'Church' Slavonic because of its association with Cyril and Methodius). Its use was permissible thanks to an 885 bull issued by Pope Stephen V that allowed Christian services to be read in languages other than Latin or Greek. The written form of the language incorporated Greek letters with some rune-like pictograms, although the language had a phonetic alphabet, meaning that each 'letter' made a sound, as in English. The short-lived but intriguing Glagolitic was eventually replaced by a standardized, more orderly and angular alphabet that Cyril's students named after him: Cyrillic, a script still used to this day among eastern Slavs from Bulgaria to Russia to Serbia.

Further confusing the story of Slavic beliefs, much of what has been discovered dates to periods when the Slavs were converting to Christianity. Ancient pagan stories have therefore, in many

INTRODUCTION

instances, been preserved only within apocryphal Christian texts. This means that some pagan rituals still survive in everyday life in Slavic communities today, but it also means that a good deal of sifting is required to separate later Christian elements from the original pre-Christian beliefs. Even more confusingly for anyone attempting to identify the original stories, the names of the gods and heroes differ, especially between the Baltic/Russian Slavic states and the southern (Yugo) Slavs.

MEET THE SLAVIC PANTHEON

The Slavic pantheon differs from its Scandinavian, German, Celtic and Mediterranean counterparts in that its form is less organized, mixing and matching gods and mythical beings. Our understanding of it today is coloured by the work of 19th-century scholars, who were generally well versed in better-known pantheons like the Greco-Roman and therefore tried to find the closest possible 'matches' or equivalents among the Slavic gods. Although it might seem superficially helpful to say that Vuk = Zeus/Jupiter, in truth it's not quite that simple. And as we will see in later chapters, the original Slavic understanding of vampires and werewolves was as two names for a single monster: vampire = werewolf.

Many of those 19th-century scholars were working in the context of their own modern states of Slavic origin – Russia, Bulgaria, Serbia and beyond – and it is worth bearing in mind that the desire for an inspiring national origin story often shaped their interpretation of the material they were researching. So when, for instance, we learn about Queen Libuše and her involvement in the foundation of the city of Prague, we might question whether this was truly her role in Slavic legend before Prague became the capital of Czechoslovakia or, even earlier, before it was an important city at all.

As a consequence of all this, the supreme god in the Slavic pantheon is identified with different forms and different names depending on which source you consult. A core group of supreme male gods can be established, but they are rarely defined in simple, straightforward terms; nor are they unambiguously 'good' or 'evil'.

Perun is the main god for most of the Slavs, the nearest to an equivalent of Zeus/Jupiter or Odin. Perun controls storms, summons thunder, hurls bolts of lightning, dwells on snow-strewn mountain tops and haunts oak trees. He is sometimes called Dažbog, god of rainstorms. He is a god of war wielding an arsenal of magical weapons: a battle-axe, a war hammer, a bow and arrows of lightning. He is the god most often cited as having appeared in person at major historical moments and in battles, so much so that he has even been listed as a conscriptor of state contracts in Russia.

Svarog is set in contrast to Dažbog as a god of the sun and of fire, similar to the Greek god Hephaestus. He exists without a body, as a god of the heavens and the atmosphere.

Svetovid, whose name might translate as Lightsight, is the four-headed god of war, but also of light and power.

Triglav, whose name means Three-Head, represents the unity of the world. He rides a black horse and is represented by the mountains and the trees. The tallest mountain in Slovenia, and by extension in all of former Yugoslavia, is named after him.

Veles might be regarded as the Slavic equivalent of Hades or Satan. He rules darkness and wet areas like swamps, wetlands and caves. He is king of the underworld. But if that sounds rather grim, hold on a moment: he is also the god of music and of poetry. It makes sense that a god of the underworld is called a 'shepherd of souls', but Veles also controls animals and livestock and is the god of wealth. As a result of the layering of Christianity within Slavic tradition, he has come to be thought of as the Devil, but since when was a mere devil also the progenitor of music, poetry and animals?

Vuk, whose name means 'wolf', is the supreme Slavic mythical animal, a totem in all Slavic mythologies. We must speak in terms of 'mythologies' plural because the dispersal of the Slavs from their likely point of origin in the Carpathian Mountains led to the splintering of

this vast group of tribespeople. In the course of travelling, pillaging, settling, conquering and being driven to or from various parts of Europe, their beliefs naturally evolved and altered in various directions. Vuk, however, remains prevalent throughout the ancient Slavic diaspora. Wolves in ancient Europe were the primary animal to be feared – to put it bluntly, wolves were the denizen of the natural world most likely to eat you. Vuk became a symbol of wisdom and power, but this god could also turn into a demon, a *vukodlak* (werewolf), as we'll see later.

Lado and Lada are twins and represent the male and female elements of love, beauty, fertility, springtime, happiness, laughter and sex – but also the underworld. A festival dedicated to them was usually celebrated at harvest time. Lada in particular resonated in the ancient world: she appears not only in Slavic mythology but also in Baltic and Finnish. There are fewer known goddesses than gods in the Slavic world, though that is counterbalanced by a good number of female heroines.

There is also an approximate equivalent to Adam and Eve – Rod and Rožanica – although this primary couple from the origin of the world are deities. They control life and its continuity: destiny, fertility and familial legacies. Of the two, Rožanica over time has tended to gain in power and ritual presence, being worshipped as the Great Mother, while her husband, Rod, has receded in importance.

All of these gods rule over atmospheric phenomena and several are polycephalic, meaning that they have two or more heads. Mokoš, a female goddess, embodies their opposites: she is associated with healing, protecting, cursing, vengeance, education, common wisdom and fertility. Her closest Greco-Roman equivalent would be Demeter.

The gods were traditionally said to gather under the Tree of the World, envisioned as a colossal oak tree, or on the top of a mountain. Under the later influence of Christianity, they were imagined meeting somewhere among the clouds. Some ritual spaces have been found dedicated to a single god, but the Slavic method of worship was much

more a part of everyday life, linked to festival days in the calendar rather than journeys to temples. To date, no information has been found about priesthood.

With so few records surviving, whether in the form of literature or cultural objects and archaeological sites, the Slavs are among the least understood of ancient peoples despite being so numerous and widespread. They certainly had a rich mythology and pantheon, but much of what we know or believe about it today is based on later inventions. The pseudo-ancient stories of ancestors concocted by scholars of the 19th century served to reinforce the contemporary idea of the 'Spring of Nations': a time when ethnic identity was transformed into national pride as old monarchies and empires, including that of the Habsburgs, disintegrated and gave way to newly formed independent nations. Each of these 'young' countries required a firm foundation story to support the belief that its people had ancestral rights over their land. For modern Slavs from Latvia to Slovenia, from Slovakia to Bulgaria, from Poland to Siberia, this meant communing with their ancient Slavic predecessors; and if there was not enough material to call upon to strengthen this connection with their roots, the myths and legends had simply to be invented.

THE SLAV EPIC

We tend to think of myths as ancient, and their origins surely are. But they have often been interpreted and reinterpreted over many generations, and the versions that we absorb organically through the cultural oxygen of our surroundings can be surprisingly new.

While modern editions of Greco-Roman myths, for example, are broadly similar to older versions thanks to the survival of ancient sources, this is not the case with Slavic mythology. The earliest written sources about the belief system of the ancient Slavs are Byzantine, so they are written from the perspective of a foreign power curious about Slavs as a potential enemy.[5] There are also relatively few archaeological traces of the Slavs. And yet there is a rich, expansive night sky of stories.

Relying on oral tradition to pass key myths down through the generations is a tenuous business, as anyone who has played the children's game 'Telephone' can tell you. The 19th-century Croatian historian Natko Nodilo in his *Old Religion of Serbs and Croats* (1884) analyses myths, oral poetry and stories he gathered in order to reconstruct the pre-Christian beliefs of his region, rather poetically describing the result as a 'sketch' made by a child's hand. Inevitably in a process like this, some elements are misheard, intentionally or unintentionally altered, forgotten. So how can stories from, say, the 7th century survive today without having been written down until more than a millennium later?

The short answer is that they cannot, and do not – at least, not in the same form. Oral traditions were harvested in whatever form they came down before being committed to paper in the 19th century. This was the method of the Brothers Grimm, who were so determined to record the 'pure' oral versions of folk tales that they paid a little girl to listen to an old woman who was known as a great font of fairy tales, but who refused to tell them to anyone but children. This little girl was a benevolent spy, adjourning from the old woman's company and stealing over to the brothers, who then wrote down, as faithfully as they could, the freshly retold tale, to be published in their now famous collection in 1812. It is thanks to this old woman's recollection of stories, which were who knows how old, that the likes of Snow White and Rapunzel survive as recorded by Jacob and Wilhelm Grimm.

Charles Perrault, an early champion of the fairy tale, took a similar approach to his work in 17th-century France. For his 1697 *Tales of Mother Goose*, he listened to traditional folk tales but did not strive to transcribe precisely what he heard. Instead he used them as starting points for his own artistic editions, making the stories of Puss in Boots, Cinderella, Little Red Riding Hood and Tom Thumb his own. Vuk Karadžić, an autodidact from Serbia working at the beginning of the 19th century, and Milman Parry, an early 20th-century American researcher of Balkan epic poetry, both employed the same 'methodology' – local brandy – to encourage people to perform for them.

Marina Warner, a scholar of fairy and folk tales (our secular mythology), makes a distinction between the two. Folk tales, she writes in *Fairy Tale: A Very Short History*, are 'attributed to oral tradition' and are linked to the German word *Märchen*, which indicates a 'genuine' oral tale – one with an origin older than anyone can remember and with no known original author. These are different from fairy tales, in German *Kunstmärchen* – with the addition of *kunst*, art, indicating that they are a literary artwork, 'signed and dated'.[6] For the Grimms and Perrault, the bones of the stories they collected were folk tales but once they were interpreted and written down, embellished and associated with an author, they became fairy tales.

Myths should, by definition, be regarded as part of the folk-tale tradition. We don't know who first 'invented' the myth. A true believer would argue that myths are not invented, but simply happen. Such true believers consider myth to be history. For a particular version of a myth, though – say, the story of Apollo chasing Daphne with amorous intent and Daphne calling upon her father, a river god, to save her, resulting in him transforming her into a tree (another version has her mother, Gaia, the Earth, transform her) – the origins may sit within Warner's definition of folk tales but the rendition we know, which in this case was penned by the poet Ovid, has become a fairy tale.

Ancient myths and legends associated with pagan pantheons run alongside folk tales. They have a sacral element, as they feature once-believed-in gods, goddesses, monsters and holy heroes ('holy' in the sense that they were aided or impeded by gods). Folk tales are not overtly religious, although they may have Christian morals to share. But in the Slavic tradition, many of the myths and legends we feel we know well are true cocktails of all three genres: myth, folk tale and fairy tale.

After Slavic myths had been committed to paper in the 19th century, they were adapted – whether subconsciously or consciously, it can be hard to tell – to suit the needs of the time. Their roots are among pagans but when they were written down their authors were named, usually signing the works and publishing them as their own; and those authors were, for the most part, Christian residents of Slavic territories on the verge of becoming independent nations. Therefore, 19th-century European themes of Christianity, the sense of unity and the right to independence and self-governance necessarily coloured the versions of the myths that were disseminated. Vampires are ancient Slavic legendary monsters but our concept of them was shaped by a 19th-century Irishman, Bram Stoker. Werewolves likewise, yet the most famous literary tale of a werewolf/vampire hybrid was penned by Alexei Tolstoi in 1839 and only published in 1884. The myth of the origin of Prague, the tale of Queen Libuše, is said to come from the 12th century, but the version taught to Czech children was written by Alois Jirásek in the 1890s. There are similar origin stories behind many Slavic myths.

To understand the complexity of Slavic myths, especially given the context of national and state consolidation and creation of collective identity and culture in which they were typically set down, it is helpful to start with one example: the most monumental work of visual art on the theme of the myth and history of all Slavic peoples. This is *The Slav Epic*, a series by the painter Alphonse Mucha. *The Slav Epic* consists of twenty huge canvases – some measuring as much as six by eight metres – painted with a mixture of egg tempera and oil. Ironically, this masterpiece of collective Slavic identity is inaccessible to the public today.

Alphonse Mucha, who was Czech, began his career in late 19th-century Paris as a distinctly art deco painter. He did not belong to any established school but was certainly at the forefront of bringing painting closer to industry: he made posters, advertisements for various products, calendars and the like. His linear, ornamental style was recognizable and popular. But Mucha saw his true artistic mission as serving the national goal of liberating Czech lands from the Austro-Hungarian monarchy. He conceived of this while working in 1899 on the design of the Pavilion of Bosnia-Herzegovina for the Paris Exhibition of 1900 – paid for by the Austro-Hungarian government. He realized then that the wealth of the United States, as well as Americans' instinctive sympathy with other nations seeking independence in the way theirs had once done, could open up opportunities, and so he travelled there on five different occasions between 1904 and 1909. In particular, he wanted to find a patron who would support his highly ambitious concept for *The Slav Epic*. He acquired such a patron on Christmas Day, 1909: Charles Richard Crane, a wealthy Chicago businessman with a keen interest in the political developments of Eastern Europe and the Slavic people. Crane would be a friend, supporter and patron of Mucha's for the next two decades.

With sponsorship secured, Mucha returned to Prague in 1910. He toured Slavic lands, from Russia to the monasteries on Mount Athos in Greece, preparing an extensive file of visual, documentary and literary material. He set up an enormous studio in Zbiroh Castle in western Bohemia in 1911 and set to work depicting twenty moments from the Slavic past, with a strong focus on Czechs: ten of his canvases showed moments from Czech history, while the other ten illustrated moments of Slavic mythical history. He finished the first, *The Slavs in Their Original Homeland: Between the Turanian Whip and the Sword of the Goths*, in 1912, and the last one, *The Apotheosis of the Slavs*, was completed in 1926. While most of the images are timeless with an ancient vibe, this final one celebrates the events of 1918, with the disintegration of the Austro-Hungarian Empire marking the moment when Slavic homelands were reclaimed by their rightful owners. As Mucha finished the canvases, each was displayed to great acclaim, and most of them were exhibited in the United States in 1921. The complete series was presented by Mucha and Crane as a gift to the city of Prague in a ceremony held in 1928, on the tenth anniversary of the city's independence from Austria-Hungary.

Unfortunately, Mucha's great work had taken him so long to paint that it was by that point regarded as old-fashioned and passé: a valid criticism, despite the beauty of the works themselves. Mucha painted in the realistic, symbolic manner typical of 19th-century academic painting, which had been overtaken between 1910 and 1928 by avant-garde movements like cubism and suprematism. All of modernism had rumbled past him while he was holed up in his castle studio.

Mucha's paintings were heavily influenced by Christianity, but in a very specific context. He chose as subjects, for instance, the introduction of liturgy in Slavonic (which also meant the introduction of literacy) for painting number 3, and a brothel converted into a convent for painting number 7, while number 14 is entitled *The Shield of Christendom*. Christian themes inhabit many of the canvases: painting number 8 celebrates the victory of a group of Slavic people repelling an attack by the military Order of Teutonic Knights at the Battle of Grunwald in Poland on 15 July 1410. Bloody clashes and wars, accompanied by the execution of so-called heretics, marked the religious turmoil in Central Europe during that period. It is interesting that Mucha's grandiose works are not allegorical: the paintings clearly separate two worlds, the real historical world and the world of myth and ritual, with the latter marked by his distortion of perspective and dimension and by the inclusion of smoke, beams of light, fog and clouds. The two worlds communicate, but without coercion and violence. The final image in the series, the theme of which is the future of the Slavs, shows the symbolic past in the background (a giant male body in suffering and pain, a clear Christological reference) and the bright future of the Slavic peoples in the foreground. Even that is not an allegory, but a direct revelation.

The theme of common Slavic origins, too, felt somewhat antiquated, rooted as it was in Pan-Slavism: a European movement for the liberation and progress of the Slavic peoples which had begun in the 18th century and continued into the 19th century. The focus of the new era, by contrast, was on those once-unified Slavs establishing independent nations upon the ruins of monolithic empires, primarily the Ottoman and Austro-Hungarian. The progressive, democratic Czechoslovak president Tomaž Masaryk was an avid supporter of modernist art and architecture who had commissioned the Slovenian architect Jože Plečnik to remodel parts of Prague Castle, transforming it from a bastion of feudalism into a cradle of forward-thinking, modern democracy. Mucha's cycle of paintings romanticizing the Slavic feudal past felt out of step with all of this. They looked backwards; they no longer expressed the spirit of the times.

During the Second World War, the paintings were hidden and Mucha was arrested by the Gestapo. He was released, but died in 1939. When the war ended, Czechoslovakia was liberated by the Red Army and gradually became a communist state dependent on the politics of the USSR. That regime favoured social realism, and it was of Slavic origin, but Mucha's work was too Christian for communist tastes. The paintings were stored in Krumlow Castle in Moravia; they were brought out of storage for a short time to be exhibited in Prague in

2012, and then again in 2018. At the time of writing, a new museum for them is being considered.

For the purposes of understanding Slavic mythology, Mucha's series does have significant value. His Slavs are culturally an extremely diverse group: while most of the canvases are related to Czech history, they also depict Croatians, Bulgarians, Poles and others. Mucha does not emphasize heroism – on the contrary, his representations of battle show its aftermath of tragedy, death and hardscrabble survival. The qualities of Slavic culture are shown first as pleasant rituals involving youths, flowers, music and trees. They then shift to more profound innovations such as literacy, law, the founding of cities, connecting cultures, and establishing a social order that differs from that of Western countries. Liberation from slavery or serfdom, literal or metaphorical, is central to Mucha's endeavour. This was the focal desire of Pan-Slavism.

Pan-Slavism as a movement had been based on a new philosophy of the collective, an intellectual response to the French Revolution. Similar concepts were used at the same time to create ideas about the Germanic race, telling a story that differed from earlier origin stories based on ancient sources. Ideas about the unity of all Slavs had also appeared sporadically much earlier, among Renaissance humanists – for example, Vinko Pribojević, a Croatian author from the 16th century – but politically, the cultural awakening of Slavic peoples and the projects of forming independent states reached a peak in 1848, with the series of revolutions collectively known as the Spring of Nations.

During an armed uprising in Prague that year, the first Pan-Slavic Congress was held: a gathering of linguists, archaeologists, writers, historians, intellectuals and students from all over the Slavic world. The armed revolt was quelled, but the ideas continued to spread. They were especially important among the southern Slavs, leading later to the formation of Yugoslavia (*jugo* meaning 'southern' and *slavija* meaning 'Slavic state'). In the 19th century, the campaign for unification in this region was dubbed 'the Illyrian movement' and was predominantly active in Croatia, then within the Hungarian part of the empire. A second Pan-Slavic Congress took place in 1867 in Moscow, but it actually promoted the imperial Russian idea of the leadership of the Russians in the Slavic world.

Apart from its deep cultural and political influence, the Pan-Slavic movement in Czech lands also formed a physical education movement with a nationalist bent called Sokol ('falcon'). From the early 1860s onwards, Sokol clubs were active in many new Slavic states, especially in Yugoslav countries before the First World War and between the wars. They represent another way in which these rising nations actively created a mythical history that supported their political ideals.

The meaning of the term 'Slavic' has been shaped over many years by Eurocentric views, by classicist canons and by Pan-Slavism. Slavic mythology was harnessed in the 19th century to the model of a mythological hierarchy of gods based on ancient, often misunderstood prototypes, and structured according to new nationalist demands. Oral tradition was mixed with approximate parallels from more firmly established mythologies and applied in ways that would resonate with contemporary ideas of nationhood among Christians. Narratives important for state use were drawn from mythological material – the idea of a glorious past, and any stories that could be rationalized to support territorial, religious, ideological and colonial ambitions or to justify historical decisions.

The creation of new state educational and cultural institutions, with their significant architecture, public exhibitions, state competitions and so on, helped these new mythological narratives and the images associated with them to become widely established and familiar. Eventually it came to seem self-evident that the ideas they represented about the ancient origins of a people were historically accurate. For instance, whether or not Prague was really established by Queen Libuše, the quantity of statues of her around the city and the teaching of her story in Czech schools led to that idea becoming accepted as truth.

The making of heroes and mixing of them with saints is a distinctive characteristic of Slavic mythology, whether in the story of Libuše; Ilya Muromets, a mythical Russo-Ukrainian epic hero who was actually canonized – likely through the melding of the fictional hero with a 12th-century monk, Ilya Pechersky; or Marko Kraljević, a 14th-century Serbian prince who became the protagonist of various folk tales in which he had a holy status. A similar process underlies the cult of personality, even in modern times: Tito, the longtime leader of Yugoslavia, acquired legendary status during his lifetime (and later, too), confirmed even by Hollywood's myth-makers when he was played by Richard Burton in a 1973 film.

The term *mythology* itself has more than one sense. As well as describing material from specific sources like folk tales and fairy tales, it can refer to the academic discourse on myths: *mytho-logy*. Linguistic and philological studies tend to dominate the latter and interdisciplinary work has, over the decades, led to a greatly improved understanding not only of the role of myth in the ancient past but also of mythological invention in the contemporary world.

The approach to the study of myths raises a number of methodological and conceptual problems. Jean-Pierre Vernant, a 20th-century French anthropologist, pointed to the arbitrary nature of myth-making and the importance of context. In the Hellenistic period, for instance, a profession existed called 'mythographer': someone who would compose an appropriate myth of origin for a powerful family or dynasty.[7] Crass as it might sound, this could take the form of a travelling god raping a local nymph, *et voilà* – the family had Hercules as their ancestor. The technique of improvising stories within the frame of some well-structured set of versification rules has been analysed in depth since Albert Lord's important 1960 study on folklore, *The Singer of Tales*. That same model can also be applied to myth-telling, which, outside the power circles of society, has traditionally been the best known and most universal kind of entertainment. Vernant regards myth, which offers space for both invention and interpretation, as the opposite of religion.[8]

Most of the myths presented in this book are accompanied by stories – new versions of the myths recorded in cultural history – to serve as a reminder of the act and practice of mythurgy, the making of myths. We hope that presenting these stories alongside the essays, which highlight interesting scholarly findings and explore the origins of the myths, will encourage readers to consider different aspects of the material – and, perhaps, to appreciate it in unexpected ways.

I

BLACK BUTTERFLY

◆

VAMPIRES

BLACK BUTTERFLY

As the clubs and hoes and threshers and rakes hailed down upon him, and the last of his breath was bludgeoned from his body, his mouth gaped open a final time and into it flew a black butterfly.

Sava Savanović was dead.

For now.

In a rural part of Serbia, quite far from the road between Bajina Bašta and Valjevo, along the serpentine route of the river Rogačica, there lies a village called Zarožje. A short walk from this village stands a birch forest that drops down sharply into a ravine. Within this fog-bound vale sits, or perhaps it would be better to say dwells, a watermill. It is cold even on the hottest summer day and in shadow even when the sun shines brightest. The vale is clotted with thick forest, tumbled boulders and a switchback stream that torques its way painfully through the vale's lowest point. This vein at the foot of the vale pushes a half-rotting waterwheel that, in fairer times, would grind grain for flour for the village of Zarožje – a scattering of farmhouses at the top of the hill – in one direction, and the village of Ovčina at the top of the hill in the other. There the black hawthorn grows. In summer, when it is smothered in white blossoms like snow, its scent summons butterflies by the hundreds. In winter, its bare, skeletal branches are speckled with red berries, each round and swollen like puncture wounds bubbling blood.

The stream gurgles its way around jagged rocks that cause whirlpools to form where they should not. By night, the vale is pitch black and pierced only by cries: of nightjars and owls and the occasional distant wolf, for not even wolves dare to enter the vale. The watermill is made of stones at its base, but their angles are awry, as if the stones themselves wish to move away from the site, each in their own direction. The upper storey is made of wood long rotted. Inside, the grindstones lie in wait, the hearthstone is cracked and the loft above, once optimistically built to hold all the grain that would be milled here, is home to no man. Yet there is still a strange congregation that gives the illusion of life to this long-abandoned, still longer godforsaken mill. For the ceiling inside, rotten and pocked with holes though it is, is covered, all the year round, in a thick and moving carpet of all-black creatures.

Butterflies.

Before the mill fell into abandonment – when there was still the hope, indeed the need, for it to grind grain for the villages of Zarožje and Ovčina – it played a key role in the second killing of Sava Savanović.

The villagers of Ovčina liked to say that the villagers of Zarožje shovelled walnuts with a pitchfork, watered their willow trees and sowed their fields with salt. The folk from Zarožje said that the folk from Ovčina stretched out their wooden boards, carried hot coals by hand and would go into the forest with an axe when they ran out of toothpicks. The leaders of each village, the *kmet*, were somehow related (they were not sure exactly how), but this did not improve their relations. The two villages were so busy either arguing with or ignoring one another that, over the course of three generations, the story of Sava Savanović was forgotten. Only one person in the village had been alive when, ninety years earlier, Sava Savanović had been killed, or as killed as a future vampire can reasonably be. Aunt Mirjana was a century old, more or less, but now she was rather less aware than more, as she was blind and almost completely deaf. She had raised children, grandchildren, nieces and nephews, great-nieces and great-nephews, and possibly some random kids who'd shown up at her door. One of her brood was a young man, just at the cusp of adulthood, named Strahinja.

He had no immediate family, so she had raised him until the first crocuses of his beard showed, at which point he set out to earn his living. He apprenticed himself to a group of men from Ovčina, on the other side of the vale from his Aunt Mirjana. They were master carpenters who travelled as far away as Belgrade to build houses for the wealthy inhabitants. Strahinja learned the trade and journeyed with them, becoming like a young brother to them. And though he endured many a joke at the expense of his origins in Zarožje, they developed a great affection for Strahinja and helped him to become a man.

When he returned to Zarožje, Strahinja set to work on his one inheritance: a ruined hut on the far edge of the village, a bit too close to the forested vale for the tastes of locals. Since it was all he had, he committed himself to working it back into a liveable state. Inspired by the folk who live around the Sava River, and encouraged by his fellow carpenters and masons, he had adopted the habit of smoking a clay pipe, which the locals considered odd for a boy so young.

Now when Strahinja returned and was working on his hut, his eye was drawn to the daughter of the kmet of Zarožje, Radojka. Her face was fresh and beautiful, bright and soft, her hair flaxen and her skin milk white. She returned his affection. Her father did not. Živan Dušman was in charge of the village, as had been his great-grandfather and so on, many generations past. He was quick and eager to anger. His belly shook and his moustache bristled. They said of him that he liked fighting as much as he liked rakija, and he was a man who liked rakija. He was the most important man in Zarožje and wanted his only daughter to marry someone of similar prominence. He was unimpressed by Strahinja, by his run-down hut, by his questionable travels in questionable company, by his weird pipe-smoking.

Eventually he forbade Radojka from seeing Strahinja. Any time she mentioned Strahinja, Živan Dušman would shout and slam his oversized fists onto the table and lock her in her room. The more he did this, the more Radojka feared him and wished to flee to Strahinja's arms.

One day, when Radojka was watching over the sheep beside the birch forest, she heard a sound behind her. She spun round to see Strahinja leaning out from behind a tree, his pipe in his smiling mouth.

'Radojka, do you think you could love me?'

'Indeed, I think I could,' she replied, blushing, 'but we can never be. My father shouts and beats me whenever I mention your name. I fear for my life sometimes. Just the other day, he overheard me talking about you to my cousin. He tore into my room and smashed all the decorations on my wall, stamping on them and throwing a beautiful old wooden antique that some shepherd had half-carved into the shape of a butterfly into the fire.'

Strahinja's smile faded. 'What if we were to run away together? To some far-off land where no one would find us, but we would have each other?'

The girl shook her head. 'I'm afraid that my father would find a way to hunt us down. He is too strong and flush with anger. I…I think it's best if we do not see each other.'

A tear wove its way down Strahinja's cheek, slid along the length of his pipe and extinguished it with a sizzle. 'For the love I have for you, Radojka, I accept. But only until I can prove myself worthy of marrying you, prove to your father that I am a good man. Or find some other way of dealing with him. Until then, farewell.'

With that, Strahinja disappeared into the birch forest and Radojka was left alone with her flock, her breast heaving with sadness and longing and concern.

Strahinja did not have a plan in place. He could not bear the thought of Radojka suffering because of him; nor could he imagine living in the same village as her and, horror of horrors, seeing her marry another. Despondent, he considered what he should do. He did not want to remain in Zarožje, but he did not know where to go instead. Should he travel afar and forget about her? His heart told him no. For want of a better idea, he decided to go to Ovčina, to visit his carpenter and mason friends. He would stay with them until he could come up with a plan.

Back at his unfinished hut, Strahinja packed his few belongings, for he didn't know how long he would be away. He packed his second set of clothes, his pipe and tobacco pouch, his warm sheepskin vest and his knife. He set off at dusk down the slope, swallowed up by the birch forest and its linear darkness.

Strahinja was young and strong, but even he did not like the feel of this vale at night. No road connected the villages of Zarožje and Ovčina, just an underused switchback path that wound down the steep slope to the ravine and a strangled section of the Rogačica River that cut through it, then up a gentler, more boulder-strewn slope to Ovčina. The further he descended, the colder it got. Though it was summer, Strahinja began to shiver. He stopped just long enough to slip on his warm sheepskin vest. He felt better for a while, but the closer he got to the river, the colder he became, until he was once more shivering.

Just as the river below came into view, his foot slipped on the loose stones and he half-fell the rest of the way until he slammed into something hard in the darkness. It was the foundation of the old abandoned watermill. Strahinja shivered, and not from the cold, as he realized where he was. He'd heard ghost stories about this mill since he was a boy, but he'd never heeded them. The path he had usually taken from Zarožje to Ovčina, when he was apprenticed to the carpenters, did not pass the watermill, so he wondered at how he could have run into it now. He had never seen it by night, and never this close. Everything in his body, apart from his mind, which was stubbornly logical, told him to flee, to run for his life. But Strahinja was a smart boy and he reasoned that there could be nothing to fear, even in the darkness, from a disused structure that was barely standing. His concerns might be wolves or the odd bear, but not an empty building.

CHAPTER ONE

He steeled himself, stood, swept off the dirt from his clothes and marched on. It was only when he had continued a reasonable distance and the night sounds of the forest – the screech owl and the nightjar and the cicadas – resumed their nocturne that it occurred to him, and only somewhere in the deep ravine of his mind, that it had been absolutely silent beside the mill.

It was difficult to find the ford of the river in the coming night, and he realized it would have been better had he set out the following morning. He eventually found the ford and wondered at how far he'd strayed from the normal footpath that linked the villages. Having once again reached the path, it did not take long for him to climb the other side of the vale. This side was freckled with boulders that looked like the battlefield of some ancient giants, hurling tremendous rocks at one another until the resulting tremors caused the earth to split open, the vale to sink and the river to rise at its base. Strahinja felt a palpable sense of relief when he saw the light of the tavern at the edge of Ovčina, and the cluster of houses beyond.

He threw open the tavern door and stepped inside, looking the worse for wear, his clothing covered in dirt, his face with sweat. But those inside were his friends and celebrated his arrival like the return of a favourite young brother. The men of the village bade him take a seat, light his pipe, take a mug of kvass and tell them what had brought him there, on the cusp of nightfall. He sat heavily, drank deeply, lit his pipe and told of his despair and his impossible love for Radojka.

His companions listened sympathetically. Their first idea was to kidnap the girl and then put up a good fight when Živan Dušman arrived to retrieve her, as he surely would, and with a posse of strong men, too. But while all those at the tavern were up for a fight, Strahinja shook his head. He did not want blood spilled on his account.

'Friends, if I could prove my worth, then Živan Dušman might accept me as I am, and all this could be settled peaceably. If only I could accomplish some task, undertake some quest that would win, if not his affection, then at least his approval.'

The men in the tavern thought long and hard. They stared at the fire in the hearth, the dance of its orange tendrils, the soft white smoke, the pulsating embers. Time passed. The owner of the tavern, a woman as strong and as broad as two men, asked Strahinja if he wanted something to eat.

'A bit of bread, perhaps,' he replied.

'Bread,' she began, 'is one of the only things in short supply. The nearest mill is an hour's walk away, so we're not a village of bread eaters, aside from your special occasions. I can give you dried meat or soup, but no bread.'

In Zarožje, he knew, grain was milled in a village further along in the opposite direction to Ovčina, using a donkey-powered mill. It was more expensive and less convenient, but bread remained a staple. Here, it seemed, it was not.

'What about the mill in the vale?' Strahinja asked.

'The watermill?' she replied. 'Best you don't ask. It's not been in use since my grandmother's time. As far as I know it's plagued with a ghost. There have been occasions when we've tried to hire a miller and get it back up and running. Last I heard, the millstones were still there, and the waterwheel was in serviceable repair. But three different men have set up there during my lifetime. Each one began hale and hearty and shortly after starting to work the mill for us, fell ill and suddenly died. There's a poison in the air or a ghost in the stones, I tell you. Why, I'm sure the kmet of Ovčina and Zarožje would pay a pretty penny in wages to a miller who brought that place back from the dead and could service our villages again. Far beyond what a miller should earn, and millers do quite well.'

Strahinja's eyes brightened. 'What if I were to take over the mill?' he suggested.

The men in the tavern grumbled in disapproval. It sounded dangerous, and they didn't want their beloved brother to risk his life. But Strahinja was adamant and they could not dissuade him. It was true, as he thought, that if he were to bring the mill back to life, it would be a boon for both villages, earn him a good wage and show both his bravery and merit to Živan Dušman. It was the best, and only, plan he had.

So it was arranged. The following day, Strahinja set back out down into the vale, which was still cold but seemed less sinister beneath the sun. His comrades from Ovčina went with him, carrying equipment to make any necessary repairs to get the mill up and running.

After kicking in the wooden door, they leapt back as a swarm of insects stormed out, objecting to the disturbance. The men hadn't time to see them properly. They behaved and sounded like bats, but they were smaller and there were so many of them that at first the men thought they were black moths – though what so many moths would be doing inside such a building, with no light or warmth to attract them, was not a question any of them could answer.

The mill was in better condition inside than it appeared from without. The stone lower floor and the wooden main structure were like a drowned corpse that had floated too long in water, the tissue peeling off but the bones still solid. Inside, the millwheel had been stopped, but when the blockage was removed it began to turn again. Beside the grindstones lay a long-disused hearth with a crack in it, a wooden bed frame, a damp, chewed blanket and a proliferation of rat skeletons, but the structure was sound enough. Above the bed a constellation of thin needles, scores of them, stuck out of the wooden wall, which was odd, but did not overtake their attention. A creaky ladder up to a wooden loft, which had once held sacks of grain waiting to be ground, was missing some rungs but seemed salvageable. The roof leaked, but that was a fixable matter. Most important was that the mill appeared to function.

The men had brought with them a small sack of wheat and one of their group, who had some experience in such things, showed Strahinja how to load the grain into place, set the grindstone and begin the process. While a few remained with Strahinja, patching up what they could to make the mill run, one comrade set off for Zarožje and another to Ovčina, to announce that the mill would be operational once more and that Strahinja had agreed to man it.

Within a few hours, the hearth was cleared and a fire set to warm the freezing cold – a cold that suggested a low-hanging mist, though there was none. The comrades returned from the villages with news that the kmet of each, Živan Dušman too, was pleasantly surprised and each had agreed to pay a miller's wage plus half again if the mill could be maintained. That meant that Strahinja could expect thrice a miller's salary and would suddenly become one of the leading men of the region, if he would but stay and work the stones. Strahinja was emboldened by this news, particularly that Živan Dušman approved, and he was more determined than ever to move ahead with his plan. So that he could prove himself, a large sack of grain from each village had been brought for Strahinja to grind to flour and bring up the following day.

Before his friends left, before dusk had set, they warned him to take care. They knew not why the last three millers had suddenly sickened and died, and they did not want their young brother to suffer a similar fate. They agreed to return the next morning to check on him and carry the flour up to the villages for him, as well as to set about healing the leprous roof. They also lent him a pair of pistols and some shot, as well as a few Turkish coins made of silver. Load one pistol with lead shot and the other with a coin, they said. The silver was too soft to kill a living man, but it was said to harm the un-living. They appeared nervous and insisted on leaving before twilight. Strahinja did not wish to keep them, though he secretly would have liked the company.

Soon they were gone, and he was left to begin his tasks. Very much alone.

Strahinja set about his work. He loaded the grain to mill in the grindstone. Since they had brought but two sacks, the work was quickly done, the sacks refilled with fresh-milled flour. Meanwhile he stoked the fire and arranged some firewood before it on the floor, roughly in the shape of a man. Over this he draped the well-chewed blanket he had found there, so that none of the logs could be seen. He loaded more logs into the hearth to last the night through. He placed his just-smoked pipe on the mantel above the hearth, and then he climbed up the rung-poor ladder to the grain loft.

From this vantage he could see down into the main ground-floor space of the mill. There was the millstone, slowly grinding as the waterwheel turned. There was the blaze in the fireplace. And there, before the hearth, was what looked like a man asleep beneath the blanket. Strahinja loaded the pistols, one with lead shot, the other with silver coins. He checked that his hunting knife was in his belt. Then he lay on his stomach in the grain loft, fighting sleep, watching and waiting.

◆

In the village of Zarožje, ninety years prior to the love between Strahinja and Radojka, there had lived a miller from a respected family named Sava Savanović. His family was among the wealthiest in the village. His grandfather had been the village leader, the kmet, and had built the mill in which Sava lived and worked. While his brother, Stanko, had married early and had many children and lived in the village proper as a seller of livestock – the family business – Sava, the odd brother, remained a bachelor far longer than was deemed appropriate or, as the villagers whispered it, normal. Sava was not old, but he was no longer young and was well beyond the age that most men take a wife. He was quite the opposite of handsome, which may have contributed to his matrimonial oversight: too tall, too gaunt, too pale. And he was quick-tempered and a great friend of rakija, but then, those latter qualifications could describe so many of the less-than-gentle 'gentlemen' of this rural, densely wooded wasteland in Serbia.

Sava's parents needled him to take a wife. The men at the village tavern teased him that he ate so much garlic, no girls would come near him. Little boys would sneak up to the mill, for that was where he both lived and worked, to spy on him as he sat by the hearth and engaged in his favourite pastime, collecting moths and butterflies. These he would capture and kill by pinching them just below the thorax, a sort of minimalist strangulation. He would then impale them lovingly with a needle and affix them to the wooden wall above his bed, which was by the hearth on the far side of the mill from the grindstone. The little boys of the village would dare each other to sneak inside if they knew Sava was out, and marvel at the mosaic of dozens of moths and butterflies pinned to the wall.

Sava was never a happy man. No one was in those parts. What was there to be happy about? Happiness did not seem a manageable goal, and the word was largely absent from conversation. He was perhaps content with his lot, milling grain for the villages on either side of the vale, sorting and caring for his collection, smoking his pipe and sipping rakija and otherwise left to his thoughts. But the rest of the world, which for him meant the villagers of Zarožje and his family, would not leave him in peace. They accused him, without saying as much, of being off, of seeking the love of those with whom coupling was unnatural. The only way he imagined quieting them was either to kill them all, which seemed impractical, or to take a wife. So he determined to marry.

The only problem was that the village was small, and eligible maidens were few. Those few expressed no interest in becoming the wife of the miller, even though he made a decent wage, as he was thought of as strange and, truth be told, he did stink of garlic. Garlic is wonderful in moderation and at mealtime, but not as desirable in other situations, like the marriage bed.

Sava's only chance seemed to be a young girl from the village named Mira, not even really of marriageable age, to be honest, but she never made fun of him nor mocked him for not having yet married. She did not appear to be repulsed by him, perhaps because she was so young that she did not think of men in such terms. She was the daughter of one of the providers of livestock for his brother,

CHAPTER ONE

a sheep farmer who owned the most heads in the village and was its kmet, Matija Dušman.

Sava began to court Mira, but not in the way young men typically courted young women. They would sit together in the field while she tended to the sheep and talk about the shapes of clouds and which of the sheep they resembled, and carve butterflies out of scraps of wood with his pocket knife. The girl's father looked upon Sava with a mixture of concern and disgust, for what could so old a man, and so strange, want with so young a girl that a father would approve? Sava felt that he might be falling in love with Mira. He could not be sure, because love was not a word that had ever really been used in his presence, and the only inkling he had of it was what was preached by the priest on Sundays – which didn't seem the same type of love at all – or what he'd heard about in epic poems with knights and princesses and such. He did know that he felt at peace when he was with Mira. Until, that is, anyone else appeared to intrude their opinion and disapproval, at which point he felt significantly less at peace than he had before this whole marriage business had been pressed upon him.

One warm summer's day, Sava emerged from the chilly shadow of the vale and into the sunlight of the fields, where he hoped to meet Mira. He brought with him his pocket knife and a piece of a black hawthorn that he had begun to whittle into the shape of a butterfly, as a gift for the girl. Hawthorn is a hard wood, but Sava was stronger than his wiry limbs and sallow face suggested, and he felt that this butterfly would last for eternity, a show of his love. He had begun the carving at home and had fashioned the hawthorn block, shaping its base into a sharp point, the tip of the abdomen of the butterfly it would one day become. He had only to carve its wings, which he planned to do while seated beside the girl, allowing her to choose the pattern on the wings based on whichever butterfly she found most beautiful.

But when he reached the edge of his forested vale, and when the pastures spread out before him in the warming sun, his brother stepped out from behind a tree. Stanko looked concerned as he approached Sava.

'I must speak with you, brother,' he said. 'The villagers ask that you stop your visits with the shepherd girl. Her father is not willing to have you court his daughter. You are too old and too strange, he says. If you approach her again, they will harm you and drive you away. Even now, in anticipation of your visit, her father and his farmhands lie in wait and will spring upon you and chase you off if you come towards her. It is a trap, my dear brother. I am sorry.'

Sava's expression did not change. He just nodded to his brother and kept walking out into the pastures towards where he thought to meet the girl. Stanko shouted after him, but it was no use. Sava continued to walk. Stanko tried to pull his brother back, but Sava turned upon him and drove his pocket knife into his brother's chest, pinning him to the warm grass until his body stopped twitching and relaxed. Covered in his brother's gore, Sava continued to walk towards Mira, who he felt reasonably certain was his one true love.

There was a crest in the grass of the pasture, like a wave trapped in the earth, and on the other side was the land of Mira's father, dotted with sheep. Sava walked to the top of the crest, a pale, gaunt, wiry man stained with blood that still dripped from his knife in one hand, the quarter-formed hawthorn butterfly in the other. The girl was seated with her back to him, watching the flock, and did not see him approach.

'Come walk with me,' he said as he stood looming above her, blocking the light of the sun. She turned with a smile, for she enjoyed his odd company. But then she saw him, awash in fresh blood. She screamed and ran. Before Sava could think, four men surrounded him, one of them the girl's father. Though Sava meant her no harm – at least, he was reasonably sure that he did not – the vision he presented suggested otherwise, as did the fresh, steaming corpse of his brother at the edge of the vale.

The men were upon him and attacked with whatever implements they had to hand. They were not soldiers and had no weapons but

CHAPTER ONE

the tools of the field. But such tools, when wielded with the proper intent, become weapons. With walking sticks and branches, with hoes and threshers and shovels, they beat poor Sava Savanović, whose only crime, as he saw it, had been to love and not be loved in return. Sava fought furiously and managed to drive the sharpened point of the hawthorn carving into the chest of the girl's father, Matija Dušman, a wound that would prove fatal. The others beat him until his body was broken and there was more blood without than within.

Just as his torqued body expired and he gurgled a last breath, a black butterfly appeared. Some of his murderers thought that the butterfly had emerged from his mouth, others that it had flown into it. Still others swore that it was a black moth, or the hawk moth with the death's-head pattern on its wings. But it didn't matter, beyond a grace note to the story to tell the boys over rakija at the tavern on a future winter's night. Dead is dead. Or so they thought.

They buried Stanko's body in the village cemetery. The young girl's father followed some days later, when the well-meaning but useless doctor of the village could not staunch the bleeding of the wound Sava had inflicted.

Some weeks later, Mira was back in the pasture with her sheep when she came upon a funny shape in the tall grass. She bent down to investigate and found that it was a wooden carving that almost wished to be a butterfly. It was made of hawthorn wood but it had been badly painted, or so it appeared, with a dark, sticky varnish. She did not know that it was Sava who had made it. She took it home and placed it on the wall above her bed, pinning it to the wood with a long, thin nail.

Sava's body was unfit for interment and was thrown into a shallow grave where the stream in the vale bent sharpest, beside a spreading elm, not far from the watermill. The mill was abandoned and shunned as a cursed place, avoided by all except for the occasional boy who accepted the challenge of his braying friends and stepped inside,

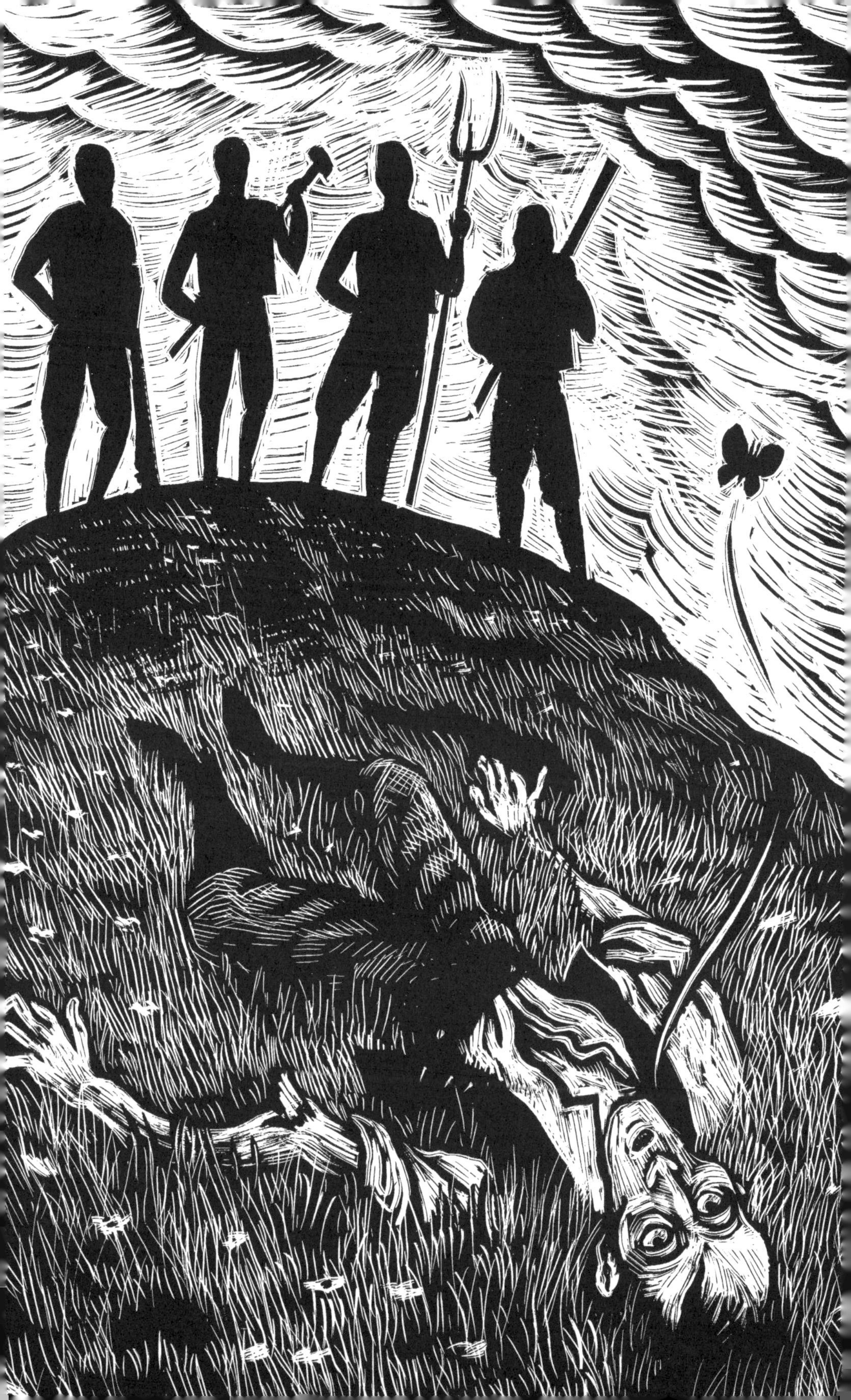

CHAPTER ONE

never to step out again. The mill was otherwise left for dead. The waterwheel stopped moving and the only sign of life was the curious proliferation of butterflies that flocked to it, even out of season.

If only they'd opted for a deeper grave...

◆

Strahinja wrestled with the ghost called sleep. The fire still licked at the hearthstone, and he struggled to keep his eyes open after a long, weary day. He did not know what to expect, if anything, in the night. Whatever had slain the three previous millers might have been disease or poison or, well, any of a number of things. But he had an inkling as to what it might be, and he would be prepared.

He opened his eyes suddenly. Had he fallen asleep? The fire was almost to embers, so it seemed that he had. How was that possible? He was angry with himself.

Then he realized that something was wrong. It was too quiet. The owls had stopped, as had the nightjars and the cicadas. Even the wind had opted to lay low. And the millwheel. It was still turning, but without a sound.

That was when he saw it. A shadow slowly expanding, elongating across the mouth of the fireplace. The mill was suddenly freezing cold, as if it had been abruptly cloaked in snow. The shadow grew and grew until its owner followed. It was a tall, gaunt man. His bald head was pale, as close to white as human skin can be, his limbs wiry, his body slender to the point of starvation, but his cheeks, only his cheeks, were engorged and bloated, rubicund like those of a baroque statue of the Christ Child in a candlelit church. His eyes were more like an animal's in the darkness, reflecting the light from the dying fire but with no light within them. He wore a long, black, soiled sheet: a burial shroud. He wore it as if it were a cloak buttoned up around his neck. The smell of damp, deep soil, caked clay, ash and rotted wood was so strong, Strahinja could barely withhold his disgust and remain still. Maybe the man wouldn't see him?

The gaunt figure stood for a moment before the hearth, seeing the pipe on the mantel, examining the form beneath the blanket upon the floor. Then, with the swiftness of a wolf, he pounced on it. He leapt back, confused, having touched not sleeping human flesh but a pile of logs beneath the blanket. He said to himself, aloud and in dismay, 'Oh, Sava Savanović! For ninety years you've been a vampire and you've never gone without supper as you will this night!'

Strahinja saw all this from above, from the grain loft, and he wasted no time. When the man recoiled, Strahinja saw his chance. As soon as this Sava stopped speaking, while still in the grain loft, Strahinja fired both pistols down at him. One harmed its target, the other did not, but one was enough. When the smoke from the powder cleared, the man was gone.

The night sounds resumed their symphony. Strahinja pulled out his knife and slid down the ladder to the ground floor. There was but one sign of the gaunt man: an oddly long, chalk-white finger capped with a talon-like fingernail, caked in soil and its tip broken, lying on the floor by the hearthstone.

Strahinja reloaded his pistols, one with lead shot, one with silver coin. He took up his pipe from the mantel. A soot-covered butterfly was seated upon it, which he shooed away. He stuffed the pipe with fresh tobacco and lit it. The smoke had never tasted so good and it helped him stop shaking. He added the logs from beneath the blanket to the fire and stoked it. He kept thinking that he saw the finger move out of the corner of his eye. He would wait for sunrise and the return of his comrades. He was not sure if the life of a miller suited him.

Finally, cocks crowed in the villages above the vale. Strahinja exhaled deeply.

It took a few more hours for the sun to puncture the mist and reach its tendrils deep down into the ravine. Strahinja heard a sound outside, but he was no longer worried. Not in the daylight. Then his comrades called to him.

'Ho, Strahinja, are you still with us?'

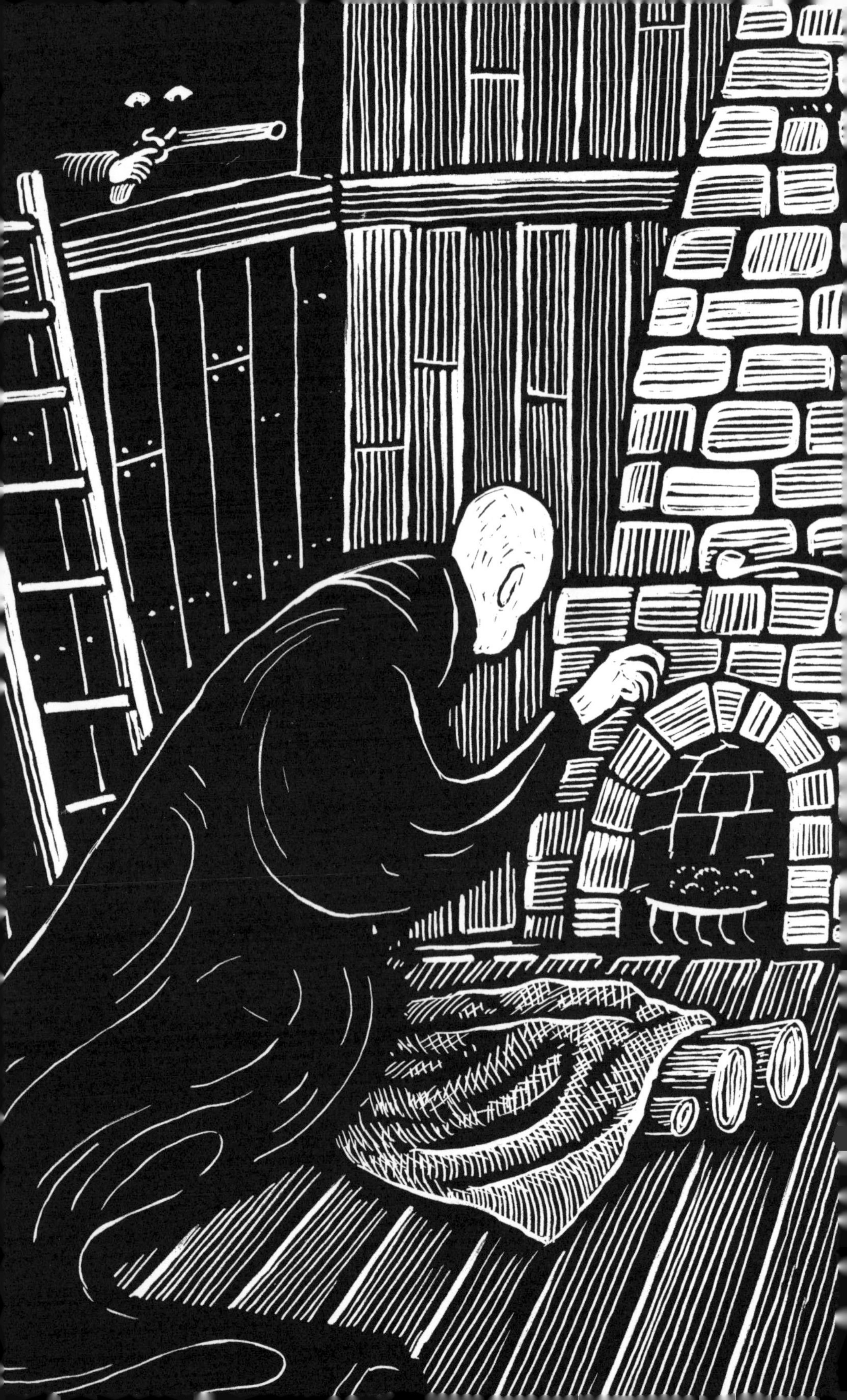

'Aye, and with a tale to tell.' Strahinja embraced his comrades from Ovčina and told them of what had happened. 'He called himself Sava Savanović. It's not a name I know, but it is something to enquire about. I suppose that the silver shot off his finger,' he concluded. 'It's there, by the hearth.' The men crowded in to see. But no finger was to be found.

'I would swear it was here,' Strahinja said, shaking his head.

'From your pallor, brother, we believe you,' one of them replied. 'And you even managed to mill the grain to flour. We'll make a miller of you yet.'

'I'm not sure I want to be, even if it would win my Radojka, if I must endure another night like this one.'

'It sounds like it can be only one thing,' another friend said. 'From what you say, it could only be a vampire.'

'I've heard of such monsters,' said Strahinja, 'but know nothing of them. I have never heard of a Savanović family in Zarožje, and I know all the families there. Whatever it is, I must put an end to it, or I'm afraid you'll have to find yourselves a new miller.'

'For that reason,' a friend smiled, 'and for our love for you, we will help you. We should speak to the priest in Zarožje. Perhaps he knows. He is more likely to remember such things than our priest in Ovčina. He only remembers where he stored his rakija.'

They set out for Zarožje, carrying the sack of flour as proof of where Strahinja had spent the night. Up the steep slope they walked, along the switchback trail through the birch forest. In the light of day each step of their ascent washed Strahinja with relief.

They went first to the village priest and told him what had happened. The priest had heard from his fellow clergy of encounters with vampires. He had read about the creatures in the chronicles penned by Baron Valvasor. He had heard of some of the rites to kill them a second time. He knew that the scent of garlic repelled them, as did the sight of a crucifix.

'We must find its den, wherever it was buried,' the priest said, for some reason in a whisper, while looking carefully around the small church. 'If you do not know where that is, then you must take a stallion, one ungelded and completely black, and lead it around. It will grow frantic when it stands above a vampire's grave. Then there are three things we must do to end it. We must first drive a stake made of wood from a black hawthorn through its chest, pinning it in place in its coffin. We must then pour holy water into its mouth, so its soul will not escape its body and find another to inhabit. Then we bury it again seven feet down, and pile atop the coffin heavy stones, so it cannot lift the lid. Then we cover it with soil scattered with holy water and plant a black hawthorn above the new, old grave. It is never truly dead. But if it is pinned in place, drowned in holy water and weighted down inside its coffin, then it can never rise again.'

'If you do all this,' said a booming voice at the far end of the church, to the surprise of all gathered around the priest, 'then I will give you my daughter.' It was Živan Dušman, his arms sternly crossed over his significant belly, his moustache bristling. He had been listening in, it seemed. 'Strahinja,' he continued, 'you have already proved yourself a man, which is more than I thought of you yesterday. But whoever marries Radojka must care for her and have a profession. If you become our miller then you will satisfy that expectation. Because I love my daughter so well, I wish her to marry someone I can be proud to call my son-in-law. If you rid the vale of this monster, I will call you son.'

Strahinja nodded. 'I accept, but we will need to work together. Have any of you heard of a Sava Savanović? I've lived here my whole life and know of no Savanović family. We must find the vampire's grave. A stallion may help but we must narrow down the search. Are there Savanovićs among the gravestones outside in the churchyard?'

One of his comrades ran outside to check. Živan Dušman spoke. 'The name seems familiar to me, but there is certainly no such family in the village today, nor has there been in my lifetime. You said that the vampire referred to himself by his name and also said "for ninety years"? Are you quite sure?'

'Indeed,' replied Strahinja. 'It was not the sort of moment one forgets.'

'Is there anyone in the village old enough to remember ninety years past?' asked one of the Ovčina carpenters.

Živan Dušman and Strahinja nearly replied in tandem: 'Aunt Mirjana.'

She was the only person over ninety years of age. How far over, no one knew, but some guessed she had lived a century. The trouble was, as Strahinja knew well, she had long ago gone all but deaf and had recently lost her sight. She was cared for by a community of her children, grandchildren and adopted souls, like Strahinja. Perhaps she would know?

A shout from outside the church summoned them. One of the comrades knelt beside a family plot with the name Savanović engraved upon the stone. It was overgrown with tall grasses and stood out at the edge of the cemetery. The others gathered round.

'The soil looks undisturbed,' said the priest, 'but I suppose it could be here.'

'I will check the village for an ungelded, all-black stallion,' said Živan Dušman.

While they waited, the priest examined the baptismal, confirmation, wedding and funeral records in the dusty church archive. He found entries under the name Savanović dating back ninety years precisely but no later. That year a Stanko Savanović had been buried in the churchyard, in the family plot. But no sign of Sava. The priest looked back further and found a number of members of the Savanović family. It was not until he combed the baptismal record from 132 years ago that he found a record of a Sava Savanović, the older brother of Stanko.

Živan Dušman returned, leading a handsome stallion. They brought the horse to the grave marked Savanović. The horse did not react in any way. They wound their way throughout the cemetery, but the horse was indifferent, calm, throughout.

CHAPTER ONE

'The monster must not be here,' reasoned the priest. 'Perhaps he did not die in this community? But if this Sava was indeed a monster during his life, and not only after it, then he would not have been granted Christian burial. Or perhaps he was a suicide or a murderer?'

'Where else can we look?' a comrade asked.

They found themselves outside the home of Aunt Mirjana. The ramshackle farmhouse was where Strahinja had grown up, and it still felt like home to him. It was busy with grandchildren playing in the yard, the older ones tending to chickens. Strahinja entered the farmhouse. Aunt Mirjana was propped up with cushions by the tiled stove at the centre of the house. She was frail and pale, wrinkled and tremored, her long, white hair braided down to her waist. Her eyes were clouded over, but when Strahinja approached, she somehow knew it was he.

'Come and embrace your auntie, my boy,' she whispered hoarsely. He approached and kissed the back of her papery hand.

'Aunt Mirjana,' he began, then hesitated. He did not want to upset her or, worse, shock her into ill health. The story of being attacked by a vampire might indeed have that effect. So he shifted his course. 'Does the name Sava Savanović mean anything to you?'

'What's that, my dear?' she replied, cupping her hand to her ear.

Strahinja repeated the question, only far louder.

Her face was as he imagined it might be had he told her about the vampire attack. Whatever colour was in her bone-toned skin drained out and she gasped, clutching her chest. Strahinja held her in his arms. Her body was like a sparrow beside him. She crossed herself and then whispered, 'He was evil. They killed him in the pasture.'

'Do you know where he was buried, Aunt Mirjana? Not in the cemetery...'

'Oh, no,' she replied. 'Not in the cemetery. They buried him at the crooked ravine, beneath a spreading elm. He...' Aunt Mirjana's body seized, as if possessed, convulsed, and then she lay back against Strahinja. She was still breathing, but he did not want to risk probing further. She closed her eyes and was soon asleep. He lowered her down to her cushions as gently as he could and left the farmhouse.

'The crooked ravine?' Živan Dušman repeated. 'There are several points down in the vale where the river bends sharply. She must have meant one of them, for nothing else near fits that description. You'll have to try them all.' He passed the reins of the stallion over to Strahinja and quickly retreated.

'First, we must arm ourselves,' said Strahinja. The sun was high in the sky as the priest fetched holy water and the processional crucifix from the church. The comrades gathered a shovel and a pickaxe while Strahinja found a black hawthorn bush and fashioned a stake from a stout branch, sharpening one end to a vicious, canine point. Thus armed, they set off, back down into the vale, with the stallion beside them.

Once again, the warm sun slipped quickly from their shoulders and the temperature appeared to drop with their descent. The footpath wound through the birch forest until they reached the ford. They determined to search for a crooked bend in the river somewhere within the vale, between where the river disappeared under the earth at one end and began at a waterfall at the other.

It took them hours to reach one end of the vale. They passed two reasonably crooked bends in the river. The first had no elm trees to be seen alongside it. The second did, and they led the stallion in concentric circles around the elm, but the horse's demeanour did not change. Finally, when they reached the crags into which the river dipped down into a cave system inaccessible to man, they determined that they must try the other half of the river.

They were tired enough when they retraced their steps and reached the ford, but they had to go on to explore the upriver territory. They walked for hours more and passed two switchback bends. The first was not far from the watermill itself, but there was no elm tree there. The second, not far from the waterfall, had two young elms beside it, but neither could have been over ninety years old. Ready to give

CHAPTER ONE

up, the party returned to the ford and the footpath in order to head back up to the village.

By now night was encroaching and the time for hunting a vampire ebbed. Eventually their path led them back to the watermill, which looked just as grim as it had the evening before. They could see the crooked bend a little further up the river but a mist had come in and choked their view, making them shiver.

'Should we all spend the night in the mill?' a comrade suggested. 'Together, for safety in numbers? Then if the vampire should return, we can attack it as one.'

None of the others liked this idea, but the priest was first to speak. 'It is unwise to try to kill a vampire by night, for they cannot truly be killed. We might only hope to frighten it away, as brave Strahinja did last night. It must be buried and trapped…I almost said buried alive, but this cannot be said of something that is no longer alive before it is buried…'

The sky was shifting to the colour of bruised flesh. They were standing together outside the mill, discussing their next move, when the stallion broke free, tearing his reins out of one of the carpenter's hands, and bolted towards the woodpile that was stacked just outside the watermill, between the mill itself and the bend in the river. The horse began to neigh and buck onto its hind legs, then smash down with its forehooves onto the ground. In wonder, the party swiftly approached. The stallion was stamping at a patch of ground that was embowered by two stacks of firewood, so it could barely be seen. At first the hooves struck muddy soil, showering it in all directions. But then they struck something different – something that made a crumpling sound.

'Whoa, whoa,' the comrades soothed. With some difficulty, they managed to seize the stallion's reins and walk him to one side. The crumpling sound had been hooves striking a half-buried tree stump. It was of huge circumference, indicating its age. One of the carpenters, who was particularly knowledgeable about wood, bent close to the decomposing stump for a moment, then looked up with a smile.

'Elm,' he said.

They set about with the shovel and the pickaxe, but it was a race with the sun. If it should set before they could perform the rite, the vampire would rise from its grave and threaten them all. The pickaxe shredded the ancient elm stump and the shovel shifted the murky soil, until a blow of the shovel returned a hollow sound. They scraped more soil off and saw that they had unearthed rough wooden planks, the roof of an amateur coffin. The priest kept looking to the darkening sky, crossing himself and whispering prayers under his breath. He draped his epitrachelion shawl over his shoulders and held the processional crucifix with both hands before him, like the weapon that it was.

'Have your tools ready,' said Strahinja. 'You know what to do. While you two remove the lid, I will pin it down with the stake and you pour holy water into its mouth. Then you slam the lid back on and we start loading large, flat river rocks to weigh it down.'

'And whatever you do,' said the priest, 'be sure not to get any of its blood on your skin.'

'We're nearly out of time,' Strahinja said. 'Do it! Do it now!'

Two of the carpenters pried open the lid with the pickaxe and slid it away.

There before them, lying in the makeshift coffin, was the pale, gaunt, tall man Strahinja had seen the night before. His chest was draped in his black burial cloth, his arms stretched out at his sides, and one leg was nonchalantly crossed over the other – a position in which no one would be buried. While the skin on his brow and hands was so white as to nearly glow in the half-light, nothing on this corpse was decomposed. It was hardly in perfect condition, but it looked to have been buried days ago, not decades. Only its cheeks were horribly flushed, incarnadine, engorged with stores of blood. It was missing one of its fingers.

'Now!'

No one moved. The whole group was so struck with terror that not one of them reacted. The only one who finally moved was Sava

Savanović. His body slowly folded upwards and forward inside the coffin, so that he was nearly in a seated position. Then he must have seen the processional crucifix, for his expressionless face twisted in agony. The priest, without thinking, swung the cross down towards the vampire and it struck him in the head. The moment it struck, the cross burst into flame and seemed to brand the vampire's face with its heat. This madness stirred the others from their stupor.

Strahinja dove at the vampire and drove the stake directly through its chest, pressing down with all his weight. The grotesque sound of the wood passing through brittle, bloodless flesh was drowned out by the horrific scream that emanated from the vampire's mouth.

'The holy water!'

Another carpenter, armed with a vial of holy water, poured it over Sava's scalded face, aiming for his open, screaming mouth. But fearing to get too close, he did not manage to spill the water directly into his mouth, but rather splashed around it. When the holy water struck Sava's skin it hissed and burned, like acid. Steam rose from the wounds inflicted and Sava convulsed in pain. From the veil of that steam something else rose. A black butterfly disgorged from Sava's throat and fluttered into the twilight air. Then the vampire lay statue-still.

Shaken and shaking, the priest retrieved the crucifix, which had not been damaged by whatever flame had surrounded it, and recited prayers. The carpenters placed the lid back on the coffin and spent the next hour layering flat, heavy river stones atop it before replacing the soil, reburying the undead.

And that was the end of Sava Savanović. The incident led to a mutual appreciation between the villages of Ovčina and Zarožje. The priest returned the next day and planted a black hawthorn bush over the grave; then, not long afterwards, he requested a transfer to a different village in a far-away part of Serbia. Živan Dušman gave Strahinja his daughter, Radojka, in marriage, and Aunt Mirjana lived to see the wedding day. But all those involved determined that it would be better to leave the watermill well alone. Instead, Živan Dušman and the kmet of Ovčina financed the building of a donkey-powered mill in the relative safety of Zarožje, provided that Strahinja would run it and deliver flour to both villages, each on alternate days. In order to carry the flour he was given, as his wedding gift, the ungelded black stallion, and his carpenter comrades gifted him the pair of pistols he'd been lent. Just in case.

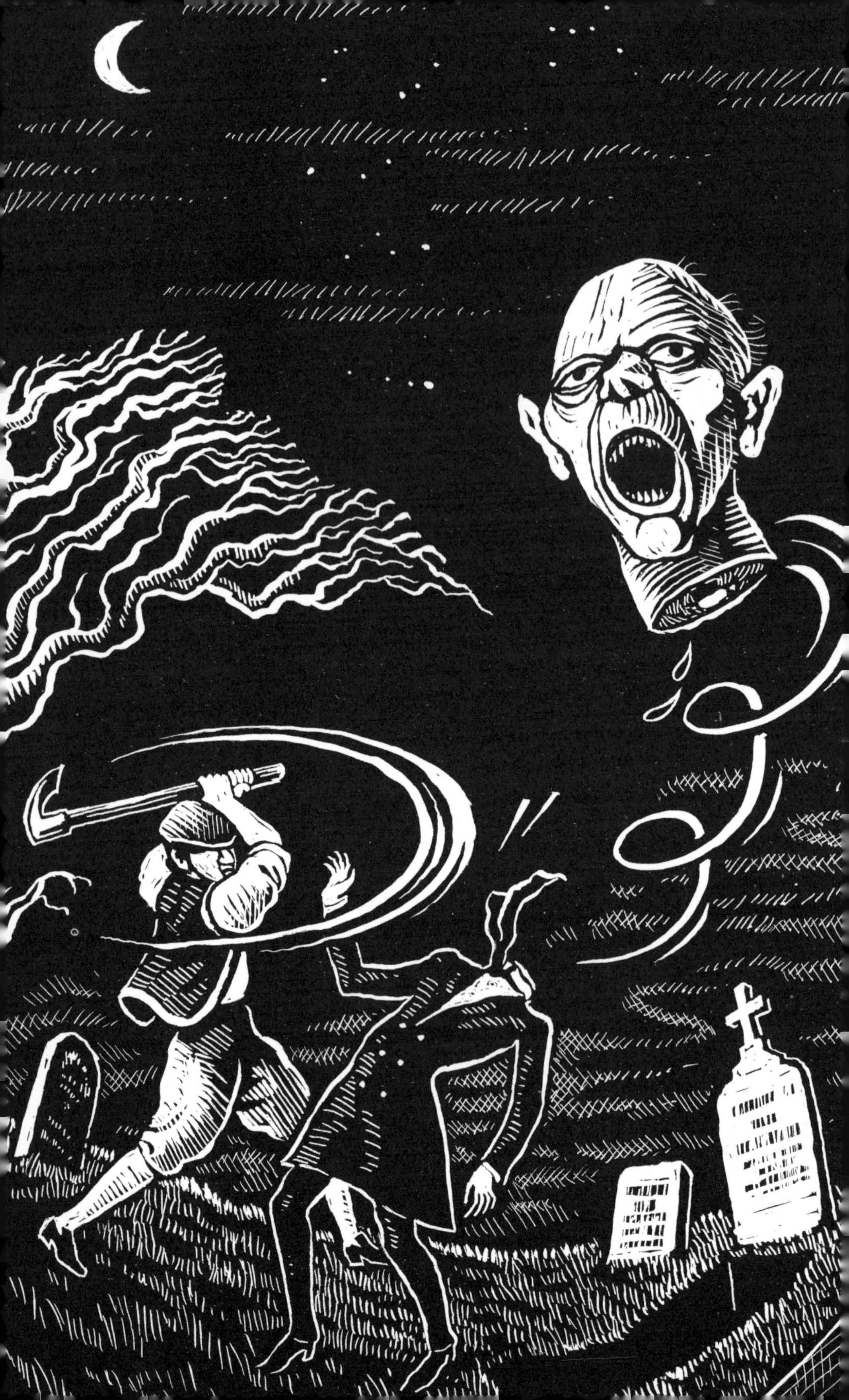

VAMPIRES

Vampires are certainly the most ubiquitous and influential of all myths from the Slavic world. They are not purely Slavic, with early stories of true belief in vampirism emerging from the Carpathian Mountains in Moldova – these territories are mixtures of Latin in their language and Slavic in their cultural traditions. It might be said that vampires are more of a Balkan phenomenon, with elements of their mythos derived from the border war zone with the Ottoman Turks.

While many might think that Bram Stoker's 1897 novel *Dracula* 'invented' vampires as we think of them today, with a nod to the fact that they had been a part of the mythology of many world cultures for centuries, this is not quite accurate. Indeed, vampires had been present in Slavic folklore for centuries. Their path led to *Dracula*, and the vampire mania of which it was the most influential part continues unabated even today. But that mania began to take off as a consequence of (primarily Serbian) folk beliefs coming under the concerned scrutiny of Austrian officials long before Stoker's work. These reports then made international newspaper headlines and intrigued the general public, inspiring the wave of literary vampire adventures that culminated in *Dracula*.

The *Oxford English Dictionary* identifies the earliest use of the word *vampire* as appearing in an essay called 'Travels of Three English Gentlemen', written in 1734 and anonymously published in 1745. Around 1725, Austrian officials had reported on a tradition in Serbia of digging up buried corpses and 'killing vampires'. Vampire lore, however, plays a role throughout Central and Eastern Europe. The actual term *vampire* is of uncertain origin, with one theory looking back to the Old Russian word *upyri*, 'to thrust violently', mentioned as a noun in a medieval Russian text called 'Word of Saint Grigoriy'.

CHAPTER ONE

Petar Skok, the greatest Croatian etymologist, describes *vampire* as an animalistic, folkloric term and suggests two combinations as to its origin. One is a loanword from North Turkish, *ubyr*, meaning 'witch', while the other is the Slavic *vampir*, literally meaning 'the one who doesn't fly'. Milan Budimir, linguist and paleobalkanologist, regards vampires as having originated as water demons, related to the word for otter, *vidra*. The Serbian word *vukodlak*, 'werewolf' (literally 'wolf fur'), was traditionally considered too frightening to speak aloud, so *vampir* was used in its place – a bit like in *Harry Potter* where, because Voldemort's name is too shocking to utter, he is referred to instead as 'He Who Must Not Be Named'. This has led to some conflation of the werewolf and vampire legends, but we'll address werewolves in a separate section.

The OED neglects to mention the first printed book to describe the practices of vampires and their hunters. This was published in 1689 and is called *Glory of the Duchy of Carniola*. Its author was Baron Janez Vajkard Valvasor, an aristocrat living in what was then the heart of the Habsburg Empire (now Slovenia) and writing in German. His work was sufficiently acclaimed and widely enough read, at least in the German edition, to win him honorary membership of London's famous Royal Society.

Valvasor was a polymath, publisher, scientist and ethnographer. He topped off an excellent education, supplemented by a home library and access to the best libraries in Europe, with fourteen years of travel, not only through Europe but also adventuring through 17th-century North Africa. He was interested in recording the folklore and traditions of his homeland, a region of present-day Slovenia called Carniola. Valvasor represents a fascinating fulcrum between absolute belief in magic and the supernatural, and a desire to seek a scientific, rational explanation for inexplicable phenomena. He genuinely, wholeheartedly believed in supernatural beings, and he was thoroughly religious (which of course requires a solid belief in the supernatural) – but he also sought scientific evidence to 'explain away' that which was universally considered the result of magic.

This is most obvious in his best-known investigation, that of the 'disappearing lake' of Cerknica, which for half the year is dry pastureland but during the other half, floods and becomes Slovenia's largest lake. Tradition had it that a group of witches performing rituals atop a local mountain controlled the flooding and draining of the lake. But while Valvasor believed in witchcraft, he was determined to find a more natural explanation, and he did so. This was part of the body of work that gained him honorary membership of the Royal Society, a generation or two before the Enlightenment made it the norm.

GIURE GRANDO

Valvasor records the story, dating from 1672, of Giure Grando, a vampire from the historical region of Istria (a peninsula in the northern Adriatic between Italy, Slovenia and Croatia). The traditions of vampire mythology, particularly the details of how a vampire can be killed, come straight from Valvasor's texts and, as we will see, are echoed in other eyewitness accounts from southern Slavic lands over the following century.

In the town of Krinck, the night after the burial of the freshly dead Giure Grando, a priest named Father George was enjoying a post-funeral meal with the Widow Grando and other relatives. On opening the door to leave, the priest saw 'the dead man sitting behind the door', at which point he fled. Giure was then spotted by numerous former acquaintances over the following few weeks, usually going from house to house, knocking on doors throughout the town. Residents of the houses on whose doors he knocked began to die, and the locals were not happy about it. Even the Widow Grando claimed to have seen him – and slept with him – before turning to the local sheriff, Miho Radetič (the first recorded vampire hunter) for protection.

A team of nine 'courageous neighbours', strengthened by quantities of 'strong spirits', set out carrying two lanterns and a crucifix. They opened Giure's grave, only to find 'the corpse's face flushed red; he turned and looked at them with a smile, then opened his mouth'. All nine vampire hunters freaked out – understandably, it must be said – and ran. The sheriff came to his senses and, Valvasor wryly comments, 'was quite annoyed to find that nine living men could not handle a single dead one and were transformed into rabbits at a single glance'.[9]

There were, apparently, several traditional methods of re-killing vampire corpses. The first one Sheriff Miho tried was to impale the suspiciously rubicund and mobile corpse in the stomach with a stake made of hawthorn. But Giure proved too resilient: the stake bounced off his stomach without piercing it.

Time for Plan B. Sheriff Miho summoned a priest who performed an exorcism rite, holding aloft the crucifix by lamplight and shouting repeatedly, 'Here is Jesus Christ, who saved us from damnation and died for us!' Giure's corpse began to weep. Another member of the team then tried to chop off Giure's head with a garden hoe, but he went at it half-heartedly. In stepped a local authority, Marshall Milasič, who used the hoe to 'send the dead man's head flying' (Valvasor is not shy about projectile body parts). As soon as it was severed, the head 'began to scream as if he were still living, and the grave filled with blood'. In a wonderfully matter-of-fact coda, Valvasor concludes the episode: 'And from that point on, Grando left his wife and other folk in peace.'[10]

Valvasor's tale is gory and vivid and he clearly had great fun in telling it. While the vampire tradition dates back far longer, with vampire-like monsters described in ancient tales in most of the world's cultures, we can credit the lively Baron Valvasor with having been the first to codify the vampire story, penned as fact, in a printed book.

PETER PLOGOJOWITZ

In the 1720s a local official, Kameralprovisor Frombald, was tasked by Emperor Charles VI with observing and reporting on the phenomenon of corpses being 'murdered' in the far reaches of the Habsburg Empire. A representative case from 1725 in Kisilova, part of Austrian-occupied

Serbia, involved a man named Peter Plogojowitz (or, in Serbian, Petar Blagojević).

Peter's death in 1725 was followed by the sudden deaths of nine other people over the course of eight days – each of whom had appeared ill for less than a single day. Several of the victims claimed before dying that Peter had appeared in their rooms and choked them. His wife, too, claimed that he had visited her after his death and requested his shoes. She moved to another village to escape him, but Peter's son then claimed that he had returned to his house and demanded food. The son had refused, and soon afterwards he became Peter's next victim.

The frightened villagers decided to disinter Peter's body to check for signs that they associated with vampires: lack of decomposition of the corpse and the continued growth of hair, beard and nails. Both Kameralprovisor Frombald and the local priest were asked to be present at the disinterment. Frombald insisted that permission must first be sought from the Austrian officials in Belgrade, but the villagers did not want to wait and (as they argued) risk more people falling victim to the vampire. The locals claimed that 'in Turkish times' – that is to say, when the area had been under the control of the Ottoman Empire prior to 1718 – whole communities had been wiped out by a single vampire.

Frombald had to acquiesce and, along with the priest, he bore witness to the disinterment of the body. He was shocked to see that Peter's corpse did indeed bear the signs the villagers had predicted. The body had hardly decomposed, the beard and hair were longer than when Peter had died, and it had 'new skin and nails', the old ones having fallen off. Not only that, but there was blood visible around Peter's mouth. This information was first published in 1728 in *De masticatione mortuorum in tumulis* by Michael Ranft, a text that sought to explain folk beliefs about vampires; then it was picked up by a popular Viennese newspaper, *Wienerisches Diarium*. According to that account, the villagers 'grew more outraged than distressed' – presumably because they had expected to find these signs of vampirism, whereas the Austrian official and the priest had not – and they drove a hawthorn stake through the corpse's heart. This caused a large quantity of 'completely fresh' blood to flow out of the ears and mouth of the body, which was subsequently burned. Ranft's text, which in proper Enlightenment style sought a rational explanation for a supernatural belief, explains:

> This brave man [Peter] perished by a sudden or violent death. This death, whatever it is, can provoke in the survivors the visions they had after his death. Sudden death gives rise to inquietude in the familiar circle. Inquietude has sorrow as a companion. Sorrow brings melancholy. Melancholy engenders restless nights and tormenting dreams. These dreams enfeeble body and spirit until illness overcomes and, eventually, death.[11]

Ranft guessed that the 'vampire' was in fact someone who had died of an infectious disease that was passed on to whoever accessed the corpse – or that the 'vampire' was the member of a family or community who had the most advanced version of a disease that was already present in the community. The first one to die was therefore blamed for the sickness and deaths of the others.

ARNOLD PAOLE AND THE VAMPIRES OF MEDVEĐA

A second case piqued the curiosity of Austrian officials in the Slavic dominion. Arnold Paole was a *hajduk* (a type of local militiaman, pronounced 'high-dook') in Medveđa, also part of Austrian Serbia. The story goes that Paole was bitten by a vampire while in Turkey before dying in an accident. He then rose from the dead and attacked locals: not only men, women and children, but sheep and cattle too. His body was exhumed, staked and burned. This case wound its way back to Empress Maria Theresa, who considered it particularly horrific and launched an investigation.

VAMPIRES

An infectious diseases specialist named Glaser was sent to Medveđa in December 1731, with a field surgeon following a month later. As Christopher Frayling notes in his history of literary vampires: 'The Austrians were occupying substantial parts of both Serbia and Wallachia, and they evidently wanted to find out more about the bizarre local customs near their garrison towns – particularly if these customs led to breaches of the peace.'[12] Glaser's account, as presented by the historian Ádám Mézes, contains various intriguing details:

> There used to be two women in the village who during their lifetime became vampirized (haben sich vervampyret), and it is said that after their death they will also become vampires and will vampirize (vervampyren) yet others.
>
> [...][The villagers] said that before getting themselves killed this way, they would rather settle somewhere else. Two or three households get together for the night, and while some sleep, the others keep watch. And [they also said that] the deaths would not cease until the Praiseworthy Administration agreed to and carried out the executions of the said vampires.
>
> [...] A woman named Miliza. Vampire (Vampÿer). Age fifty, lay for seven weeks. Came over from the Turkish side six years ago and settled in Medveđa. She[...]was never known to have believed or engaged in anything diabolical. However, she told the neighbors that in the Turkish land she had eaten of two lambs which had been killed by vampires and therefore, after her death she would also become a vampire. It was on this utterance that the common folk based their steadfast opinion. In fact, I have also seen such a person. And because [Miliza] was known to have had a dry, haggard body, was of old age and lay buried in the moist soil for seven weeks without any garb, she should have already been half-decayed. Nevertheless, she still had her mouth open,

light, fresh blood was flowing out of her nose and mouth, her body was bulging, and was suffused with blood, which appeared to be suspicious even for me. And these people cannot be wrong, [because] by contrast, after the opening of some other graves, [in which the cadavers] were of a younger age, used to have a bulkier constitution in life, and died of a shorter and easier sickness than those old people, [the younger bodies] were decayed the way regular corpses are supposed to be.[13]

Johannes Flückinger, the field surgeon, published his own report the following year (1732) with the title *Visum et Repertum* (Seen and Discovered); in it, he describes a total of eleven bodies being exhumed, eight of which were judged to be vampiric. Part of what made these grotesque accounts so compelling was the ostensible reliability of the officials, who wrote them up as objective observations of local traditions. Flückinger's report states: 'I affirm, together with the assistant medical officers dispatched to me, that all these things took place just as we have reported them at Medveđa, in Serbia, on 7 January 1732.'[14] His account is signed by himself – 'Johannes Flückinger, Regimental Field Surgeon' – and four others.

To be clear, none of these officers claimed to have encountered a vampire, simply to have observed an absolute belief in vampires among the local populace. As Mézes explains, their investigations were 'born out of a practical and urgent pressure to make sense of the public health situation in Medveđa and to be able to give an expert opinion for further judicial action'.[15] There is an element of patronizing colonialism to the accounts of 'civilized' Austrian military men reporting on the barbaric practices of Slavic rural peasants, and religious differences would also have coloured their views: the Austrians were almost exclusively Roman Catholic, while the locals who believed in vampires were Orthodox. The Catholic focus on not violating the dead abhorred the idea of disinterring a corpse from a graveyard and, effectively, killing it again.

Nevertheless, coupling reliable narrators with a vampire story implied that vampires might really exist, and the story snowballed from there, making its way to England. According to the writer and antiquarian Horace Walpole, King George II believed in it – and in vampires more generally. Walpole wrote: 'I know that our late King, though not apt to believe more than his neighbours, had not doubt of the existence of vampires, and their banquets on the dead.'[16]

THE TRANSNATIONAL VAMPIRE CRAZE

These accounts soon spilled out beyond the confines of Austria-Hungary. The French Benedictine monk and intellectual Antoine Augustin Calmet wrote about vampires in his 1746 *Dissertations on Apparitions of Angels, of Spirits and of Revenants and Vampires from Hungary, Bohemia, Moravia and Silesia*. This was an early, extensive compilation of vampire stories (with an analysis of their role in mythology), cultural legends and questioning accounts of historically documented cases. The book was so popular that it was republished in 1751 with further studies and accompanied by letters sent to Calmet in praise of the first edition. Calmet considered the possibility that vampires do exist, though he did not state a conclusion.

An article entitled 'Political Vampyres' in the May 1732 number of London's *Gentleman's Magazine* summarized the understanding of vampires first in terms of historical accounts – but this was used as a stepping stone to an analogy with politicians 'feeding' off the lifeblood of their constituents:

> This account of *Vampyres*, you'll observe, comes from the Eastern Part of the World, always remarkable for its *Allegorical Style*. The States of *Hungary* are in subjection to the *Turks* and *Germans* .... These *Vampyres* are said to torment and kill the *Living* by *sucking out all their Blood*; and a *ravenous Minister*, in this part of the World, is compared to a *Leech* or *Bloodsucker*, and carries his

CHAPTER ONE

> Oppressions beyond the Grave...must gradually drain the Body Politick of its Blood and Spirits....Paul Arnold [a mangled anglicization of Arnold Paole, the Serbian vampire], who is call'ed a Hajduke, was only a *Ministerial Tool*, because it is said he had kill'd but 4 Persons; whereas, if he had been a *Vampyre* of any Rank, we should probably have heard of his *Ten Thousands*....*As to the driving A Stake through the Heart of Arnold, at which he gave a horrid Groan*, this seems an argument that the whole Story is a Fable, us'd to convey a satirical Invective against some *living Oppressor*....The Blood which Arnold lost might figure the making him refund the *corrupt Wages* which he had suck'd out of the Veins of his Countrymen....Private Persons may be *Vampyres*...but nothing less than the Power of a *Treasury* can raise up a compleat *Vampyre*.[17]

Voltaire also drew analogies between vampires and political or official figures: 'Kings are not, properly speaking, vampires. The true vampires are the churchmen who eat at the expense of both the king and the people.'[18] Thus the 18th century saw vampires as so ubiquitous a concept that they'd become idiomatic, while true accounts of belief in vampires in remote Slavic communities filtered in, titillating in their horror. A French newspaper, *Gazette Française*, on 26 October 1770 published a news piece indicative of the rampant interest in vampires throughout Europe:

> The madness of Vampires, which caused such a sensation in Hungary many years ago, has just broken out again in a little town on the borders of Moldavia, accompanied by events which are as horrible as they are bizarre. The plague having entered the town, a few impostors persuaded some of the lower class of persons that a sure way of keeping the contagion under control was to tear out the teeth of the plague-ridden corpses and suck the blood out of the gums. This disgusting practice caused many

people to perish, despite the care that the Police took to prevent it from taking place.[19]

Efforts were made to explain away vampires in scientific terms, as per the rationalism of the Enlightenment. The most probable explanation for the origins of the very genuine and ubiquitous belief in vampires in rural Slavic communities, from Istria to Serbia to Moldova, likely stems from the unfortunate frequency of premature burial. Poor understanding of medicine resulted in not infrequent incidents of people being declared dead when they were not, in fact, quite there yet. Fear of premature burial was so widespread that high-end coffins were designed with bells attached, so that, should a victim wake to find him- or herself buried in a coffin but still conscious, they could ring a bell and summon assistance. Some prematurely buried individuals might manage to break out of their tombs before suffocating and it is easy to imagine how the sight of someone recently buried and mourned, now staggering around a graveyard covered in blood (likely their own, if they had smashed their way through a wooden coffin and a layer of soil), might have prompted imaginative supernatural explanations. There are likewise scientific explanations for why hair and nails can continue to grow after death, and why some corpses may appear bloated and flushed crimson. Suffice it to say that there were likely some true anecdotal accounts linked to premature burial that acted as sparks to the bonfire of vampire legend in these rural communities. The 'solutions' to these problems can be explained practically: staking a corpse in its grave would pin it down, so that it could not wander about and wreak havoc. Burning the corpse would likewise render nocturnal perambulations impossible.

VUK KARADŽIĆ

While Baron Valvasor was the most important chronicler of folk legends and habits in the lands of Slovenia, that role in Serbia goes to Vuk Karadžić. It is difficult to overstate the importance of Karadžić as an ethnographer covering a region that extended well beyond contemporary Serbian borders and touched upon Bosnia, Montenegro and parts of Croatia – between Valvasor and Karadžić, the traditions of the southern Slavs are well covered. His banishment from Serbia in the 1810s, after he got on the wrong side of the despotic ruler Miloš Obrenović, led him to settle in Vienna and as a consequence he became all the more influential. There in the heart of the Austro-Hungarian Empire, as the city's leading Serbian intellectual and writer, he was called upon by Austrians to explain Serbians (among other things, he was a significant source for Leopold von Ranke's important text *The Serbian Revolution*), and in turn his fellow Serbians looked to him to better understand themselves. He was in regular touch with leading European cultural figures including Goethe, Alexander von Humboldt, Jacob Grimm and the great Montenegrin poet Petar Petrović Njegoš.

His influence was particularly felt in the field of linguistics. In 1850 a treaty of languages was signed in Vienna, fixing one language for both Serbs and Croats: so-called Serbo-Croatian. That treaty endured a storm-tossed history; today the two states, both originating in former Yugoslavia, claim linguistic independence. The same goes for Bosnian and Montenegrin, although in practice the languages are (nearly) identical; those who claim that they are different do so for political reasons. So too did Karadžić's writing in Serbian feel like a political action. He wrote in a vernacular that he called the 'language of shepherds' to distinguish it from highly formal Church Serbian.

Karadžić was particularly remarkable in that he was self-taught and had none of the advantages from birth that were prerequisites for most scholars. He received numerous honorary degrees from European universities, but never a traditional one. His writings were divisive. He produced a new translation of the New Testament, which the Serbian Orthodox Church refused to accept as valid. Much of his extensive writing was not published until the 1970s, more than a century after his death.

VAMPIRES

For our purposes, Karadžić's recording of Serbian ethnography is important because of its influence on the Austrian conception of the Slavs within their dominion. Karadžić wrote on many folk traditions, including werewolves and vampires. The two best-known Slavic mythological monsters are sometimes conflated in his work – notably in the *Serbian Dictionary*, written in collaboration with Jernej Kopitar, a Slovenian censor at the Vienna court, and first printed in Vienna in 1818.

> A werewolf is a man who, forty days after his death, is inhabited by some devilish spirit, and he returns to life ('vampirizes', becomes a vampire). Then he rises from the grave by night and sucks blood from people in their homes. An honest man cannot become a vampire unless a bird or any other animal wanders across his corpse. Therefore, the recently deceased are always guarded so that animals do not cross them. Werewolves usually appear in winter, from Christmas to Spasovdan (when Christ rose from the grave; part of the Easter tradition). When people start dying in large numbers in a village, rumours swirl that a werewolf is in the graveyard (and some will swear that they saw him, wearing his funeral shroud draped over his shoulder at night), and they start guessing who became a vampire. Sometimes they take a young black stud horse without patches on its hide, and they lead him to walk over graves in which they suspect the werewolf could lurk. They do this because they say that such a stud will not and could not walk over the grave of the werewolf. If they are convinced that they've identified the grave, it happens that they open the grave. All the villagers gather with hawthorn stakes (for he only fears a hawthorn stake – a saying goes 'let him find hawthorn and madder on his way', because hawthorn grows above madder), and then they open the coffin. If they find a man who did not decompose, they run the stakes through him, throw the remains into a fire and let it burn. They say that sometimes they'll find a werewolf who

grew fat, bloated and rubicund with human blood (a saying goes 'red as a vampire'). A werewolf might visit his wife, especially if she is pretty and young, to sleep with her and they also say that a child conceived with a werewolf would be born without bones. In times of hunger, a werewolf is often seen around mills, wheat and corn reserves.[20]

There's a lot to unpack in this short passage, but perhaps most striking is the consistency of Slavic legends and traditions, from the case of Giure Grando in Istria to Serbia and beyond: of unexplained deaths in remote villages (for vampires in folk traditions are rural or village apparitions, not urban monsters); of graves opened to reveal bloated, red-cheeked, intact corpses; and of eliminating suspected vampires by impaling them with stakes of hawthorn wood.

Karadžić is also the source of an explanation for the use of hawthorn stakes as a preferred weapon. In the Balkans, the blood-red berries of the hawthorn tree are used in traditional medicine for heart problems. Hawthorn wood is very strong, so it makes for a sturdy stake, but its association with fixing problems of the heart is likely also significant in terms of piercing the heart of a vampire. A Serbian saying recorded by Karadžić can be roughly translated as: 'This guy could be hurt only by a hawthorn stick' – referring to someone who is physically and psychologically very tough. Hawthorn (*glog* in Serbian) was also employed as a preventive measure against vampires: a branch of hawthorn would be suspended over the head of a deceased person laid out at home prior to burial. There were recorded instances that were a step more grisly: sometimes a thorn from the hawthorn tree was forced into the bellybutton of the deceased. Thorns were likewise stuck into the earth above the graves of those who, it was feared, might rise again. A hawthorn branch might be fixed to the door of a home as a sort of vampire repellent, and a piece of hawthorn wood might be incorporated into a protective amulet worn by children. It was a Slavic tradition to present sacrificial objects before a hawthorn tree: cakes, flowers, herbs, even horseshoes. This was linked to an ancient belief that hawthorn trees might be home to demons, who would remain in the tree if offerings were brought to them; if not, they might get a bit peckish and venture out into the village. They were thought to fear metal, so the horseshoes were meant to hem them in to the tree.

An ancient cosmological myth in Serbia says that the whole world sits upon a hawthorn tree, which is constantly being bitten by a black dog. When the dog bites deeply into the tree, the tree starts to fall; this is the origin of earthquakes. But, as a later Christian addition to this myth explains, Saint Peter then shakes his stick and the hawthorn tree is once again set upright, ending the earthquake.

Hawthorn was not resonant only for Slavs; Germanic tribes used it in burial practices, as recorded by Tacitus. The hawthorn tree was said to mark the division between the worlds of the living and the dead. Ancient Greek and Roman traditions also mention hawthorn as effective in fending off demons and witches, and in preventing the dead from reappearing.

Karadžić demonstrates his bold independence by using the words for werewolf, *vukodlak*, and vampire, *vampir*, interchangeably in the *Serbian Dictionary*. The very appearance of the word *vukodlak* would have shocked some readers. Karadžić's own Christian name, Vuk, means 'wolf' in Serbian and was given to him as a sort of a talisman to protect him from demons who, his parents believed, were killing newborns in the family. The word itself was a totem that helped him survive.

SAVA SAVANOVIĆ

The story of Sava Savanović is the most famous of Serbian vampire tales – and as we have seen, Serbia was the cradle of vampire lore. In 1973, while Serbia was still a part of Yugoslavia, the tale was adapted into what is now regarded as the first Serbian horror film, *Leptirica*.

However, the best-known version, based on local oral legends, is that written by Milovan Glišić, a beloved 19th-century writer and

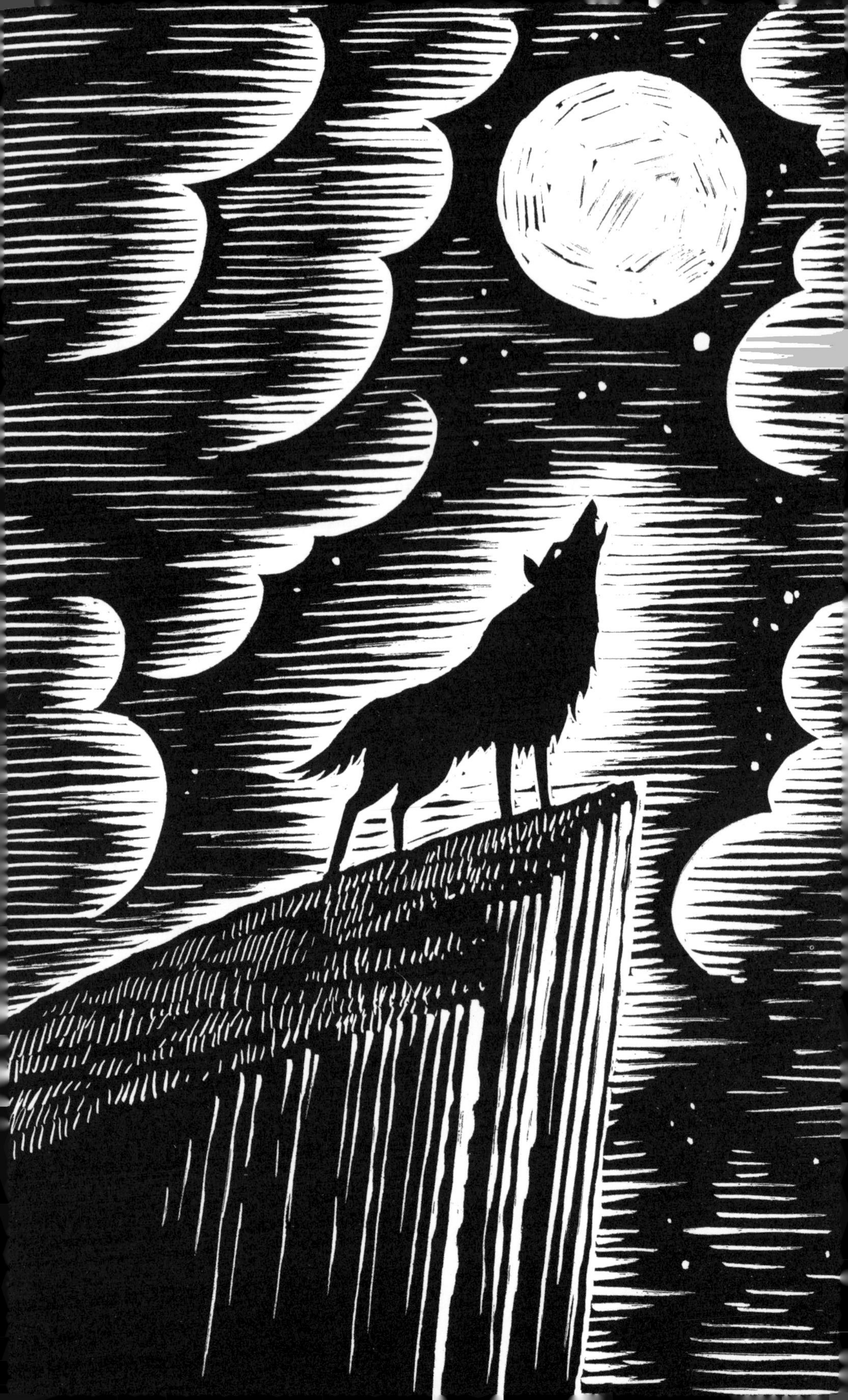

translator from French and Russian who has been called 'the Serbian Gogol'. Glišić knew Vuk Karadžić and admired him; he filled his vampire story with resonant references to Karadžić's ethnography, intermingled with the traditions of northern Slavic writers like Gogol. It first appeared in 1880 under the title 'After Ninety Years'. While it features some of the elements we now typically associate with vampires (silver inflicting damage while other metals do not; hawthorn stakes), in other ways it diverges from the familiar *Dracula*-influenced concept.

The mill that has for nearly a century been associated with the story is located three kilometres from the road that links Bajina Bašta and Valjevo (where Glišić was born) in the Rogačica river valley, and was still in active use as recently as the 1950s. Even after that it remained a site of touristic interest, and in 2010 some locals began planning to repair it and make it into a proper tourist attraction; however, it collapsed in 2012 before renovations could begin. Municipal authorities, with a dry sense of humour, announced that Sava Savanović was finally free to find a new home. The project was renewed in 2018 and, at the time of writing, is still under way.

STOKING THE VAMPIRE LEGEND

The popularization of vampire lore can safely be described as a craze that continued throughout most of the 19th century and was then revived in the second half of the 20th. It's not our purpose here to trace the cultural interest in vampires beyond its Slavic origins, but it is worth noting that it was authors from the British Isles who first brought this curious, marginal belief to the attention of a wider public. We should also mention in passing some historical figures whose renowned cruelty led to them being called 'vampires', but in this context the term was used more as a general slur – rather like calling someone a 'demon' or the 'devil incarnate' – than as a literal accusation of vampirism. One such example is the Hungarian-Slovakian countess Elizabeth Báthory (1560–1614), who was said to bathe in the blood of virgins to maintain her complexion. She was accused of torturing and murdering some 300 women and girls. She may have done this – the evidence is circumstantial and based on testimony given under torture, so it would not stand up in court today – but although she will pop up in a search for 'vampires', her story is more accurately one of (alleged) serial, wanton sadism.

The first work of vampire fiction proper was penned in the early 19th century by twenty-year-old John Polidori, who briefly served as personal physician to Lord Byron. The oft-told origin story of two of literature's most famous monsters begins during a rain-soaked holiday in Switzerland in June 1816, at the Villa Diodati overlooking Lake Geneva. Byron, his friend and fellow poet Percy Bysshe Shelley, and a handful of relatives and companions took a holiday there together, drawn by the famously sublime, sweeping views of the Alps, but the poor weather obliged them to stay inside.

They came across a French translation of a German book of ghost stories (*Fantasmagoriana, or a History of Apparitions, Spectres, Revenants, etc.*, translated by Jean-Baptiste Benoît Eyriès) at the villa. Inspired by it, they decided to invent their own supernatural stories to tell one another. Percy Shelley's young wife, Mary Wollstonecraft Shelley, was part of the group and developed what would become the most enduring creation of that dark and rainy night: her novel *Frankenstein*. Byron came up with a sketch of a story about a vampire, featuring a British aristocrat who joins a young man on a trip to Turkey and dies in a graveyard there – but not before promising to return from the dead a month later. Polidori purloined this idea, although his version of the origin story frames him as an innocent. As Christopher Frayling describes: 'Polidori had rewritten, and expanded, Byron's story during "two or three idle mornings" to while away the time in the summer of 1816, while Byron and Shelley were otherwise engaged. He left his manuscript behind in Geneva and thought no more of it. Someone then sent this to a publisher in London, without his consent, or so he subsequently claimed.'[21]

Polidori was fired by Byron soon afterwards. In England that year 'The Vampyre' was published by one Henry Colburn, who had recently enjoyed commercial success publishing *Glenarvon* by Lady Caroline Lamb, a former lover of Byron's who modelled her fictional Glenarvon on him. It was a year of bestsellers linked to Byron. Part of the trick was that 'The Vampyre' was marketed as a secret story by Byron, who was then at the height of his fame: the published version had a cover featuring the initials 'L. B.', so the public largely assumed that it was his work. It was even included in some later collections of his writings. The story was an immediate success, much to Byron's confusion and annoyance, and its renown spawned what might be called the first wave of vampire literature.

Polidori's vampire is called Lord Ruthven. He is described as having a 'dead grey eye', his face is a 'deadly hue', and he rises from the grave in that Turkish cemetery to exsanguinate London high society. If a pale aristocrat from the Balkans returning from the dead and terrorizing England sounds familiar, it should: what began with Byron and Polidori was picked up with delight by a fascinated Victorian public. Many copycats (or should it be copybats?) followed. 'The Vampyre' lived on, turned into a hit stage play and innumerable spinoffs and alternative versions, but always largely maintaining the idea of the vampire as aristocrat. In short, the popular literary form of the vampire has always been based on Lord Byron himself, a serial 'devourer' of women. The sexual aspect of vampires as incubi – men who come to your bedside in the night and suck on you, ingesting your bodily fluid – seemed to hold great appeal for Victorian readers. A sensational serial novel of the 1840s called *Varney the Vampire* continued the tradition and was a significant influence on Bram Stoker, Irish theatrical manager of the era's most famous stage actor, Henry Irving (who may have served as partial inspiration for Count Dracula).

Stoker's 1897 novel *Dracula* firmly established vampires, and the title character above all, in the popular imagination around the globe. He drew upon the story of a real-life Hungarian warlord, Vlad Tepes, in his depiction of the vampire Dracula (a name derived from the Romanian for 'dragon'), who can be killed in limited ways – the most famous of

CHAPTER ONE

which is to have a wooden, ideally hawthorn, stake driven through his chest in an echo of Tepes's nickname 'the Impaler'. Impaling was a Turkish execution method inherited from the Byzantines in which a victim was pierced through the abdomen with a sharpened wooden stake and then fixed into the ground. Tepes, while in prison in Turkey, had duly noted the benefits of intimidation and fear offered by this technique, and consequently adopted impaling in his later campaigns against the Turks. He reigned from 1448 until 1477, pre-dating by two centuries the historical record of vampire traditions – but it can be assumed that those traditions were centuries, if not millennia, old.

Scholars have identified many of the books Stoker read while working on *Dracula*. He learned about Vlad Tepes, for instance, from the *Account of the Principalities of Wallachia and Moldavia* (1820) and *General History of the Turks* (1603). It is unlikely that he read Karadžić or Valvasor (even now, Valvasor's writings are not available in English), but the earliest printed vampire stories had already spread throughout Europe. Stoker probably heard of the Serbian vampire Arnold Paole through a version of the story that appeared in Robert Southey's 1801 vampire book, *Thalaba the Destroyer* – so direct access to primary sources was not essential to an understanding of the key vampire stories and traditions. The concept of a vampire hunter who is also a doctor, like Stoker's Abraham van Helsing, seems to have been inspired by accounts of the medically qualified Austrian officials who were sent to investigate Paole.

As ideals of womanhood changed during the late 19th century, female vampires began to appear in various cultural contexts. Some were succubae, female demons who appeared in their victims' bedrooms while they slept and fed on their life energy. Edvard Munch's haunting 1893 painting *Love and Pain* was immediately given the nickname 'The Vampire', though not by the artist; and in literature, the lesbian vampire came to the fore in Sheridan Le Fanu's story 'Carmilla' (1871). Later, during and after the catastrophe of manliness known as the First World War, the vampire femme fatale became such a familiar figure that the word was shortened to 'vamp'.

Vampires are now so ubiquitous that they must surely qualify as a Jungian archetype, a much-beloved monster breed that has been en vogue to varying degrees ever since the 18th century. In the 20th century, British newspapers reported on the appearance of a vampire in the centre of Belgrade, throwing stones at passers-by. Expressionism embraced vampires, most famously in F. W. Murnau's 1922 film *Nosferatu*. By the beginning of the 21st century, you couldn't bite a neck without bumping into one of pop culture's many vampires, whether in the *Twilight* series, *Blade*, *Interview with a Vampire* or *True Blood*. While *Buffy the Vampire Slayer* and *Abraham Lincoln: Vampire Hunter* may have come and gone, there remains no shortage of vampires in the age of streaming, whether you like them camp (*Van Helsing*, with its slogan 'Slay all day') or more sophisticated (*Preacher*, in which vampirism is more an intellectual device than an excuse for rampant bloodletting).

Vampires are frequently referenced in any context where one entity flourishes by draining the life force of another. While their origin stories are southern Slavic, northern Slavs appropriated the idea and embraced its allegorical potential. Karl Marx's *Das Kapital* includes, in chapter 10, the lines: 'Capital is dead labour that, vampire-like, only lives by sucking living labour, and lives the more, the more labour it sucks.'[22] Perhaps Marx had read Vuk Karadžić, because he too conflates analogies about vampires and werewolves, describing 'the werewolf's hunger for surplus labour' and observing that 'the prolongation of the working day quenches only in a slight degree the vampire thirst for the living blood of labour'.[23] As noted by Christopher Frayling, in the same chapter Marx references a historical anecdote about a 'Wallachian Boyard' who leeched much of his peasants' labour to pay for his own feudal estate. This Wallachian Boyard was, in fact, Vlad Tepes.

Today, belief in vampires remains alive and well. In Serbia – even in the metropolitan capital, Belgrade – it is still not customary for mourners at a funeral to leave the cemetery en masse. After the service, the assembled will depart in different directions as a precaution to confuse the dead, lest they decide to rise, follow and take revenge. Only afterwards will the party reassemble at a predetermined place, usually a tavern. But before they go, they believe that it is important to laugh at a funeral – a tradition that was present in ancient Greece as well, because loud voices and sounds are efficient at keeping malevolent souls away.[24]

A forced laugh, perhaps, before setting off with a stout hawthorn walking stick by your side.

2

AT STAKE
◆
WEREWOLVES

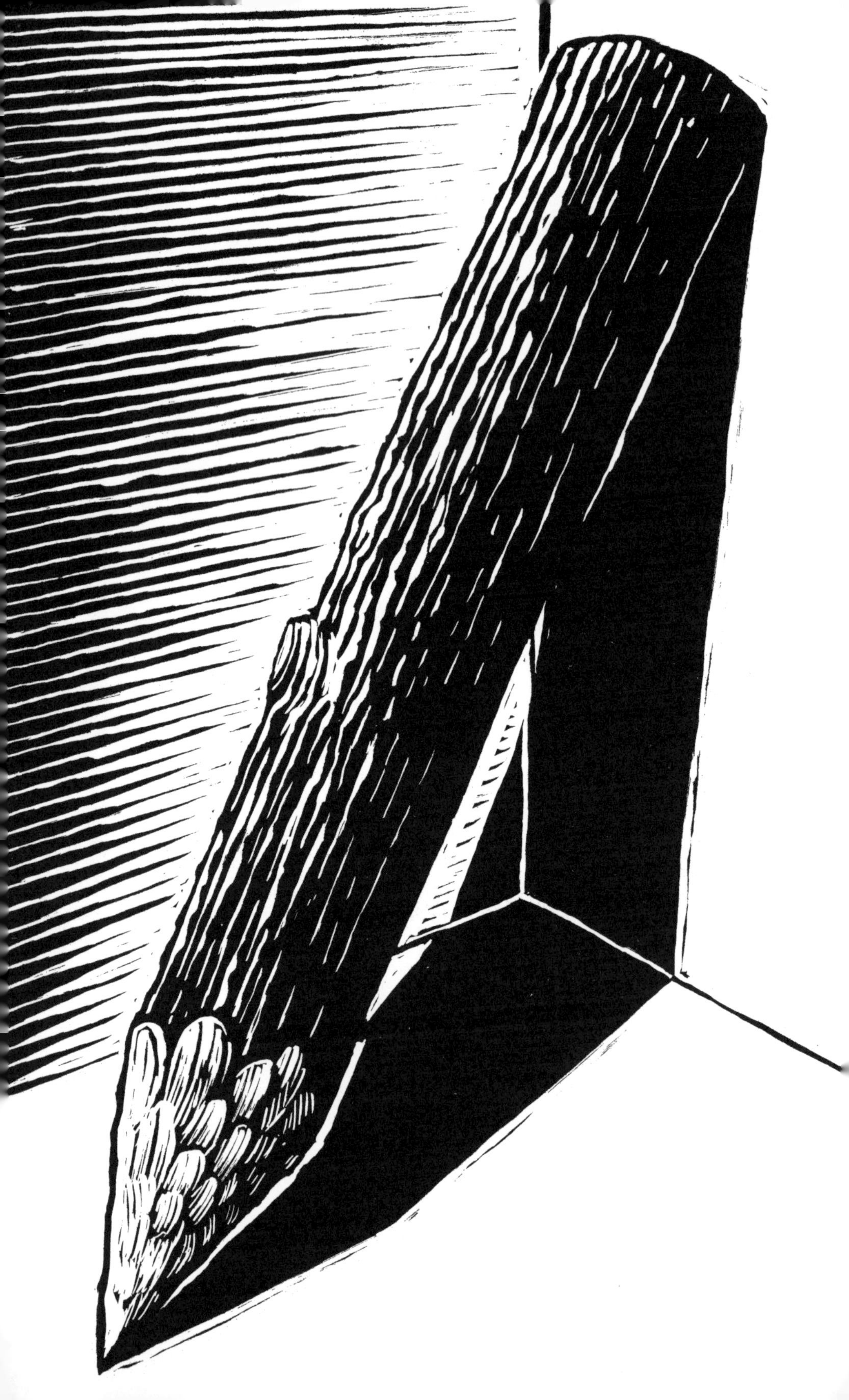

AT STAKE

'Where is the stake?' he cried. 'Where did you hide the stake?'

He turned to the thing before him. 'What have you done with my boy? Give me back my son!' As he spoke the blood drained from his face, making him as pale as the creature at which he screamed. 'The stake, where is the stake?! I'll have the head of whoever hid it!'

◆

'Woman,' Đorđe suddenly asked his wife, making the family jump in their seats. 'What time did he leave?'

The wife turned to him. 'At eight o'clock. I heard the monastery bell.'

'Good,' Đorđe replied. 'It's not yet time.' His eyes swivelled back to the long, lonely white road that lanced through the aspen forest.

A pendulous silence was broken by one of the children tugging on his mother's apron. 'When is Grandpa coming home?'

His mother recoiled and smacked the young boy, who began to cry.

Đorđe turned, red-faced, to their guest, the Marquis d'Urfe. 'Please accept our apologies, Monsieur Marquis. You see, if he comes back too late, then we will know that he is...A *vukodlak* cannot enter into a household unless his name is spoken on the day of his arrival, and he is invited in. My children do not know this, but now...'

'A *vukodlak*?' the Marquis replied in halting Serbian. 'Your father?'

Đorđe kept his eyes on the white road, bounded by wisps of mist, while he spoke. 'We are honoured by your presence, and you are welcome at our humble inn, but you pass through our village at a bad moment. Ten days ago, my father...'

His wife gasped, but he hushed her with a gesture. 'It's too late anyway, Zorja, the boy has already said his name. My father, Gorča,

CHAPTER TWO

set out to join a local militia hunting for a Turkish bandit called Alibeg who has been terrorizing our land. Before leaving, he called me and my brother, Petar, over to him and said, "My sons, I'm going up to the mountains to join the brave men who are chasing this dog. Wait for me for ten days. If I do not return by the tenth, say a mass for my soul, for I will have perished."' Đorđe paused and took a long breath before continuing. '"But if – God forbid – I should return *after* ten days, for your own sakes, do not let me in! If this happens, I command you to forget that I was once your father, no matter what I say or do. You must impale my heart with a hawthorn stake, for I will be a cursed *vukodlak* returned to murder you all." Today is the tenth day.'

The Marquis looked around the room. It was the kitchen of a small inn in a village called Our Lady of the Oak, halfway between Bosnia and Moldova, where he had been sent on a diplomatic mission from Versailles. Having worked as an ambassador in the past, the Marquis spoke some Slavic languages and could get by among the locals. This village was tumbledown, without a cobble on its streets, just a clutch of houses within a clearing in the aspen forest. Its only landmark was at the very edge of the village: the monastery, manned by a few elderly Orthodox monks, which gave the village its name.

The Marquis had stopped once before at this same village and stayed at this same inn. What had made him detour to reach it this time was his affection for a daughter of the family, Zdenka. Her beauty had haunted him since his first visit and he had been delighted to find her just as lovely, and still unmarried, when he arrived this morning. But it seemed he had chosen the wrong time to come. And now he would have to stay at least two days, until a new coach and horses could be sent to fetch him and bring him on to his business in Moldova.

Around the table sat Petar and his wife; Đorđe's wife; their young sister Zdenka; and four children under the age of ten. Đorđe paced. The chair by the fire, belonging to the patriarch of the family, sat conspicuously empty.

'I am sorry for your troubles,' said the Marquis as politely as he could. 'But what is a *vukodlak*?'

Petar looked up from the table, where he had been sharpening a hawthorn wood stake to a fine point with his pocket knife. 'It is a word we normally do not say. Sometimes we called them *vampir*. It means "the one who wears the wolfskin". They are the result of a curse. Vuk, the god of our ancestors, brought us power, and our predecessors worshipped wolves. But among the wolves there are also demons. *Vukodlaki* are men who have been killed by other *vukodlaki*. They do not die as most men do. They are not devoured, but are drained of their blood. They then become bloodless wolf-men and are known for slaying their own...' But here Petar's voice trailed off.

'They cannot be killed as you would kill normal men,' Đorđe continued. 'If they are cut, they do not bleed and their wounds heal – unless they are cut with silver, which acts like a poison in them.'

'Or unless the weapon remains within them, to prevent the wound from closing,' Petar resumed, holding up the stake.

The Marquis was a man of enlightenment and these local folk tales seemed charming but meaningless to him. Still, he could feel the tension in the room, and it infected his body even if his mind did not believe.

The old monastery clock tolled the first of eight strokes. The family froze, all eyes locked on the road through the trees beyond the dirty, skin-thin windowpane.

'Is that him?' Đorđe whispered.

In the distance, a lone figure walked the road towards them.

'It's him, God be praised,' Zdenka cried. 'He's not too late...Is he?'

'God protect us,' said Petar, 'how do we know if ten days have passed?'

They looked once more, terror in their eyes, as the figure loped towards them. It was suddenly far closer than seemed logical for the time that had passed. It was now close enough that the Marquis could see a tall, bone-thin old man with a full, silver moustache curved on either side of his nose, like a scimitar. He limped painfully, leaning on a stick, a long musket strapped across his back and a burlap sack over his shoulder.

Đorđe's eyes hardened. The children jumped up and made for the door to greet their grandfather, but Đorđe slammed his fist upon the table. They stopped and returned to their seats.

Then Gorča's face appeared in the window.

'Well?' he said. 'Will no one stand to greet me? Will no one invite me in? Don't you see that I'm wounded?'

'Help your father,' the Marquis said in an involuntary flush of compassion. 'Bring him a drink, can't you see he's about to faint?'

Đorđe glared at the Marquis but nodded. He crossed to the door, threw it open, but said to Gorča, 'Father, show me your wound. I want to help you, believe me, I do...'

'Can't you see the blood?' said Gorča. 'And the wolves. They were following me. I barely got away, but...'

There was blood staining his shoulder, which seemed to reassure Đorđe. Then, from the forest beyond the village, rose a canon of howls that made the Marquis's skin crawl.

'*Volkovi*,' said Zdenka. 'Come in, Father, and close the door behind you. They smell your blood. They hunt you.'

'Thank you, my child,' Gorča said. He limped inside, pushing past Đorđe, who was not sure whether to bar him entry or embrace him in compassion.

With difficulty, Gorča sat at the table. The family looked to his chair by the fire, then back at him, confused.

The grandchildren came to embrace Gorča.

'But you're cold as bone,' said one.

'Tell us of your adventures,' said another.

Gorča nodded. 'I will tell you what happened to me in the mountains, but some other time. I'm tired. But I can tell you this. The bandit Alibeg is no more, and it was by my hand that he perished. I have brought with me proof, if anyone dares to doubt it.'

With this, he opened the burlap sack that he carried on his shoulder. Out of it, onto the table, rolled a severed head. Its eyes were rolled back into its skull, and its Turkish-style moustache was caked with gore.

Gorča looked down on it with pride. 'Hang it over the door, so that all who pass will know that Alibeg is dead and the roads are free of bandits. Other than the Sultan's Janissaries, of course.'

Petar obeyed. He was hiding something behind his back. The Marquis realized it was the hawthorn stake. He watched as Petar secretly passed it to his wife, then picked up the severed head by its hair and carried it outside.

The Marquis was relieved to be shown to his room as night swiftly descended on the village. Despite his fervent logic, he was shaken by what he had seen and heard. He washed in a shared bath and returned to his room. A door nearby was open. Through the doorway, he could see Zdenka removing her blouse from her shoulder.

'Marquis.' The voice startled him. It was Đorđe. 'Your room is this way, sir.'

The Marquis lay in bed. He was the only guest at the inn, but the walls were thin and he could hear the family speaking.

'The neck, did you see it?'
'Yes. It looked torn, not sliced cleanly.'
'As if it were cut not with a sword, but...'
'...Gnawed.'
'I'll keep watch tonight. The old man is asleep and looks peaceful, but...'

Fatigue triumphed, and the Marquis closed his heavy eyes.

◈

Then he was awake again. He was in that state between slumber and alertness, when one is not sure if one dreams. He thought that the door to his room was open, although he was certain he had closed it. It seemed to him that there was a silhouette, tall and thin, standing in the doorway. He imagined that it must be Gorča, but he could

CHAPTER TWO

not tell. The Marquis remained perfectly still as the silhouette drifted towards him. Now it loomed above his bed. He could smell cadaverous breath. Surely this must be a nightmare! Terrified, he willed himself to wake.

And wake he did. He breathed heavily, covered in sweat, but he saw that he was alone in the room and the door was closed. He exhaled in relief, until he looked to the window.

There, his face framed within it, pressed up against the pane, was old Gorča, staring in through the window with all-white eyes.

The Marquis stifled a scream and had the presence of mind to remain still, pretending to sleep, as if he had seen nothing. This required a supreme effort but it appeared to work, as Gorča peeled his face away from the glass. He must have been only checking that the Marquis slept.

Then he heard a voice from the room beside his own, which belonged to one of Đorđe's children, a boy of about ten.

'Little one, you cannot sleep?' It was Gorča's voice.

A child replied. 'No, Grandfather. I want to hear about your adventures.'

'What do you want to know?'

'How you fought the Turks! I want to go fight the Turks, too, like you.'

Gorča laughed without mirth. 'You know I brought you a *yatagan*, a Turkish dagger, that I took from Alibeg. I'll give it to you... Tomorrow, maybe.'

'No, Grandfather, please, please give it to me now!'

'Very well, little one. But let's go outside. I don't want to wake your father, he would be cross with me.'

'Yes, yes! I promise not to make a sound!'

The Marquis heard the creak of the bed as the child rose. A moment later, the door to the inn was shut.

Instinctively, the Marquis leapt out of bed and tore to the door, determined to save the child, but it had been locked from the outside!

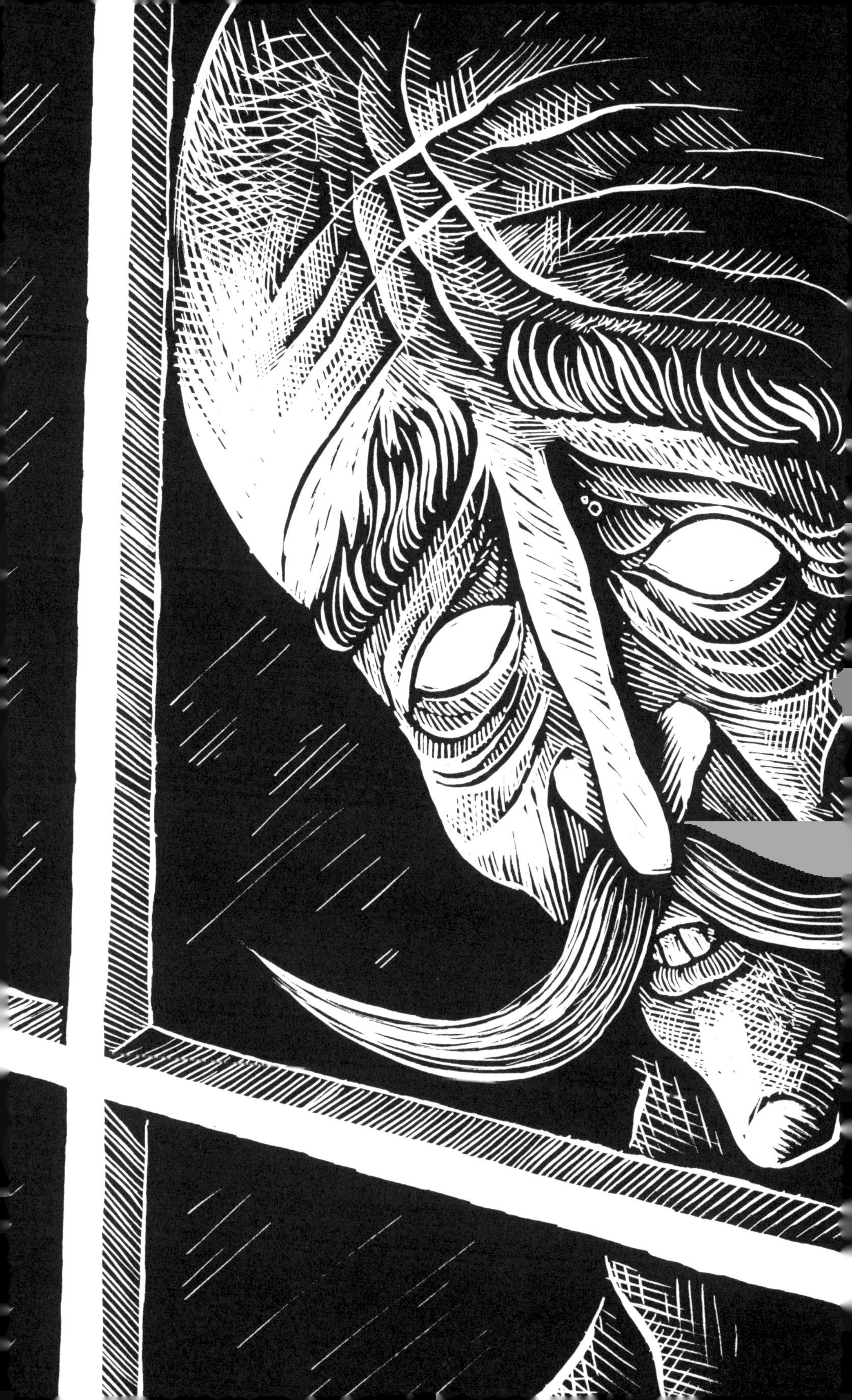

CHAPTER TWO

He began to hammer on the wall with his fist and shout: 'Wake! Wake! The old man has taken your boy!'

This stirred the others, and someone tried the Marquis's door. Finding it locked, he smashed it open with his shoulder. It was Petar.

'He took the boy outside!' the Marquis shouted.

The family gathered in the front room, all but Đorđe, who was already outside. A moment later he returned, bearing his son in his arms.

'He was by the roadside, at the edge of the forest. He's alive but unconscious,' Đorđe panted.

'The old man?' Petar asked.

Đorđe shook his head.

The boy recovered and showed no signs of injury. He remained in bed throughout the following day, but the Marquis was told that it seemed as if all was well. The Marquis, needless to say, had not slept well but was otherwise unharmed. Had it all been his imagination?

As he ate a humble breakfast of soured milk and buckwheat spoonbread, he overheard Zdenka and Petar's wife quietly speaking to each other in the next room.

'...But if you consider the facts, then none are damning,' Zdenka said. 'He returned home before the bell tolled eight times. He did take the boy outside, but no harm was done.'

'Then why has he fled? Or gone back to the mountains?' the wife asked.

'You know that Father never tells us his comings and goings. My point is that, while he was acting strangely, we mustn't forget that he had just returned from fighting a terrible bandit. He has not shown any reason for us to condemn him! There is no evidence that he is a...'

'This much is true. He has always been reasonable to the family. I don't believe that he would hurt us. Not as long as he is Gorča. But your brothers think otherwise. When...if he returns, they will surely kill him. They are certain that he is no longer Gorča.'

The Marquis heard Zdenka begin to weep. 'Murder our own father? Just like that? We mustn't let it happen, Ana, we mustn't.'

'What can we do?' Ana asked. 'Your brothers are men. They decide all.'

'I know,' Zdenka sighed. 'It would be useless to try and talk them out of it. What if they cannot find the stake?'

Just then the door opened and in walked Petar and Đorđe. They took seats at the table with the Marquis. They banged on the table, and Ana and Zdenka brought them their breakfast. Zdenka looked at the Marquis, her eyes lingering, before she returned to the kitchen.

By sundown, there was still no sign of old Gorča. The Marquis retired early and lay in bed, unable to sleep. This time he was not thinking of danger, but rather of the loveliness of Zdenka. Before long, his eyelids grew heavy, but just before sleep could embrace him he felt the room grow cold, as if a wind blew in, though the curtains did not stir. His eyes flew to the window and there it was: the ghastly pale face of old Gorča, eyes white and teeth more like a dog's than a man's, pressed against the pane.

He must warn the family! The Marquis tried to rise from his bed but found that he could not move; it was as if his limbs were tied down and a weight placed upon his chest. He looked back at the window, now empty, but then heard a tap on the glass – in the room adjacent to his own.

'Is that you, Grandfather?' the child's voice asked, as it had the night before.

'It's me,' came a whispered reply that the Marquis was surprised he was able to hear. 'I've brought you your little *yatagan*.'

'But I mustn't leave my bed, let alone go outside. Papa forbids it!'

'Oh, you needn't even leave your room. Just open the window so you can give your grandfather a kiss, and I will pass the hard-won blade to you.'

The Marquis struggled again to rise and warn the household as he heard the child's footsteps patter over to the window. Now he was

CHAPTER TWO

able to break the invisible bonds that had lashed him down before and he sprang out of bed, pounded on the door and shouted, 'He's back! At the window! At the boy's window!'

The family awoke and threw their doors open. The Marquis followed, his door unlocked, and he ran to the room next door. Đorđe and Petar knelt beside the boy, who lay upon the floor beneath the open window.

Đorđe looked up at the Marquis. 'You're certain it was he?'

The Marquis, words caught in his throat, nodded sternly.

The boy bore no signs of injury, but he was dead.

◆

The family was in anguish, but the Marquis saw that Zdenka was alone in her sadness. Her brothers had their wives and remaining children; this angelic young woman had no one. So the Marquis sat with her that evening, speaking in comforting tones, and their affection grew throughout the night. Zdenka recognized that circumstantial evidence pointed to her father being responsible for the boy's death, but without proof she couldn't bring herself to allow her brothers to murder him. The Marquis, lost in her eyes and in sympathy for her, agreed, though he could not explain what he had seen – that horrible, white-eyed face at the window with the mouth of a beast.

In the morning, the Marquis's coach was due to retrieve him and bring him on the next leg of his journey towards his diplomatic mission in Moldova. But he determined to remain at least for the funeral, which was to be held that day.

The boy was buried in the monastery graveyard. The Marquis remained by Zdenka's side, comforting her as best he could and within the boundaries of acceptable decorum. Their affection did not go unnoticed by the family, but they were so distracted, not to mention distraught, that they said nothing about it.

After the funeral, the family and the Marquis sat at a wooden table in front of the inn, taking a lunch of bread and cheese, largely in silence. Only the younger children seemed unaffected by what was happening. They played in the yard, pretending to fight the Turks with little wooden swords. That is, until Zdenka's face ghosted, she raised her hand and pointed to the forest.

'Father...' she whispered.

They all turned to see Gorča emerge from the trees, as if from curtains on a stage set. He walked slowly towards them, no longer limping, a beard having grown remarkably swiftly, catching up with his scimitar moustache. He moved with assurance, without hesitation, without a projection of guilt. Before the family knew it he was upon them, and took a seat at the head of the table.

'Welcome, Father,' Zdenka said, as much to herself as to anyone else.

Petar and Đorđe made meaningful eye contact before Đorđe spoke. 'Father, we would like you to say grace.'

Gorča shook his head.

Now Đorđe stood and fiercely smashed his fist upon the wooden table. 'Your grandson is buried! You will say grace this instant and make the sign of the cross!'

'Please do it, Father,' Zdenka pleaded, 'or else...'

'He refuses,' said Petar, 'because he *cannot*.'

Đorđe ran inside and emerged just as suddenly.

'Where is the stake?' he cried, before turning to Zdenka. 'Where did you hide the stake?'

He swivelled to face the thing that had once been his father. 'What have you done with my boy? Give me back my son!' As he spoke the blood drained out of his face, making him as pale as the creature at which he screamed. 'The stake, where is the stake?! I'll have the head of whoever hid it!'

As if by summoning, two of the youngest children emerged from behind the house, still pretending to duel – one a Turk, one their grandfather. The Marquis's eyes homed in on them and suddenly he noticed what they were playing with. Each held a length of

CHAPTER TWO

wood, pretending that it was a sword. One used a stick of firewood. The other...

Đorđe saw it too, and ran at the boy. He seized the hawthorn stake and rushed back towards his father. Seeing the stake, Gorča sprang to his feet with a scream – more like a roar than anything that could emerge from a human throat – and sped off for the forest at a pace unbelievable for a man of his age, or indeed for any man. Đorđe pursued him, vanishing into a thicket of aspen trees.

Just before night fell, a coach arrived for the Marquis. Neither Gorča nor Đorđe had returned from the forest, and the family was distraught. Petar had assumed the position of interim patriarch and was preoccupied with his wife, Đorđe's wife and all the children. This left Zdenka once more alone. She and the Marquis had now spent hours together and their bond had deepened. The Marquis tried to convince himself that this budding love he felt was but an illusion. He could not do so. Then he tried to imagine Zdenka, a Slavic peasant girl without a word of French, somehow becoming wife to an aristocratic ambassador of the French royal court. It was an impossible love. Several times he thought to ask her to accompany him, but propriety and logic prevailed. He was an enlightened gentleman, after all.

So they bid a formal farewell. The Marquis left with the situation far from resolved. The blanket of night pressed down as he mounted the coach and was driven away.

He travelled on to Jassy, where his diplomatic mission required him. The situation there led him to remain for months. His business finally ended and, having achieved what was expected of him, he was recalled to France.

Throughout this time, Zdenka had never been far from his mind. The longer he was away, the more certain he had become of his feelings. On his way back to France he took the same route by which he had come, so that he could be sure to see her.

It was near sunset when his coach pulled past the monastery of Our Lady of the Oak towards the centre of the village. The Marquis was eagerly anticipating his first glimpse of Zdenka, hoping that she would be equally glad to see him – that he had remained in her thoughts and, more importantly, in her heart, as she had in his.

Suddenly a hooded figure ran in front of the coach. It pulled to an abrupt halt, the horses whinnying and the coachman cursing. The Marquis leaned his head out of the coach window to see what the matter was. His ear was immediately struck by a chorus of howls, as if they were surrounded by hundreds of wolves.

The lamplight struck the hooded figure, casting him in white. It was a monk, his beard cascading out from beneath the hood.

'Turn back!' he shouted. 'The village is damned. No one remains. No one alive!'

'What do you mean?' replied the Marquis, his heart racing. 'You live, do you not?'

'Only within the monastery, sir,' the monk replied. 'There we are safe. They cannot enter. Drive on, or shelter with us for the night and then be gone.'

'I must go on to the village,' said the Marquis, though his coachman clearly felt otherwise.

'I would say God be with you, sir,' the monk said, shaking his head, 'but if you enter the village, God will not follow.'

'I thank you for your concern,' said the Marquis, 'but I must...'

His words were drowned out by another volley of howls that sounded even closer than before.

'I am not afraid of wolves,' the Marquis continued.

'Nor am I,' said the monk. 'If it were only wolves...'

'I volunteer that I am afraid of wolves, and more besides,' said the coachman. 'I feel it would be wise to heed this monk's warning and spend the night within the monastery, my lord.'

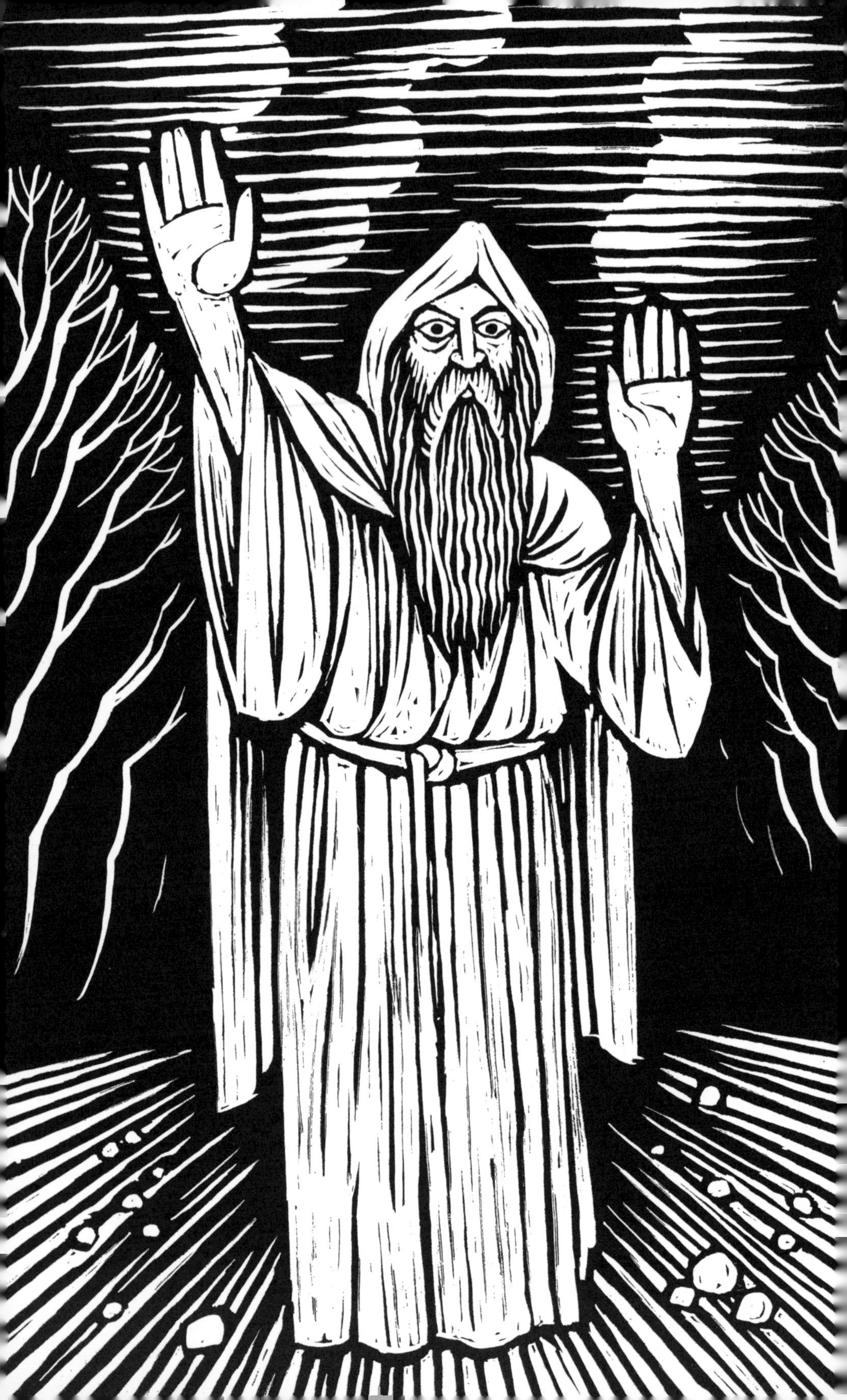

'Nonsense,' the Marquis replied, impatient. 'Especially if there are wolves, then I must go on to see...to see a family in the village that is dear to me.'

'Then let me save at least one of you,' said the monk sadly.

The Marquis was frantic, but not with fear for himself. He had to see Zdenka, to make sure that she was safe, to make sure that she loved him, as he had never been more certain that he loved her.

'Stay here,' he said abruptly to the coachman. 'I will retrieve you when I've seen this...family.'

He stepped down from the coach. He was about to close the door behind him when he thought to also take a pistol with him. Turning back, he saw the monk looking at him with pity.

'For wolves,' said the Marquis.

'You do not have enough bullets,' said the monk, 'nor the right kind.'

The coachman handed the Marquis a lit lantern, and the monk blessed him. 'Does the blessing from an Orthodox monk work for a Catholic Frenchman?' the Marquis asked, half in jest.

'No amount of blessing, no matter the faith, will help you there,' said the monk. 'Farewell.'

The night felt very cold and dark, the lantern very dim, as the Marquis stood alone on the long, white road that lanced through the aspen forest. He walked ahead to the village, the sound of howling now absent and the night eerier still for the silence.

When he came to the village, he saw that it had changed immensely. The humble houses appeared uninhabited. Smoke rose from not a single chimney. It was as if the whole had been abandoned. But he did spy a single dim light – and it was inside the inn.

He rushed ahead, ran past the wooden table in the garden. He knocked on the door, never noticing the head that was still nailed to the threshold above – now merely a skull.

The door opened. There, seated at a table beside a single candle, was Zdenka. She looked just as beautiful as the Marquis remembered.

CHAPTER TWO

'Zdenka,' he said, moving towards her. 'Are you all right? Are you pleased to see me?'

She looked up at him, expressing no surprise at his arrival. 'So very pleased,' she said.

'But what happened to the village? Where is the rest of your family?'

She looked like she was crying but shed no tears.

'It is horrible,' she began. 'And it is Father's fault.'

'You mean that Gorča lives?'

'Oh, no,' she continued. 'He is well and truly buried. A stake driven through his heart. But he drained the blood of Đorđe's son, as you will recall.'

'Yes, I'm so sorry. We buried him the day I left.'

'Indeed. So you can imagine our surprise when he came back the next night, crying at the window, calling to his mother, saying he was cold and wanted to come in. This was before Đorđe returned from the forest, where he had chased our father. You cannot blame the child's mother. She may have seen him buried with her own eyes, but it was only hours earlier. We all thought that he had been deemed dead prematurely and, most horribly, buried alive. But he had managed to burst out of his coffin and clear the earth above him. So, of course, she invited him in. No sooner did he cross the threshold than he attacked her and drained her blood. Petar managed to scare him off and he fled to the woods, running *on all fours*. His mother was buried soon afterwards. For a while.'

'My poor Zdenka, this is horrible. I'm so sorry that this has happened to you.' The Marquis drew closer to her, wishing to embrace her. 'Let me take you away from this place. You shall marry me, if you'll have me. We can go away immediately. I would not want you to stay another minute in this cursed place.'

'Oh, I will have you,' she said, without emotion.

Then the howling in the forest, until now absent, resumed. Suddenly the Marquis, whose heart thundered faster than his mind, began to piece things together.

'You say the boy rose from the grave and attacked your sister-in-law the very night I left?'

Zdenka nodded.

'And where is the rest of your family?'

'Oh,' said Zdenka slowly, 'they are very close. Very close indeed.'

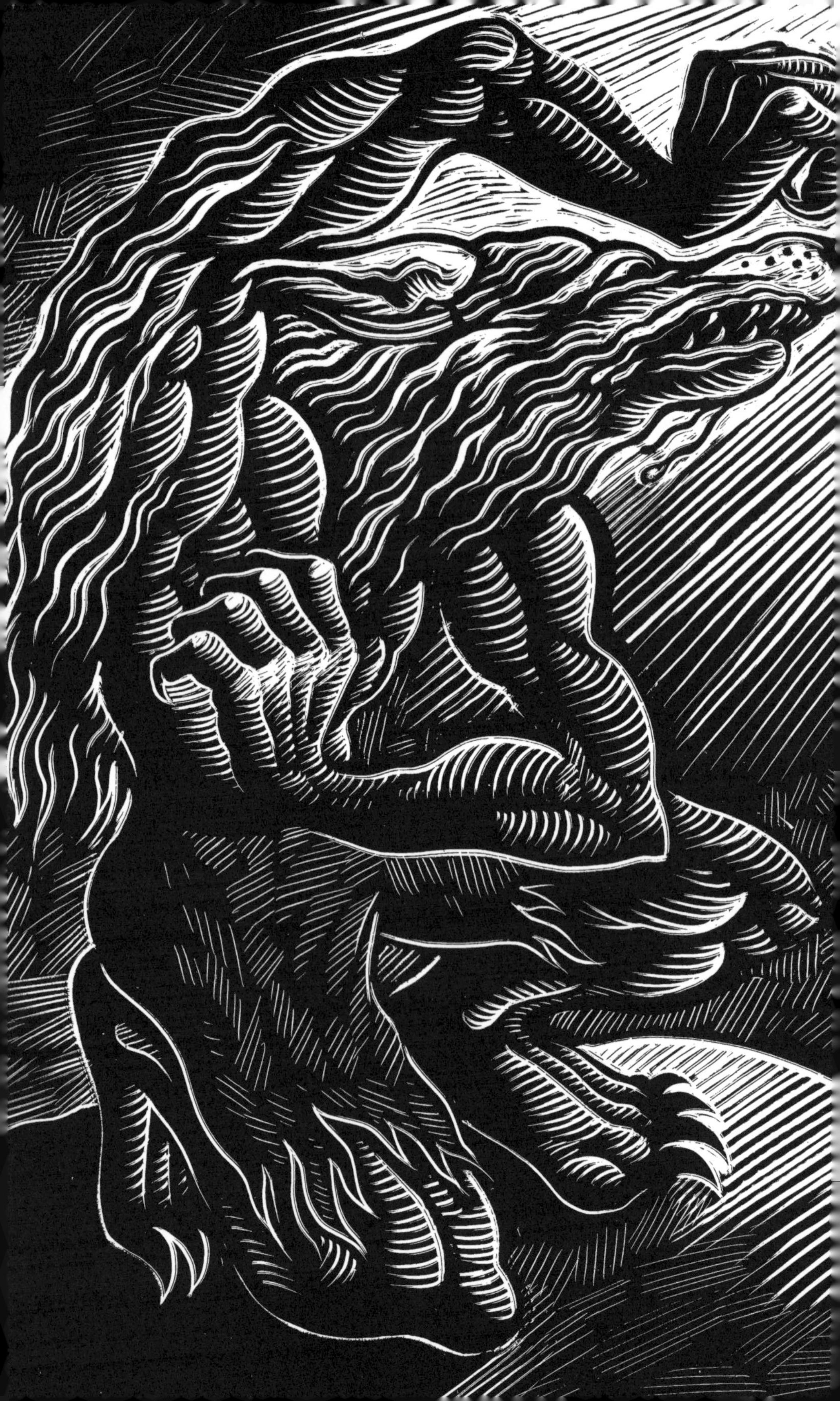

WEREWOLVES

Count Jan Potocki was one of Poland's most revered writers and Enlightenment intellectuals. His masterpiece, *The Manuscript Found in Saragossa*, first published around 1805, is considered among the nation's greatest works of prose storytelling, in the vein of the *Arabian Nights*. Hailing from one of Poland's wealthiest aristocratic families, Potocki was a world traveller and polyglot who wrote his masterwork in French. He was educated in Switzerland, served as captain of the engineers in the Polish army and was recruited as a Knight of Malta and a Freemason.

On 23 December 1815, this brilliant, worldly man absconded with one of his mother's silver teapots, made out of it a bullet, had this silver bullet blessed by a priest and then shot himself in the head with it. Jan Potocki was entirely convinced that he was doing the world a great favour and saving many lives by taking his own, because Jan Potocki believed that he was a werewolf.

While in the modern, Western imagination werewolves and vampires are distinct mythological monsters, in Slavic legend they are inextricably linked. It could be argued that they are two words for the same mythical monster. Many pre-20th-century stories, even those ostensibly including the term for werewolf, *vukodlak*, describe what we would today call a vampire. That includes the legend presented here, which draws upon an 1839 story called *La Famille du Vourdalak* (roughly translated as 'The Werewolf Family') by Alexei Tolstoi. Tolstoi's story has also inspired several classic horror films including *Black Sabbath* (1963, starring Boris Karloff, which in turn inspired the naming of the rock band) and 1972's *Night of the Devils*, as well as a BBC radio production. But while a wolf does appear, the actual threat comes from creatures we would identify as vampires. Recall that the Serbian word *vukodlak* was considered too terrifying to utter, so *vampir* was used in its place; we chose this legend because it reflects that typically Slavic blurring of the line between vampire and werewolf.

The fluid nature of the vampire/werewolf figure can be better understood once you appreciate the exceptional position of the wolf within Serbian mythology. In the Slavic world, not only is the wolf the main totem animal of Serbs and other southern Slavs but the wolf god, Vuk, is their supreme god – the cosmic ruler, to which various origin stories are related. There are countless male and female names, as well as names of places, incorporating the word 'wolf'. Serbia's rich linguistic and ethnographic literature explains that *vampir* is a replacement for the 'sacred' name of werewolf, *vukodlak*. The term *nepomnik*, 'the one who should not be mentioned', is another alternative to the unmentionable werewolf, as is the simple *vuk*, a wolf. Vampires in Slavic legend can take the form of a wolf or a black dog. The Slavic demon Psoglav ('Doghead'), who appears in legends in Bosnia, Montenegro and Istria, has a dog's head, a horse's legs and only one eye.

We also see an interweaving of pagan Slavic legend into the nascent Christian traditions adopted by southern Slavs from the 9th century onwards, eastern Slavs from the 10th, and western Slavs between the 9th and 12th centuries, owing to the cultural and missionary work of two brothers from Thessaloniki, Cyril and Methodius (both later canonized). They invented the Cyrillic alphabet and spread Christianity along with literacy among the Slavs. The Devil, in the Christian Slavic tradition, often looks like a *vukodlak*. Saint Christophor is meshed with Psoglav, represented with a dog's head in some frescoes and icons in Serbia, Macedonia and Greece. This figure is also linked to an apocryphal story about Roman soldiers who were fighting a dog-headed tribe, when one of the prisoners converted to Christianity. The Romans tortured and killed him, and he became a saint with the name of Christophor. He is not the same figure as Saint Christopher in the Catholic tradition, but as their names are so similar it is easy to see how the stories have melted together.

A short version of *vukodlak*, *kudlak*, means 'butterfly' in Dalmatian; the butterfly is also one of the vampire's forms, as seen in the story 'Black Butterfly' in this book. A *vukodlak* is able to attract clouds and change weather, and one of his synonyms is *zduhać*, a demon (sometimes a human magician) who can affect the weather – in some legends, vampires can transform into fog. *Vukodlak* usually appears with the full moon, but in some stories he is a solar deity.

A wolfskin was a key component of many Slavic rituals and holy days all over the Balkans. These holy days included a whole week of wolf-related festivities called *Mratinci*, held in November. Youngsters wearing wolfskins would appear before the house of a maiden who had been promised in marriage. Petar Skok offers a convincing semasiology, or linguistic meaning, for *vukodlak* – 'the one who skins' (it could also mean 'the one who is wearing the skin').[25] In his book on vampires, Nick Groom offers the less convincing etymological combination of *vuk* (wolf) and *dlaka* (a hair).[26]

According to Sabine Baring-Gould in his 1865 *Book of Were-Wolves*:

The Serbs connect the vampire and the werewolf together, and call them by one name, vlkoslak. These rage chiefly in the depths of winter: they hold their annual gatherings, and at them divest themselves of their wolf-skins, which they hang on the trees around them. If anyone succeeds in obtaining the skin and burning it, the vlkoslak is thenceforth disenchanted.[27]

These Slavic rituals of *Mratinci* are the probable origin of the concept of the wolf-man, a human who becomes a wolf/man hybrid, as opposed to transforming into a wolf proper. The donning of a wolfskin was a shamanistic practice of the pagan Slavs. The shaman would take on the role of the wolf, singing and dancing, in a ritual likely augmented with alcohol or hallucinogenic herbs. This wolf-man was

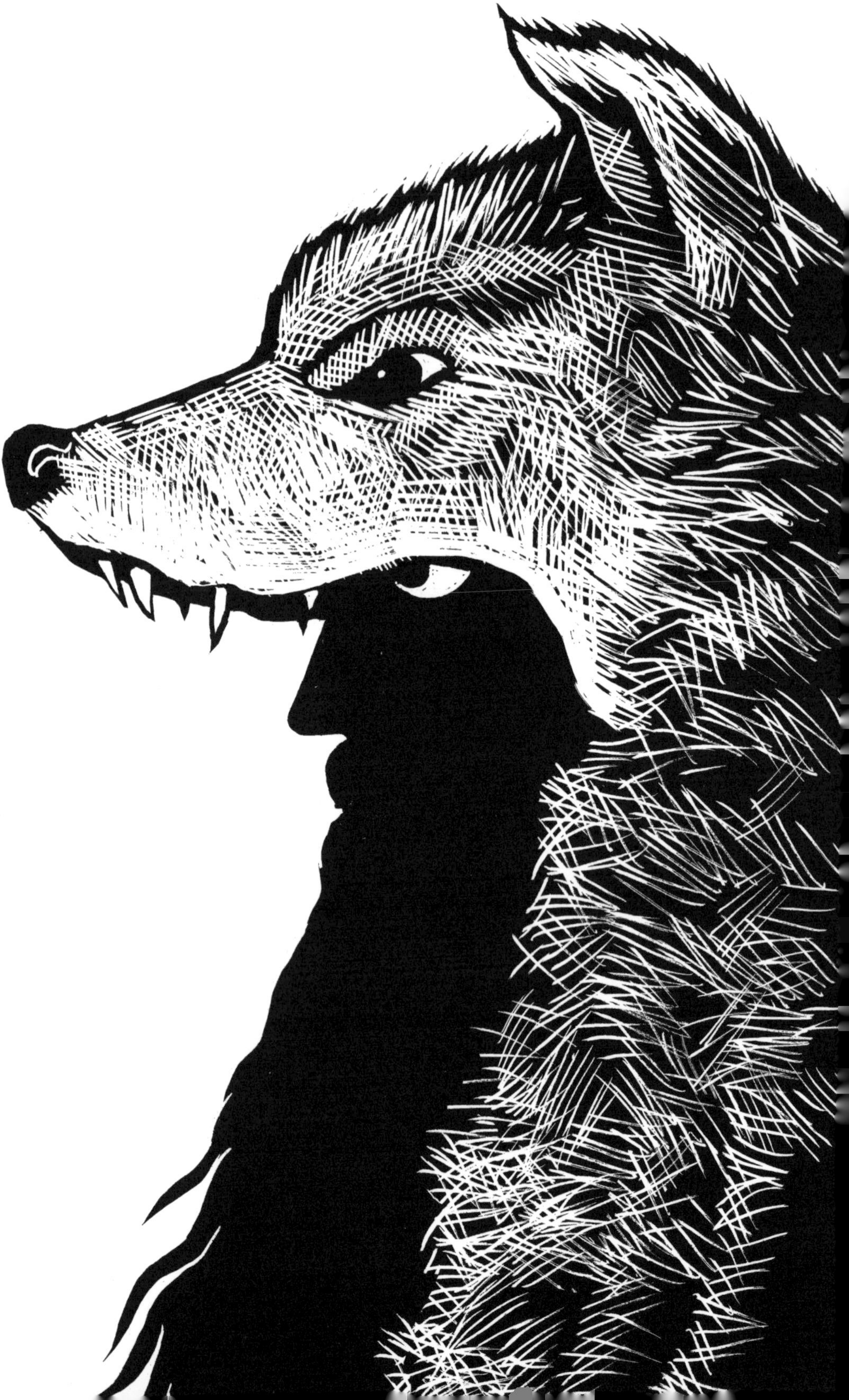

taken up as the Hollywood concept of a werewolf, from Lon Chaney in *The Wolf Man* (1941) to *An American Werewolf in London* (1981) and beyond. The difference between the ancient Slavic idea of a vampire and one embraced by Western pop culture is small, while the Slavic werewolf is very different from the pop-culture version. The closest union of the two appears, probably unwittingly, in the *Twilight* books and films, in which forever-teenaged vampires are locked in an eternal struggle with forever-teenaged werewolves who transform into giant wolves, not wolf-man hybrids.

Jan Potocki suffered from what is called 'clinical lycanthropy', a recognized psychiatric syndrome in which the patient is wholly convinced that he or she is a werewolf. This (presumable) misconception cost him his life. In order to understand the term *lycanthropy* we must first go back to ancient Greece, where many a legend can be found of humans transforming into wolves, before seeing where the Slavic tradition adopted a version of this linked to Vuk, the wolf, the king of the Slavic pantheon, and the idea of the anthropomorphic wolf-man – as opposed to an animagus, a man (as we shall see, there are traditionally no female werewolves) who can transform, or who is cursed to transform against his will, into a wolf.

ORIGINS: GREEK AND SLAVIC

The earliest written reference to wolf-men is provided by Herodotus, who describes a tribe of Scythians. The werewolves in early Slavonic literature were not bad, nor did they harm people while they were in lupine form. Bojan (Baianus), a son of Tsar Simeon of Bulgaria (893–927), allegedly knew how to change himself into a wolf or other animal by magic at any time.

Všeslav Brjačislavič, 11th-century Prince of Polock and a wizard (*volchv*), also became a wolf at night; the 12th-century Russian heroic epic poem *The Tale of the Campaign of Igor* describes how Všeslav ruled during the day and never slept. By night, he supposedly prowled around as a wolf. This may actually refer to the physiological condition called hypertrichosis – when the fine layer of hair present during the foetal stage does not go away after birth but continues to grow, the patient will exhibit extreme and excessive hair growth, sometimes even on the face. Such patients appeared to be 'wolf-men', and it is possible that Vseslav suffered from this condition. But it is so rare, by one account with as few as fifty known cases worldwide, that it is difficult to determine whether it was prevalent enough to influence cultural beliefs.

According to the poem, Vseslav once ran from Kyiv to Tmutarakan until the cock crowed, at which point he ran faster than the sun. His mother gave birth to him using magic and he was born with the caul, a newborn's membrane, on his head. He wore this membrane as an amulet for his whole life, a common practice in many cultures.[28]

Volga (a name derived from *volchv*, wizard) Svjatoslavič, who fought against the Tatars and became the hero of an Old Russian epic poem, could also change into a wolf. Volga, probably inspired by Vseslav or another historical figure, was the son of Marfa Vseslavevna ('daughter of Vseslav'); his father was a dragon or a snake. When he was ten years old he could change into a pike, a falcon or a grey wolf. He was an excellent hunter and, like Vseslav, he did not sleep at night.

There was a popular belief that the 15th-century Despot of Serbia, Vuk Grgurević Branković (1440–1485), was a werewolf, although Vuk was and remains a common Serbian name. After the fall of the Serbian Despotate, he fought against the Turks in the service of King Matthias Corvinus of Hungary. Thanks to his courage and victories, he was described as the Fiery Dragon Wolf (*Zmaj Ognjeni Vuk*) and became a subject of Serbian heroic poems. Thus he has two biographies, one historical and the other mythical. In the popular conception, these two can merge. Like Vseslav, Vuk was born with unusual bodily characteristics, namely hair on the palms of his hands (this is possibly apocryphal, but it may indicate hypertrichosis). Like Volga, he was said to be a dragon's son or to have lived among dragons. The similarities between these Russian and Serbian heroes, Volga and Vuk, point to an older Slavonic tradition upon which both are based.

It is important to understand that while other European cultures saw wolves and werewolves as inherently bad, dangerous enemies, the Slavs did not perceive the wolf only as negative. They regarded it as an animal with the power to protect. Parents gave their children wolf-related names in the hope of protecting them against evil and bringing them strength, health and happiness. In pagan tradition, a name conferred powers and could dictate the fate of the child to whom it was given.

In the territory of Slovakia, wolf names given to children as early as the 9th century include Vlkina, Vlčen, Vlko, Vlkan, Vlčuta, Vlkoslav, Vlkas, Vlkašin, Vlk and Vlčík. Later, however, like the majority of Slavonic names, these were replaced by biblical ones. The werewolf – in Slovak, *vlkolak* – spread into other languages including Greek, Albanian, Romanian and even Turkish.

In Slavonic tradition, a living person could become a werewolf in three ways: voluntarily, with the help of magic spells, a wolfskin belt or water from a wolf's footprint; by being cursed; or by being born a werewolf – for example, born at the time of a new moon (not a full moon), having a wizard as a father, or being born feet first. Any anatomical anomaly, such as slightly excessive body hair, eyebrows that grow together, teeth present at birth, or remnants of a tail, could be regarded as the sign of a werewolf. Prior to the Enlightenment and its scientific focus, every deviation from the norm was rationalized by pointing to magic or unclean forces and evil beings.

In his thoroughly gruesome tale *Vlkolak*, 19th-century Slovak folklorist Pavol Dobšinský tells of a cannibal father of three daughters. The youngest flees from him and finds protection with the king, who marries her. They have two children. Then, one night during a storm, they give shelter to a beggar – her father in disguise, of course – who cuts the throats of both children and plants the bloody knife on the woman, his daughter. On the advice of the beggar, the king has her hands cut off, the bodies of her children are wrapped in a sheet and tied onto her back, and then she is driven away (be grateful this is not the legend we've chosen to retell here).

However, the story has a happy ending. The werewolf-like father dies; his daughter finds her hands in a magic spring, and they reattach to her arms. The water from the spring also revives her dead children. The king, her husband, recognizes that she was innocent and they live happily ever after (she is apparently very forgiving). In this story, the 'werewolf' does not have anything in common with a werewolf as we typically think of it – he does not change into a wolf, but only has wolf-like characteristics. Here, the werewolf is a man, but he is also a psychopathic, violent serial killer and a cannibal with possible tendencies towards incest.

MEDICAL EXPLANATIONS

It is not the focus of this text to consider scientific explanations for belief in the supernatural. But it is worth noting the medical conditions that may have initiated belief in werewolves.

Clinical lycanthropy, the diagnosis of Count Jan Potocki, is defined as a mental illness in which the patient believes himself to be an animal. Which animal this is has much to do with the patient's cultural background and self-image. That Jan Potocki thought he was a werewolf, in the modern sense of a wolf-man capable of running rampant, uncontrolled and murderous, is in keeping with the popular culture of his time and background. A person with clinical lycanthropy can likewise think that they are an animal proper – an example is the character of Renfield in Stoker's *Dracula*, who thinks that he is a spider and is diagnosed in the novel as a 'zoophagous' (animal-eating) maniac. This concept is founded on the classical belief, reflected in texts including Plato's *Republic*, that the consumption of human flesh by a human – cannibalism – would transform the consumer into a werewolf. Its origins can be found in the Greek myth of King Lycaon, recorded by Hesiod and popularized in Latin in Ovid's *Metamorphosis*. Lycaon, an archaic king of Arcadia, tests the omniscience of Zeus by serving him a meal that includes the flesh of Nyctimus, the youngest of his fifty sons. Zeus recognizes immediately what has happened and, to punish Lycaon, brings Nyctimus back to life and transforms Lycaon into a wolf. In a 16th-century engraving by the German-born Dutch artist Hendrick Goltzius, Lycaon is shown as a wolf-man with the head of a wolf and the body of a human.

In the 7th century CE, just as the Slavic tribes were settling into the regions they largely occupy today, a Byzantine physician in Alexandria called Paulus Aegineta wrote that hypertrichosis, which is sometimes rather callously referred to as 'werewolf syndrome', was caused by an excess of black bile. That believing oneself to be an animal, or capable of turning into one, was associated with depression is poetic. Of course, this is not the case of clinical lycanthropy: hypertrichosis is the physiological condition of having excessive hair, not the belief that you can turn into an animal. The patient feels 'out of body', no longer themselves, turning into someone or something else. While it should not be assumed that Slavic peoples were reading Byzantine medical books, it is easy to forget that the western fringes of the Byzantine Empire ended where the territory of the Slavs began. The physician Galen, who hailed from Pergamon in what is now Turkey, wrote on clinical lycanthropy in the 2nd century CE, describing a patient with a ravenous appetite and other wolf-like qualities. It is in his text that the term *lycanthropos* is recorded, from the Greek λύκος, *lukos*, 'wolf' and ἄνθρωπος, *anthropos*, 'human'.

In the 7th century the Peloponnesian peninsula was largely Slavic, and that tradition endures. We tend to think of the Balkans as part of the former Yugoslavia and forget that Greece is part of the Balkans. While the number of Slavs reading Greek texts would have been very limited, there would have been cross-pollination of cultural, scientific and medical ideas; the ancient Greek legends of wolf-men would have been heard by Slavs, and may have been woven into Slavic myths. Whether this was the case or the Slavic beliefs evolved independently cannot be definitively determined.

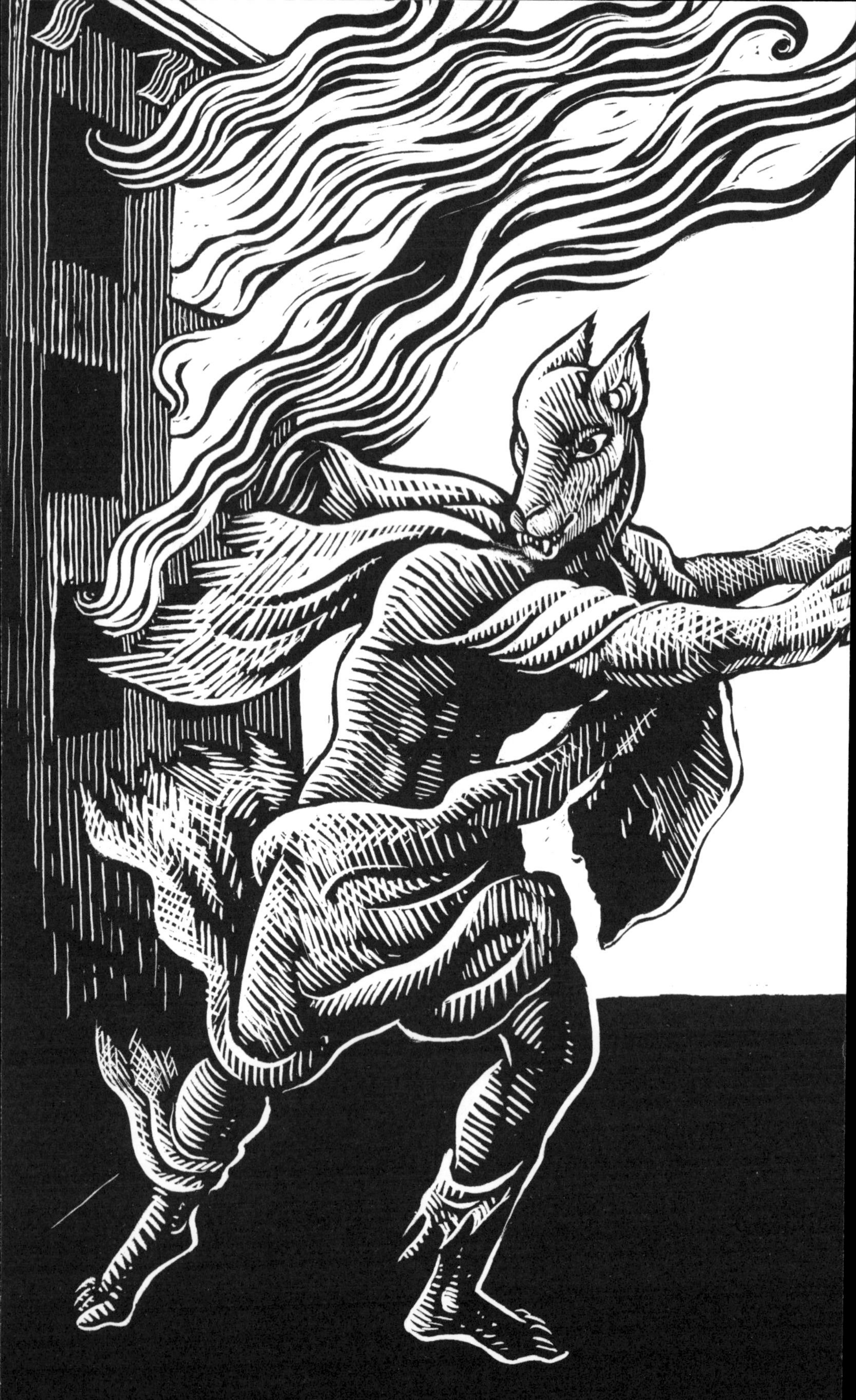

Clinical lycanthropy remained in the vocabulary of physicians. It is mentioned in 1563 by Johann Weyer, a Lutheran physician in Germany who describes such patients as overly melancholic, with symptoms including dehydration, sunken or dim eyes and pale skin. Lycanthropy appears again in the 1597 *Daemonologie*, the philosophical treatise on necromancy and black magic penned by none other than King James VI of Scotland. James believed in witches but did not believe that men actually transformed into wolves; rather he suggested that they suffered from, as he termed it, a 'superabundance of melancholie' that made them act like wolves. In this text he refers to the ancient Greek belief and the term lycanthropy, but goes on to write (presented here in modernized English):

> ...to tell you simple my opinion in this, if any sick thing has been I take it to have proceeded but of a natural superabundance of melancholy, quite like as you read that if he's mad, some think themselves pitchers, some a horse, and some any kind of beast or other, so suppose I that it has to do with the imagination and memory of some per lucida intervalla that has likely occupied them that they have thought themselves very wolfish indeed at that time and so counterfeited their actions, in getting on their hands and feet, pleasing to devour women and girls, begging and snatching... and using sickly actions and so to become beasts by imagination...[29]

The most interesting point here is that James does not consider werewolves to be part of the pantheon of 'real' demons he describes in his treatise on Christian demonology, but rather people suffering from a misunderstood mental affliction. This is a very modern take from someone who genuinely believed in witches and fairies. It reflects a widespread belief among learned men of that period, likewise mentioned in a previous book, 1584's *The Discoverie of Witchcraft* by Reginald Scot, which states: 'Lycanthropia is a disease and not a transformation.'[30]

The link to lupine behaviour when the moon is full has origins in Slavic legend, but is also an objectively observed medical phenomenon. The term 'lunacy' derives from the Latin *luna*, or moon, and refers to the fact – observed by physicians since at least the late 13th century – that humans are more prone to unstable mental behaviours when the moon is full. The Greek *selēniazomai*, referenced in the New Testament, means 'to be epileptic' and comes from the Greek word for moon, *selēnē*. The Old English word *monseoc* literally means 'moon-sick' and *monaðseocnes*, meaning 'month-sickness', describes a sickness coming once a month with the moon. Doctors to this day note a higher incidence of unstable behaviour when the moon is full, without knowing how to explain this phenomenon.

RENAISSANCE WEREWOLF TRIALS

Running parallel to the horrific witch trials of 16th-century Europe were werewolf trials – significantly fewer in number, but nevertheless a recorded phenomenon. The most famous of these, in the late 1500s, concerned a German farmer called Peter Stumpp. Stumpp, dubbed 'the Werewolf of Bedburg', was accused of witchcraft, cannibalism and lycanthropy (literally turning into a wolf, as his accusers conceived of it) as well as wolf-riding and wolf-charming. His case was popularized in a riveting and gory sixteen-page pamphlet published in London in 1590, describing his crimes and elaborate execution. His name varies across accounts – he may have been nicknamed Stumpp (like the German *Stumpf*) because of his stump of a left hand, which had been cut off.

Under torture, Stumpp claimed to have practised black magic since the age of twelve and used a magical belt to transform into 'the likeness of a greedy, devouring wolf, strong and mighty, with eyes which in the night sparkled like fire, a mouth great and wide, with most sharp and cruel teeth and mighty paws'.[31] Removing the belt would turn him back into a human. The pamphlet goes on to describe how, for a quarter of a century, Stumpp had been 'an insatiable bloodsucker';

he confessed to having killed and eaten fourteen children, including his own son, and two pregnant women, with the foetuses described as 'dainty morsels'. All of this must be taken with a shovelful of salt, as with all confessions made under torture, but Stumpp was executed along with his daughter and his mistress.

In Livonia (currently Latvia and Estonia), at least eighteen trials are recorded between 1527 and 1725 in which a total of eighteen women and thirteen men were accused of having transformed into werewolves to wreak havoc on the locals. There were also accusations of people turning into werebears. The imaginative Gret of Parnau testified in 1633 that, while Kanti Hans and his wife had transformed into wolves, a woman working with them to make trouble had taken the form of a bear. In 1696 one Greta, daughter of Titza Thomas, testified to having seen a local girl, Libbe Matz, leading a pack of eleven werewolves hunting in the woods near her native Vastermoisa. In 1651, a man called Hans was brought to trial in Idavere for having been a werewolf since the age of eighteen. The court record indicates that he had found a dog's teeth-marks on his leg, the wound having been inflicted while he was in werewolf form. Whether those on trial suffered from clinical lycanthropy or simply confessed under the duress of torture is difficult to say, and it is also possible that the historical record elaborates on the truth of what happened.

There is a case of a 'good' werewolf from Livonia. In 1692, in the town of Jürgensburg in present-day Latvia, an eighty-year-old man named Thiess of Kaltenbrun testified to being a werewolf who, with a team of fellow werewolves, descended into Hell three times a year to do battle with witches and wizards under Satan's command, in order to ensure a good harvest. The court made a concerted effort to force Thiess to confess that he'd been in the service of Satan, and therefore could be executed as a witch, but he never did. He was sentenced not to death, but to what would have been thought of as a slap on the wrist in the context of witch trials: a mere whipping.

CHAPTER TWO

These werewolf trials are linked to a figure of Bavarian folklore called *Wolfssegner*, or wolf-charmer. A wave of concern about these wolf-charmers swept Bavaria and Austria in the 17th century, coinciding with a period of unusual cold dubbed the 'Little Ice Age'. During this phenomenon it was recorded that wolves thrived in the Bavarian Alps, emboldened by the conditions to terrorize rural locals. Some believed that an evil spell called a *Wolfbann* could prompt a wolf to attack a victim, while the *Wolfssegen* was the countercharm, to defend against wolves. Those selling these wolf charms were regarded as grifters trying to scam peasants into paying them. Even so, the heightened level of concern about wolves in this period – in lands that were firmly part of the Habsburg Empire, which at that point also extended well into the Balkans – was such that, in Vienna, a special prayer called *Wolfssegen* was chanted after mass on Christmas night, meant to commemorate the eradication of the danger posed by wolves when Vienna was walled in.

It is easy today to forget that in Europe, wolves (and much more rarely, bears) were the primary animal danger to humans. It is no surprise, therefore, to find a rich mythology surrounding them and any humans who might align with or transform into them.

MODERN WEREWOLVES

The early 19th-century fad for vampires extended to the vampires and werewolves of Slavic lore. The Russian word *vurdalak* – meaning 'vampire', but clearly linked to the Serbian *vukodlak* – entered the language thanks to Alexander Pushkin's 1836 poem *Wurdulac*. This drew on John Polidori's story 'The Vampyre' and in turn inspired the work of Prosper Mérimée (*Lokis*, 1868). The works of Nikolai Gogol (*Evenings on a Farm Near Dikanka*, 1831–2), Alexei Tolstoi (whose literary offering we adapted here) and Mikhail Bulgakov (*Dog's Heart*, 1925) also include some vampire/werewolf motifs. Orest Somov, a Ukrainian writing in Russian, was a famous author of gothic tales including *Werewolf* (1829), as was Alexander Kuprin (*Serebrjanyj volk* or *Silver Wolf*, 1901).

Within the wider landscape of Slavic culture, Poland was perhaps the most prolific source of werewolf narratives, from Mikolaj Rey's short 16th-century text on the topic through the various works of 19th-century writers Adam Mickiewicz, Jan Barszczewski and Tomasz Olizarowski. Mickiewicz, during a lecture in Paris, described these monsters as a reflection of the Slavic soul.

A mention in the *Alexandreida*, a 14th-century Czech epic poem, of beings (*vědi*) that devour people is regarded as evidence of belief in vampires/werewolves in the Czech lands. Czech literature likewise has a tradition of werewolf stories, including Jan Neruda's famous short story 'Vampýr' (1871). A number of 20th- and 21st-century Czech female authors have also chosen this topic, including Jenny Nowak (Jana Moravcová), whose cycle of novels about *Dracula* connects the horror with historical fiction, and the 'Czech Anne Rice', Daniela Mičanová.

Slovenian, Croatian and Serbian literature is likewise rife with werewolf stories. Fran Wiesthaler published five Slovenian werewolf stories in *Ljubljanski zvon* magazine in 1883. Janez Trdina has a story of *vlkodlak* in his collection *Fairytales and Stories about Gorjanci*, and Franček Bohanec includes one in his collection of Slovenian people's stories (1966). In Croatian literature, Đura Sudeta's novel *Mor* (1930) is an allegorical narrative about the human relationship with nature, prophetic about future ecological catastrophes. The literary presence of werewolves in Serbia can be traced to a fairy tale by Joksim Nović Otočanin ('Vrzino kolo i Zlatni i Alem-grad', or 'The Devil's Dance in the Round and the Golden and Diamond Town', 1864).

The trend in both the Slavic world and in literature at large has only accelerated in recent decades, to the point where werewolves – usually in their wolf-man hybrid form, transforming against their will when the moon is full and slayable only with silver bullets, à la Jan Potocki – are universally familiar. They appear in popular narratives from the film *Teen Wolf* (which cleverly references the Greek myth of Lycaon) to *Harry Potter and the Prisoner of Azkaban* (with its good-hearted werewolf teacher, Professor Lupin), to the *Hotel Transylvania* animation franchise. The overlap with vampires remains only in the sense that both mythical monsters exist in the same realm of gothic fantasy, where they are liable to encounter one another and possibly duel for predominance.

Werewolves, like vampires, have become symbols as much as fantasy creatures. The quirky British clergyman Montague Summers, prolific author of gothic stories and literary criticism, wrote a series of studies on the occult, among them *Werewolf* (1933). There one may find an account of a sort of reverse werewolf, or rather werebear, in a Russian story Summers had heard. In it, a bear is kept at the tsar's court for entertainment, made to drink vodka and dance. The bear manages to escape to Siberia, where he finds a shaman who makes him human, capable of taking revenge on the tsar's family.

The bear's human name?

Vladimir Lenin.

3

THRESHOLD

◆

LIBUŠE AND WOMEN

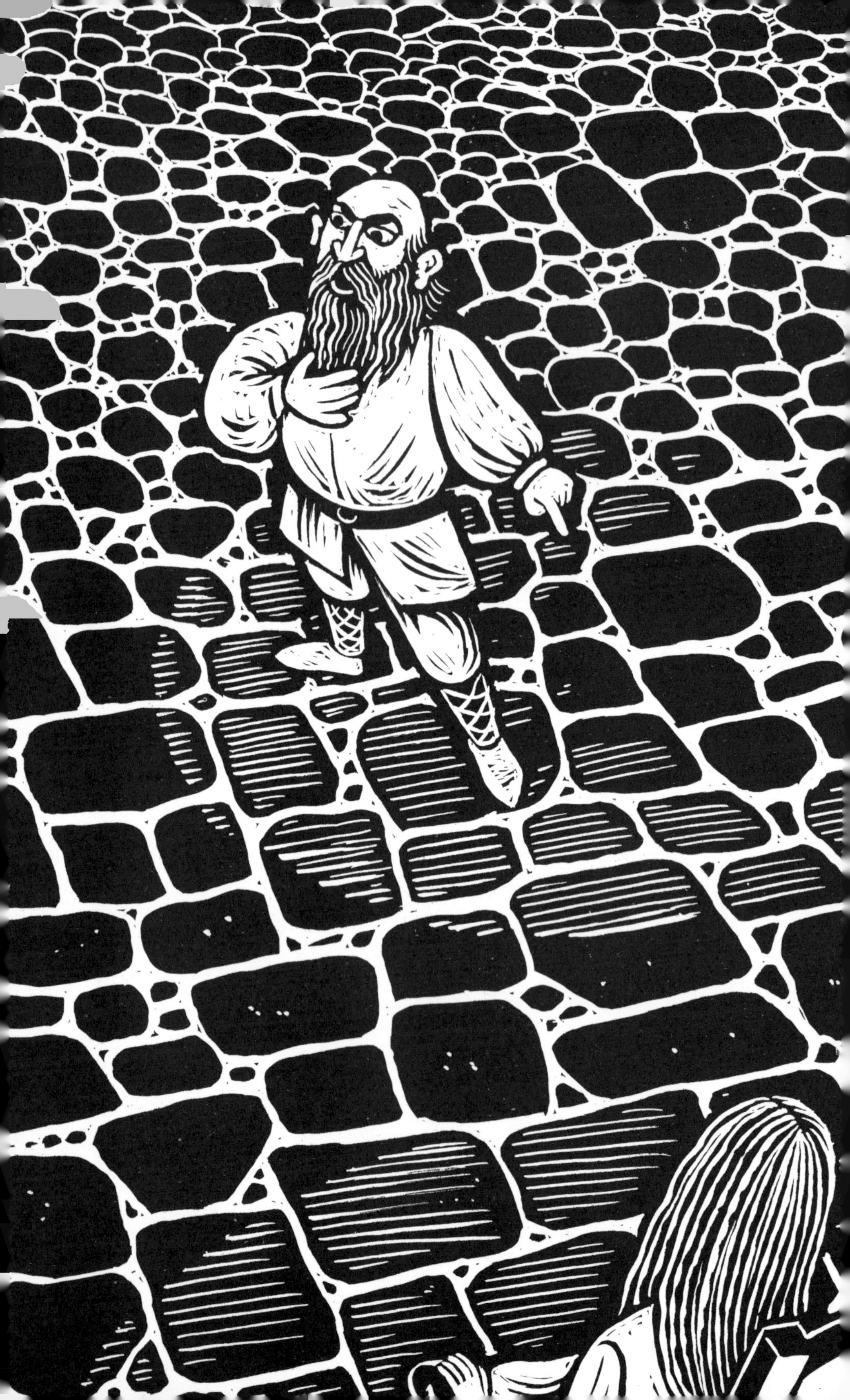

THRESHOLD

Libuše looked up into the eyes of her beloved, still breathing hard after their stolen moment of love, body to body, at the threshold of happiness but without hope of crossing it.

'Must it remain only this?' she whispered. 'Our love hidden away because of the misfortune of our birth?'

Přemysl met the gaze of his queen, embracing her as they lay upon a bed of moss in the sheltering forest. 'Though I daresay I have the heart of a king, and love you with the strength of iron, I was born into the body of a farmer. It would take a wondrous alchemy to forge a crown from an iron plough.'

'Indeed,' Libuše said, more to herself than to her love.

◈

Long ago, long before the written word was invented, there lived a good king called Krok who had no sons but was proud of his three daughters. King Krok established an academy where the wisest men in his land taught religion, hymns, prophecy and magic. But because this was a time before writing, all that was taught had to be memorized, and so it was committed to song, and spoken from tutor to pupil.

Of all the subjects taught at the academy, magic was considered of the greatest importance, as it was a gift from the gods. Whenever he was in need of advice, Krok would travel alone to a secluded glade deep in the forest and ask the gods for guidance. Once they came to him and told him to move away from the small castle in which he lived with his daughters, and instead to find a spot along the Vltava River to build a new one. Krok did as he was told, gathering the important men of the tribes under his dominion. They travelled the shore until they found a suitable place, upon a steep cliff that looked down

CHAPTER THREE

upon the rushing river below, where a spring of fresh water bubbled to the surface through the rock that would serve as his foundation. There he built a castle that would become his capitol and he called it Vysehrad, which meant High Castle, for so it was. Krok ruled there for thirty good years.

During that time, he raised his three daughters, Kazi, Teta and Libuše. All three were beautiful and wise. Kazi was gifted with the art of medicine. She knew how to heal with herbs and plants and magic, and she healed the sick of her father's kingdom from her own castle, Kazin. Teta was the high priestess of their religion, which she practised from her castle, Tetin. And the youngest daughter? Libuše, who lived at a castle called Libušin, bore the gift of prophecy, or so she said. At times she would fall into a trance and make predictions that would inevitably come true. When this happened, the people feared her, but because she was kind and beautiful and wise, she was the most admired of her sisters. When King Krok died, it was Libuše who was chosen to inherit his throne and become queen. And so she moved to Vysehrad and, for a long while, the people were happy with their queen.

In that land, there were no courts, and so it fell to the ruler to determine disputes among the people. Queen Libuše was wise and just, and she would sit beneath the vast linden tree in the courtyard of the castle, upon a platform covered with carpets, surrounded by the twelve wisest men of the realm, and hear the cases presented.

Once, when Queen Libuše's heart was sore with longing for her secret love, she sat in judgment as two neighbours argued over where one's land ended and the other's began. Having heard the arguments of each man, she consulted with her twelve advisers and, in all objective fairness, decided in favour of the younger of the neighbours.

As she did so, the older neighbour's face grew red and his mouth foamed into a rage, as he screamed at her, tearing the air with his voice: 'What kind of justice can we expect from a woman? You're all long on hair and short on brains!' He turned to the twelve wise men and continued, 'Let her sew and spin and bear children, but not rule and judge. Where else in this world does a woman rule over men? Our kingdom is a laughing stock among nations!'

All those assembled were dumbfounded. Silence echoed. Though it seemed that some of the wise men would speak, Libuše subtly gestured for them to remain seated. A flush came to her cheeks, which those around her read as shame and sorrow, though her eyes glimmered. She rose and addressed the crowd.

'You are right! I am a woman and I rule like a woman, not with a rod of iron, but with compassion, which you mistake for weakness. You do not deserve such a ruler. If it is iron you want, iron you shall have. I will let the people choose a man and I shall marry whomsoever they choose.'

Having said this, she left the shocked crowd and retired to her castle. She summoned her sisters, Teta and Kazi, and retreated to a secret, private garden in a hidden corner of the castle where none but the three sisters could go. There she stood before a gilded wooden statue of the god Perun, its head cast of solid silver, its beard of gold. Libuše did not kneel before it, but stared into the statue's cast eyes until darkness fell and her sisters arrived. Then the three sisters spoke in secret until dawn bled over the horizon.

That morning, Queen Libuše summoned the heads of the tribes over which she ruled to gather on the day after the harvest. When that day came, chieftains arrived from far and wide, wondering who would be chosen to marry their queen. Trumpets were blown to summon the meeting to order and all turned to Libuše, on her throne, flanked by her sisters. She spoke.

'You all know why I summoned you. You did not appreciate the freedom I gave you, so the gods inspired me to tell you that I shall rule you no more. You want a man to rule you. You want someone to drag your children away from you to serve him, to kill and die for him. You want a man who will tax you the way you deserve to be taxed, taking your best cattle and horses. You want to serve a hard master and to pay for it. None of this have I asked of you, and yet…You want

CHAPTER THREE

to be dominated rather than shamed by having a woman ruler. So be it! You will choose your king, but do so carefully and wisely, for it is easy to place someone on the throne and far harder to pry him off it.'

The assembled demurred. When she put it like that, they were no longer certain that they wanted an iron king. Libuše saw their hesitation and continued.

'If you wish, I can advise you on who to choose.'

This brought them relief and they shouted, 'Tell us! Advise us!'

Libuše nodded. She stood, her eyes clouded, her body trembled and, as some would later recall it, she seemed to rise up just off the ground and hover in the air. In a voice that seemed to emanate not from her throat but from some chasm deep within her, she said, 'Beyond the hills winds a small stream called Bilina. Where its banks bend there is a tiny village called Stadice. One hundred and twenty paces past the village, as you walk upstream through a narrow valley, you will find a field. In that field you will find your future king. He is disguised as a ploughman with a broken bast sandal and a pair of oxen, one brown with a white head, the other brown with a white stripe along his back and white hind legs. You will know him because he will be using his teeth to their best effect when no one else does and then he will dine at an iron table. Go to him, bring clothing befitting a king, tell this man that I have summoned him and it is the will of my people that he should marry me and become king. Our descendants will rule here forever. You will not have to ask the way. Take my white horse – she will lead you, you need only follow.'

With that, Libuše's vision ceased and she was once again one with her body. She sat back on her throne, weary but with a spark in her eyes.

Marvelling at the precision of this vision, the gathered chieftains assembled a retinue, gathered clothing befitting a future king and rode away from Vysehrad, led by the queen's white mare. The mare led them beyond the hills, along the Bilina stream and into the village of Stadice. One hundred and twenty paces beyond the border of the village, they entered a narrow valley and found a field stretched beside the road. There the white mare stopped. There were several men around, gathered beneath a tree taking their lunch, but one man, regal of bearing despite his humble clothing and position in life, stood alone, sawing off a branch of a hazel tree.

A member of the retinue pointed to him and turned to the others. 'Behold,' he said, 'which of the men here is using his teeth to their best effect?' He laughed to himself. 'While the others chew their meal, this man chews through wood with the teeth of his saw!' And the others saw that this was true and agreed.

'And look what sits in wait for him,' another of the retinue said. He pointed to a pair of oxen yoked to an iron plough that was halfway through tilling the field. The oxen were both brown, one with a white head and one with a white stripe along its back and white hind legs. They approached and saw that one of the straps on the man's bast sandal, a type of shoe made of plaited strips of linden, was torn.

'This is our king, as the prophecy foretold,' said one of the retinue. 'But I am not sure that our queen will like him.'

They approached the ploughman.

'What is your name, good sir?' they enquired.

'Přemysl,' he said in a strong voice. 'And who wishes to know?'

'We are the emissaries of your queen, Libuše. She has sent us to inform you that it is the will of the people that she marry you and that you become our king.'

Přemysl was in awe, but managed to hide his emotions. 'I have been expecting you,' he began, inventing as he went, 'for I saw all this in a dream, but thought it nothing more than fantasy. Would that you had come a little later, when I would have finished tilling the field. You came too soon and this warns of famine in our kingdom. Do you still wish me to come?'

'Oh yes, our king.'

'Very well. Then let us take a meal together, as a king among his chieftains.' At this, Přemysl turned his plough onto its side to act as a table, and he laid out a humble meal of bread and apples.

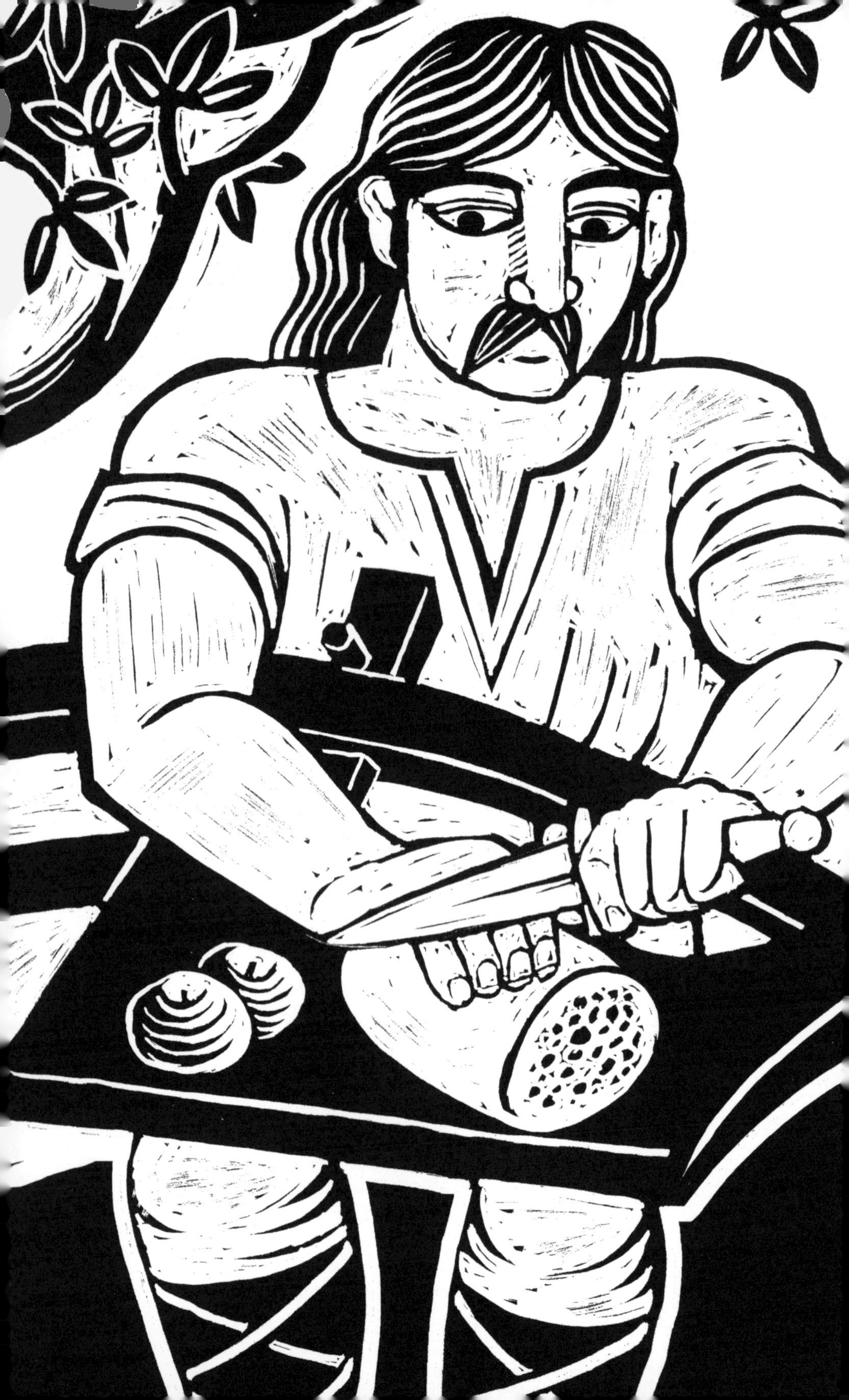

'Behold,' one of the retinue whispered to the others, 'he eats at an iron table.'

The retinue presented Přemysl with the clothing they had brought. He struck the hazel branch he had sawn from the tree into the field, freed his oxen and dressed in princely attire. Přemysl was about to discard his broken bast sandal, but instead held it up and handed it to one of the retinue. 'Let this function as a relic and proof of the story of how your king was chosen by the gods from among the humblest of men.'

And so it was. Přemysl followed the retinue back to Vysehrad, riding the queen's white mare. He and Libuše were wed and lived a long, happy life together. They founded a new capitol, which they called Praha, meaning 'threshold', for it was the point of entry for a new nation, the Bohemian Czechs. Přemysl became known as the Iron King, but for his strength, for he was just. There was indeed a famine in the land, as he had predicted, but it soon passed. That hazel branch he had planted in the field sprouted three young branches, but two of them withered, the villagers said, though one flourished. And so it would be with the offspring of Přemysl and Libuše. They had three sons. Radobyl and Lidomir died, but Nezamysl lived strong and inherited what became the Přemyslid dynasty.

As for the hazel branch, it is said that it continued to grow into a tree. In appreciation for the village having provided a king, the people of that village were exempt from paying taxes in perpetuity – beyond the requirement of paying a pint of hazelnuts each year, a tradition continued for centuries and still present under the reign of the Holy Roman Emperor Charles IV.

And the bast sandal? It was kept on display in the castle as a reminder that a peasant had risen to the throne, that his successors must never forget this, and that their duty was to serve and defend the peasantry. It became a custom for Přemyslid kings of Bohemia, while being crowned in royal attire, to wear bast sandals beneath their robes.

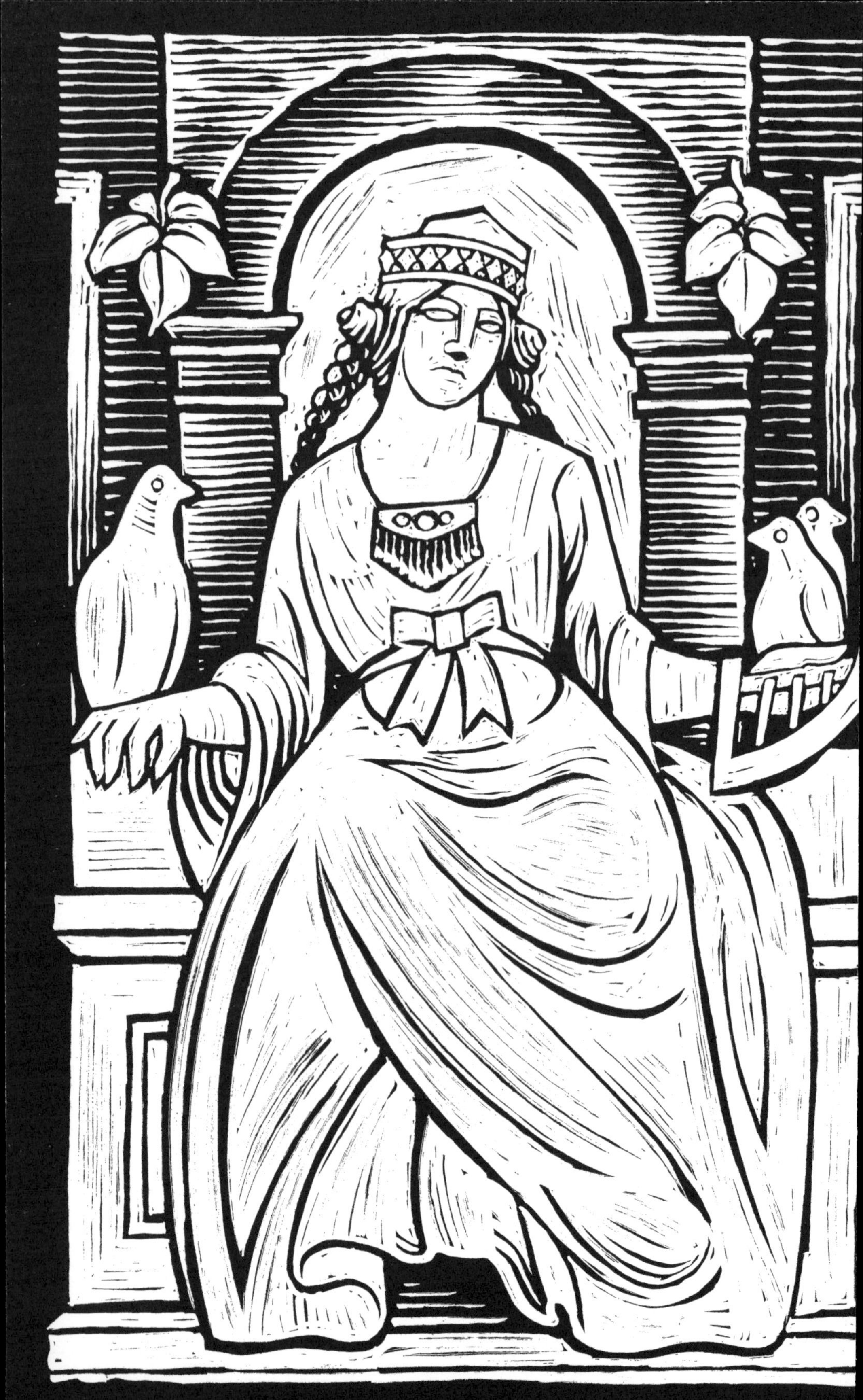

LIBUŠE AND WOMEN

The tale of Queen Libuše is said to date back to the 12th century, but it's a version from the 1890s that most Czech people know best.[32] According to the jacket copy on a modern edition of Alois Jirásek's *Old Czech Legends*, the stories were written 'before Czech independence and in an age of patriotic upsurge and romanticism. They quite naturally reflect a glorification of the Czech past. While the details of the legends are necessarily archaic, peopled by kings and noblemen, ghosts and magic, the themes are universal. Now, at the dawn of a new era of Czech independence, they provide a fascinating new perspective on the contemporary situation.'[33] That edition was published in 1992, as Czechoslovakia was giving way to the independent, democratic Czech Republic.

The myth of Libuše tells of a woman who decides where to build a city that will become the font and fortress of a new state. This future city has a symbolic name: Praha (Prague), which means 'the threshold'. Ancient myths include many founders, as well as a few architects – Romulus and Remus founding Rome, Ilos founding Ilios/Troy – but women founders are few and far between. Mircea Eliade, a renowned 20th-century Romanian historian and scholar of myths about builders, does not mention women at all. There was, however, an ancient cult of founding cities involving the goddess Tyche ('luck' in Greek) during the Hellenistic period after Alexander the Great's death, when his higher military staff were founding cities and states all over his swiftly assembled empire. Tyche is usually represented wearing a crown that looks like a fortress, a wall around the city. It seems likely that the Libuše story – or at least the part about founding Prague – is a mythurgical construct typical of a time when the state was in need of history.

CHAPTER THREE

There are founding myths associated with other cities. The emblem of Ljubljana, Slovenia's capital, is a green dragon; it comes from a mythical account in which Jason, returning home with his golden fleece, stopped there with the Argonauts to slay a dragon. Argonauts are also said to have dug the foundations of Emona, the ancient name for Ljubljana – although this is not supported by archaeology, as Emona was really a Roman military outpost that developed into a city. Ancient origin stories have often been affixed to newly founded places, ideas or even tourist items as a way of lending them the illusion of authority, propriety, ownership and endurance.

In the absence of such myths, architecture can achieve a similar goal. Capitol buildings and courthouses in American cities, often built in the late 18th or early 19th centuries, were designed to recall ancient Athenian architecture: all Corinthian columns, cornices and domes, pediments and marble floors. The aesthetic associated with ancient Athens symbolically conveyed ideas of enduring democratic rule. Without the need for anyone to create a foundation myth, the architecture silently attested to it. Totalitarian regimes such as fascism, Nazism and Soviet Stalinism often aspired to give an illusory impression of collective unity by copying the style of ancient buildings or depicting muscular bodies in monuments.

In the case of Prague, a founding myth was developed possibly in the 12th century or even earlier and then, centuries later, set down in writing in a form that is now considered definitive. It shifted from the category of folk tales (author unknown) to become a fairy tale (authored by Jirásek), but it was also adopted as mythical history – a tale that had been recounted so often, it became an ingrained story. Even so, few who thought carefully about it would consider it truthful, given its supernatural elements.

Several statues of Libuše can be found in Prague. There is one nonchalantly poised between two balconies on an art nouveau façade in the city centre (Karlova Street), watching with some curiosity the flow of contemporary street life far below. While Libuše is a positive figure, there is also a negative version of a woman builder in the story of a historical person, Irene Kantakouzine, known as Jerina. Jerina was a Byzantine princess married to the 15th-century Serbian despot Đurađ Branković. She has become a figure of evil, dubbed Jerina the Cursed, allegedly because she imposed taxes and forced her subjects to labour at building fortresses. Several epic poems about her in Serbian have been preserved and various fortresses, especially Smederevo Castle on the Danube, are still associated with her.[34]

It was a Byzantine custom for wealthy women to establish abbeys or monasteries, and women *ktitors* are therefore known all over the Balkans (*ktitor* being a modern Greek reading of *ktetor*, 'founder' or 'donor to monasteries'; they are often represented on frescoes carrying models of the buildings they sponsored). Widows would often retire to abbeys, bringing their remaining wealth with them and donating it to the institution as a sort of dowry. A widow who was rich enough might build an abbey herself.

A kind of inversion of the woman builder figure is that of the 'built-in' or walled-in woman, representing a collective memory of human sacrifice known among Slavs in funerary rituals and generally reserved for widows. There are many oral poems, ballads and epics on this topic, extending from present-day Montenegro and Serbia to Greece and Romania. 'The Building of the Skodra (Skadar) on the Bojana River' is the most famous of them.[35] In it, three newly wedded brothers unsuccessfully attempt to build a fortified city, until a prophecy reveals that only the sacrifice of a bride will make the building possible. The youngest and most devoted of the brothers' wives is to be the victim: she is referred to only as Gojkovica ('wife of Gojko'). The prophecy requires her to be walled into a tower of the fortifications, with a small window in the stone left open so that her baby can feed at her breast while she is dying. There is a similar story about the Arta Bridge in western Greece.[36] Such a horrifying and misogynistic ending is, alas, part of the patriarchal tradition that, in less gruesome fashion, required Libuše to take a husband in order to satisfy her people. Rather depressingly, mythical women must frequently be marginalized or sacrificed for the good of the people.[37]

These myths reveal the power of the fertility rituals that are always present in constructing and guarding a habitat. They are as important to the process of creating bridges and roads as they are for nations and cities. While the myth of Mokoš/Baba Yaga features a mobile home for the goddess – a log cabin on chicken legs – a Slovenian myth from the Karst region features a combination of the Roman sibyl and a devil goddess on a flaming carriage, Šembilja, who thunders along trailing tongues of flame, preferring Roman roads for her wild rides.[38]

Slavic deities that dwell in homes, like the Russian Domovoy and Kikimora (male and female household gods, respectively),[39] can be connected to deities and spirits in different mythologies that take care of the home and the hearth: the Greek Hestia and the Roman Lari among them. The Slavic home protectors, who are not always benevolent, demand small gifts – a cup of milk left for them at the threshold, for instance. Kikimora sometimes dwells outside the home, in a bog or a forest.[40] In Dalmatia, the coastal region of Croatia, it is still common today to leave a cup of milk by the threshold of one's home for a resident snake, which will then protect the home from other snakes. The threshold and doorway are, ritually, the most important part of a home, along with the roof. The door is a point of transition while the roof is inhabited by the spirits of ancestors. This is shown by the early 20th-century Serbian scholar and translator Veselin Čajkanović in his study of the role of the groom's mother in Serbia, Bosnia and Herzegovina, who, during the wedding, climbs onto the roof and dances to attract spirits to come and bless the marriage.[41]

In light of all these elements, Libuše as the founder of a city named 'Threshold' might be regarded as the household deity of Prague. All too often, however, the female protagonists of Slavic myth must be sacrificed – either peacefully, like Libuše, simply abdicating power to a husband she did not need, or violently, as in the case of Gojkovica. The role of the woman builder is dangerously close to that of the built-in woman.

4

DO NOT WEEP

THREE VERSIONS OF THE GREAT GODDESS

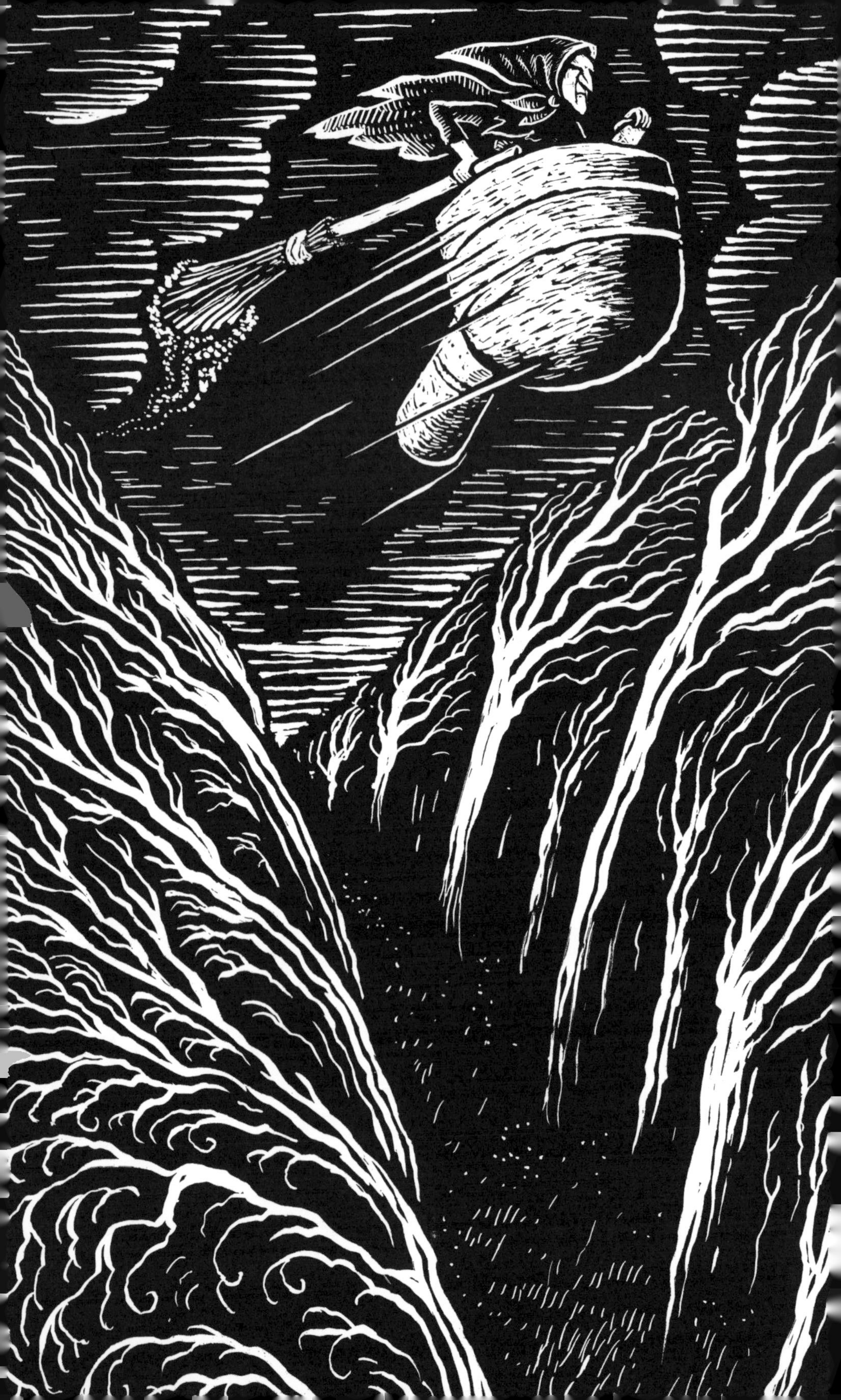

DO NOT WEEP

Wander, my child, across three times nine kingdoms, thread the links in a chain of mighty mountains, and you will come to a remote tsardom where a merchant once dwelt. Twelve years had he been married but in all that time, no son was born, merely a single daughter. But like you, my child, this little girl was as beautiful as the moon, and so they called her Vasilissa the Beautiful.

When Vasilissa was eight years old, her mother grew sick and her condition worsened. Fearing that she would soon die, she called her beloved daughter to her. Vasilissa had once rejoiced when called to her mother's bedroom, where the two would kiss and embrace and laugh upon the great bed. But now she moved with solemn weight upon her, for she could feel the darkness that approached and could guess what this summons meant.

Seeing Vasilissa's face, hesitant and on the verge of tears, her mother tried to raise her own strength to pass it to her daughter. She called her over to the bed.

'My little Vasilissa, my dear one, look who lies in the bed beside me.' And she pulled aside the blanket to reveal a tiny wooden doll that she had carefully and secretly made as a gift. When the blanket was drawn away and the wooden face stared up at Vasilissa, the little girl could not help but smile, even though the face of the doll did not smile back. In fact, the doll had no face at all: its head was just a rounded egg of wood, without markings upon it.

At the sight of her daughter's smile, Vasilissa's mother felt a touch of peace.

'Vasilissa, I am dying, as I see that you know. My time with you has been the most beautiful time of my life, and I am only sorry to leave you so soon. But a part of me will always remain with you.' At

CHAPTER FOUR

this Vasilissa began to cry, but her mother touched her shoulders softly, as if they might crack, and went on, 'Remember my words to you and be certain to fulfil my wishes, and you will keep my blessing with you always.

'I have made this doll for you and it is my gift to you. Keep it with you at all times, and never, never show it to anyone. If you feel sorrow come upon you, or if evil threatens to harm you, then go into a dark corner where no one can see, remove the doll from your pocket and give it something to eat and to drink.' Vasilissa's teary eyes widened as her mother continued, 'The doll will begin to move on its own. It will eat and drink a small amount and then it will look up at you. Then you may talk to it, tell it your troubles, express your fears, speak your sadness, ask its advice, and it will be there for you, to advise you and even help you in your time of need.'

Vasilissa took that wooden doll from her mother's hands, pale, blue and cold as the ocean, and clutched it to her. Her mother kissed her daughter for the last time, made a blessing upon her and fell asleep, never again to wake.

Vasilissa was wracked with sorrow. Her mother had always been her only companion, for her merchant father was often away, she had no siblings and no children lived nearby. Now she was wholly alone. She took to her bed, pulled her blankets above her head and wept until she felt that every strand of feeling, every cup of tears that her small body could produce, had been purged. All that remained were exhaustion, fatigue and loneliness.

In her sadness, she had been clutching the wooden doll to her, hugging it as she would have liked to hug her mother, and it slowly dawned on her that, through this doll, a part of her mother might still remain with her. So she shook off her upset as best she could, pushed aside the blanket and took the doll into a shadowy corner of her bedroom. She sat it upon a stool there and stole away to the kitchen to fetch something to eat and something to drink. She returned with a crust of black bread and a tiny cup of kvass, the drink made from black bread, and she placed them on the stool beside the doll.

The doll did not move.

Vasilissa grew fearful that even this legacy of her mother would fail her, never to appear. But she fought back her hammering heart and said aloud, 'Take this meal, my little doll. A bite to eat, a drop to drink and hear of me my sorrow. My beloved mother has died, and I am so lonely.'

There was a long pause, my child, but do you know what happened? The doll's blank, egg-shaped wooden head suddenly lifted up. Its wooden arms slowly, almost mechanically, shifted and reached out for the crust of black bread and the cup of kvass. The doll brought the food and drink to its invisible mouth and both bread and drink disappeared, eaten away into nothingness, vanishing although there was no mouth to be seen. When the doll was done, she placed the empty cup back upon the stool and raised her head up towards Vasilissa. Upon that once-blank face, my child, now burned a pair of fire-orange eyes, looking up at Vasilissa. And then the doll spoke, with a voice like a mother's whisper in the ear of a sleeping baby.

'Do not weep, Vasilissa. Sorrow stalks by night but flees the morning light. Lie back in your bed, close your tired eyes, hold me close to you as you would like to hold your mother and welcome sleep. The morning light is wiser than night.' Then the fire-orange eyes extinguished, and the doll's face was once more a blank curve of wood.

Vasilissa nodded, lifted the doll to her, clutched it tight and climbed back into bed. Sleep overtook her, welcome sleep, and when she woke, her sorrow had inched back in slow, begrudging retreat.

When Vasilissa's father returned from his travels and found his wife gone, he wept and mourned and retreated into himself. He was not there for Vasilissa when she needed him most, as indeed he had never truly been there, even when he was at home. Vasilissa was used to this and had expected no more from him. She was her own rock, small and humbled against the pull of the wake of sorrow, but she

CHAPTER FOUR

would have to hold fast, because she knew that no one but her mother would have been able to help her, and her mother was no longer.

Her father mourned for a respectable amount of time, one day longer than was prescribed by tradition, and then turned his attentions to finding a new wife. While he was poor of compassion and warmth, he was also wealthy, owned a goodly home and several horses, and generously – and visibly – donated to the church every Sunday, at least on the Sundays when he was neither travelling nor asleep. This all suited many women perfectly, and there was no shortage of potential new wives. Vasilissa's father's eye fell upon a widow his own age with two daughters of her own who, he thought, might be good companions for Vasilissa, and would provide extra hands to work around the house. The widow was particularly beautiful, but while Vasilissa's father had a heart short on compassion and warmth, the widow did not seem to have any heart at all. Just a hollow, tin fist where her heart should have been.

Vasilissa learned this within days of the widow's arrival at their home. She overheard her new stepmother telling her daughters that they would remain in this family only so long as the merchant father spent most of his time abroad and the money was ample. Vasilissa tried to warn her father during one of the few moments when the two were alone, but he would hear none of it, for women have ways, my child, of diverting a man's attention from what it should be focused upon, and the stepmother was well versed in such traps.

That the stepmother should dislike Vasilissa made little sense, aside from the fact that her own daughters, somewhat older than Vasilissa, were plain of face and crow-like, while Vasilissa was the most beautiful girl anyone in their village had ever seen, or imagined that they ever would, with the beauty of a raven. First, the stepmother dismissed the merchant's modest staff from the house: a married couple, one maid and one butler, who had been all Vasilissa could call family since her mother's passing. Vasilissa knew that her stepmother had done this simply to save money so that she could keep more for herself, but she

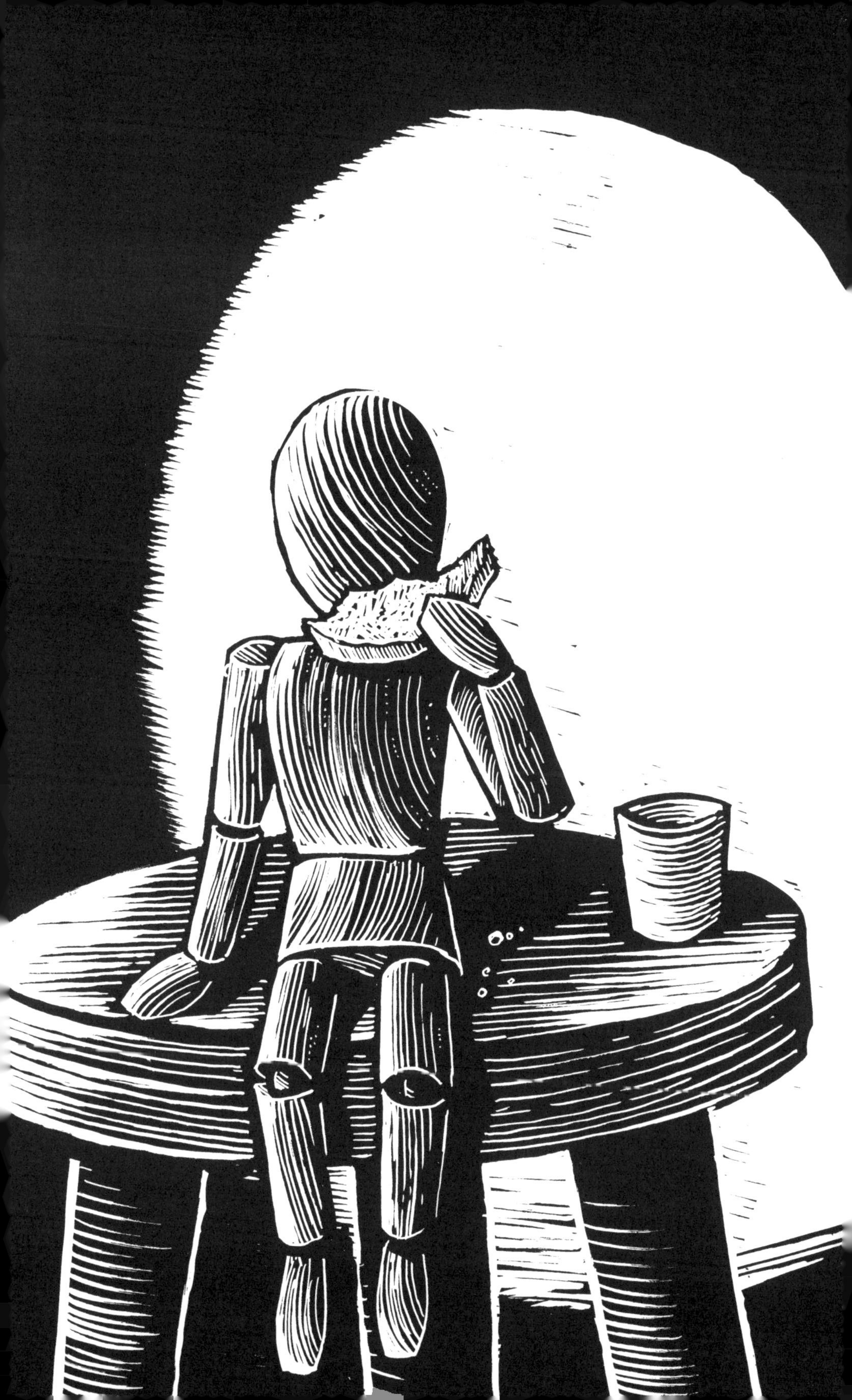

could not convince her father of the stepmother's ill intentions. The housework fell not on the stepmother's two daughters, as Vasilissa's father had imagined, but onto Vasilissa herself.

Envy encouraged Vasilissa's new stepsisters to pour both scorn and chores upon her, for they wanted not only to poison her good spirit, but also to wilt her beauty to amplify theirs. They instructed her to work outdoors, to tan her milk-white skin, and made her lift, sweep and drag so as to thin out her idyllic softness and bring out her bones. But their efforts failed, for Vasilissa's goodness could not be siphoned off, and her beauty was neither burned away by the sun nor starved by toil.

The stepmother and her daughters were mad with confusion. No matter how arduous or complex the task, Vasilissa was able to complete it, and she never appeared the worse for wear. They came up with ever more arcane tasks. Once they emptied a pot of boiled lentils into the still-hot ashes of the kitchen hearth and told Vasilissa to pick them out again, every one, before the ashes had cooled. When they returned from whatever idle, boring, hard-hearted women do all day, the pot was once more filled with lentils and the ashes remained warm as wolf's breath.

Vasilissa was able to achieve all this thanks to her great secret.

As soon as her stepmother and the daughters were out of sight, Vasilissa would find a shadowy corner and remove the tiny doll from a hidden pocket she had sewn into her dress. She would give the doll a small amount to eat and a small amount to drink, and say, 'Take this meal, my little doll. A bite to eat, a drop to drink and hear of me my sorrow.' Then she would explain what she was obliged to do. The doll would consume some food and quaff some drink with that mouthless wooden face, and then the fire-orange eyes would glow.

'Do not weep, Vasilissa,' it would say in her lost mother's voice. 'Sorrow stalks by night but flees the morning light. I will assist you in your tasks. The morning light is wiser than night.' Then the doll would do whatever the girl had been tasked with. When the work was done, the fire-orange eyes would extinguish and Vasilissa would place the doll back into her hidden pocket. There was no joy in Vasilissa's life, but at least the little doll prevented her from collapsing with suffering. In the form of the doll, a sliver of her mother remained with her, keeping her afloat in the storm.

In this sorry state, years passed. The stepmother and her daughters never stopped pouring work upon Vasilissa, but their jealousy grew stale out of habit and no longer bit at them each time they set eyes upon her beauty. Eventually Vasilissa reached the age when thoughts naturally turn to marriage. All the young men from the village and beyond stopped by the house when her father was in, to ask for Vasilissa's hand in marriage. Not one came to enquire after the stepmother's two daughters, even though they were older than Vasilissa and, by rights, should have been married off first. Whenever Vasilissa's father considered a young man to be a good choice, the stepmother would say, 'The elder daughters are first to wed, or you will never be welcome in my bed.' And that was that. Each suitor poured fuel on the stepmother's envy and hatred, and the only option for escape that appeared open to Vasilissa – marriage to, she hoped, a young man who would at least be kind, if not truly good, for one should not hope for too much – remained blocked. If not for the tiny doll hidden in her dress, that relic of her now long-lost mother, Vasilissa would have sought to take her own life.

◈

For the past few months, the merchant father had encountered rough times. Thrice had ships bearing goods he wished to sell been dashed upon the rocks by storms at sea. He pooled the last of his finances and decided to make one more investment, all or nothing, to save his status and home. To do so, he would have to travel abroad for some time, much longer than his usual trips.

No sooner had his horse and carriage vanished over the horizon than the stepmother sold their house and all its contents, packed and

CHAPTER FOUR

moved away to a far-off place, a gloomy, shadow-stricken cottage at the edge of a briary forest, where the father would not be able to find them. Vasilissa was unable to do anything but follow meekly, for she could see no escape as a young, unmarried girl whom no one would believe, without a penny to her name or a friend in the world aside from that tiny wooden doll.

The stepmother was foul and vile of heart, but she was not a murderess, and she saw a material benefit in Vasilissa. Any work Vasilissa was given, no matter how difficult, would be completed swiftly and thoroughly. The stepmother had tested the limits of Vasilissa's capabilities. Once, she asked her to chop firewood sufficient for the entire winter: the next morning, row upon row of logs were lined up neatly, each chopped to precisely the same size. The stepmother was no fool. She could see that some magic was about, although she could not figure out what it was. In any case, the figuring out was less important to her than the benefit of that magic, for Vasilissa would do *anything* the stepmother needed done, and that was a powerful tool.

That said, should some accident befall young Vasilissa, the stepmother would not have been bothered. With all the money she had made from selling the merchant father's estate, she could easily afford to hire a maid and butler so that she would still never have to lift a finger.

It was her two daughters who wished Vasilissa would disappear, for they remained ever in her shadow. Plain and crow-like, they were ignored by suitors even here at their new home in a new land. The daughters wished more than anything for Vasilissa to vanish, because they saw in her raven beauty their only obstacle to finding husbands.

And so the stepmother began to set Vasilissa tasks that required her to venture deep into the briary, darkling forest behind the cottage. Often she asked Vasilissa to gather mushrooms. The reason for this was that the stepmother had learned that the forest was home to a horrible witch by the name of Baba Yaga. This ancient, evil crone was said to feast on children just as mortal men eat chickens. The

DO NOT WEEP

comparison was a poetic one since, the story went, Baba Yaga lived in a hut perched on hundreds of severed hen's legs that, through her enchantment, could walk about, moving the hut this way and that at her bidding.

Should Vasilissa bring us mushrooms and fulfil all the other chores, thought the stepmother, I shall be content with the work provided. But should Vasilissa encounter Baba Yaga and fall victim to her, I shall be just as content, and my daughters even more so. And so it went that, almost every day, Vasilissa was sent on an errand into the forest.

Now, my child, you might think that surely Vasilissa would run into Baba Yaga, or that the ancient witch would smell her delicious flesh and hunt her down. That is what would have happened – but every time Vasilissa entered the forest, no sooner did she step inside the shadow of the thorny trees than she would take the tiny doll from her pocket, offer it a crumb lifted from the pantry and a thimbleful of kvass, and the doll would brighten its fire-orange eyes and come to her aid.

'Do not weep, Vasilissa,' it would say in her lost mother's voice. 'Sorrow stalks by night but flees the morning light. I will assist you in your tasks. The morning light is wiser than night.' The doll would provide whatever the stepmother had required and keep Vasilissa away from the ancient witch.

The two daughters were not satisfied. They did not recognize the value of keeping Vasilissa alive to work for them and wished only for her to disappear, for they imagined that, with her gone, they would find the happiness that had eluded their sour hearts. Finally the stepmother, growing tired of her daughters' complaints, made a plan to force Vasilissa to encounter the ancient witch.

One evening in autumn, the stepmother summoned Vasilissa and her two daughters to the sitting room. She assigned each of them a task: one daughter must make lace and the other a pair of hose, while Vasilissa must spin a wicker basket full of flax. They had to finish by dawn and set to work by the light of a single candle, for darkness had

CHAPTER FOUR

fallen. While they worked, the stepmother carefully extinguished all the other candles in the house and poured well water onto the fires.

The two daughters, having been given the easier, faster tasks, naturally finished first. One of them, as she stood to leave the room, pretended to trip and knocked over the candle, dousing the flame as she fell upon it. Vasilissa would have to finish spinning the flax without light.

'What a shame,' said the other daughter.

'Yes,' said the first, 'while we have finished our work, Vasilissa has not, and cannot do so without fire to light the candle. Vasilissa, you must go and fetch fire and bring it back here, so you can finish your work.'

'But where shall I find fire in the middle of the night?' Vasilissa asked innocently.

'The only house near to ours is the hut in the forest where Baba Yaga lives. You must go. Now. And never come back, unless you have flames in your hand!'

The daughters chased Vasilissa out of the house and into the dark maw of night. The cold autumn air whipped cracked, dried leaves about her face, blowing her soiled white dress into ragged veils behind her as she pushed through the wind towards the yawning black forest.

Rain began to hammer down, as if clapped into action by a strike of thunder, and Vasilissa ducked under the shade of a hawthorn, its trunk like an arm, its branches a claw. She shivered against the cold rain and pulled the tiny doll from its hidden pocket. It was a good thing she had kept some crumbs in that pocket, because she hadn't had time to go to the kitchen before her stepsisters chased her from the house.

'Take this meal, my little doll. A bite to eat...' But she had nothing to offer for the doll to drink. No kvass, no wine, no beer. Then she looked to the skies. She cupped her palm and caught the rain. 'And a drop to drink,' she continued, relieved, 'and hear of me my sorrow.' The tiny doll began to move in her hand and its eyes of fire began to burn. 'My stepsisters have cast me from the house,' Vasilissa said, barely whispering without weeping. 'And I cannot return without fire, and the only fire nearby is at the hut of the ancient witch, Baba Yaga, who will surely eat me. What am I to do?'

'Do not weep, Vasilissa,' the doll said in her buried mother's voice. 'Sorrow stalks by night but flees the morning light. I will assist you. Go to the witch's hut, and I will ensure that no harm befalls you.' Vasilissa nodded, placed the doll back into her pocket, pulled the hood of her cloak over her head and ran into the tar-black forest.

Now, my child, imagine a forest at night. A dark forest, full of twisted roots and claw branches and trunks like arms. Now picture it in the midst of a downpour, water falling from the sky so thickly that you could scarcely see if you were out in the open – but the rain is deflected by the canopy of the trees, and so it falls in slashes like liquid knives. Oh yes, it was hard going through the forest, and truth be told, Vasilissa did not know the way. She trusted only that the doll would guide her.

She could not imagine that anyone else would be in so bleak a forest by night, especially in a rainstorm, and so she was very much surprised to hear a sound in the distance like that of a horse's hooves pounding a path. Yes, indeed, it did sound like a horse at a gallop. And she was even more surprised when, coming up suddenly from behind her, emerging like a flash from the shadows, a horse with a cloud-white hide dashed out and past her. A man rode the horse, but he wore a hood against the rain. It happened so quickly that Vasilissa could not see him well, but she knew he had worn all white. It took an additional moment of thought for her to register surprise and to doubt her own memory when she realized that both his white attire and his horse's white coat had been unblemished by mud and untouched by the rain, as clean and white as if freshly laundered.

She shook her head, unsure what to make of it. And so she pressed on...until she heard the hoofbeats again, coming back. Now she slipped behind a boulder in order to get a better look at the white horseman, and was even more surprised to see that the horse that

CHAPTER FOUR

suddenly galloped past was not white at all – instead it was a scarlet red, wholly unnatural and unlike any horse she had ever seen. So scarlet was it that she wondered if it was the same horse all bloodied, but the scarlet colouring did not drip or clump like gore. It appeared to be the natural colour of the beast. She thought that it was the same man riding this horse, the same stature and hooded, but this man's attire was likewise scarlet from head to toe.

As the horse and horseman passed, Vasilissa marvelled as the rain suddenly stopped and she saw the sun begin to rise, turning the sky as red as the horse. She had not realized she had been wandering the whole night through. Once she might have been worried that she had failed at the task cast upon her by her stepsisters, but she was no longer so naive. They wanted to be rid of her, and the task had been but a pretext. They could wait.

However, she was still lost in the forest, and the breaking sunlight barely penetrated the thicket of branches that made the forest floor dark even in daylight. Vasilissa began to wonder if the doll had finally failed her, but she had no food to offer it in order to bring it to life once more. Just as she was about to give up and collapse from exhaustion, she spotted a clearing in the wood ahead. She approached it cautiously, her heavy legs tripping over undergrowth, her hooded cloak weighted down with the rain. She tumbled forward when her foot caught a root and stopped herself behind the trunk of a beech tree, the last one before the glade opened up.

In the middle of the glade stood a dilapidated little hut. Its walls were cracked and peeling like rotting, sunburned skin. Its thatched roof was tangled and marled. It had no windows, but smoke slithered up from a central chimney and melted into the sky. It was, as legend had stated, supported by hundreds of chicken legs, which made a skirt around its foundations and kept it from touching the ground. But these could barely be seen because of the fence around the hut.

This fence was thrice as tall as Vasilissa and was made entirely of bones. Oh yes, my child, if only they had been from chickens. The

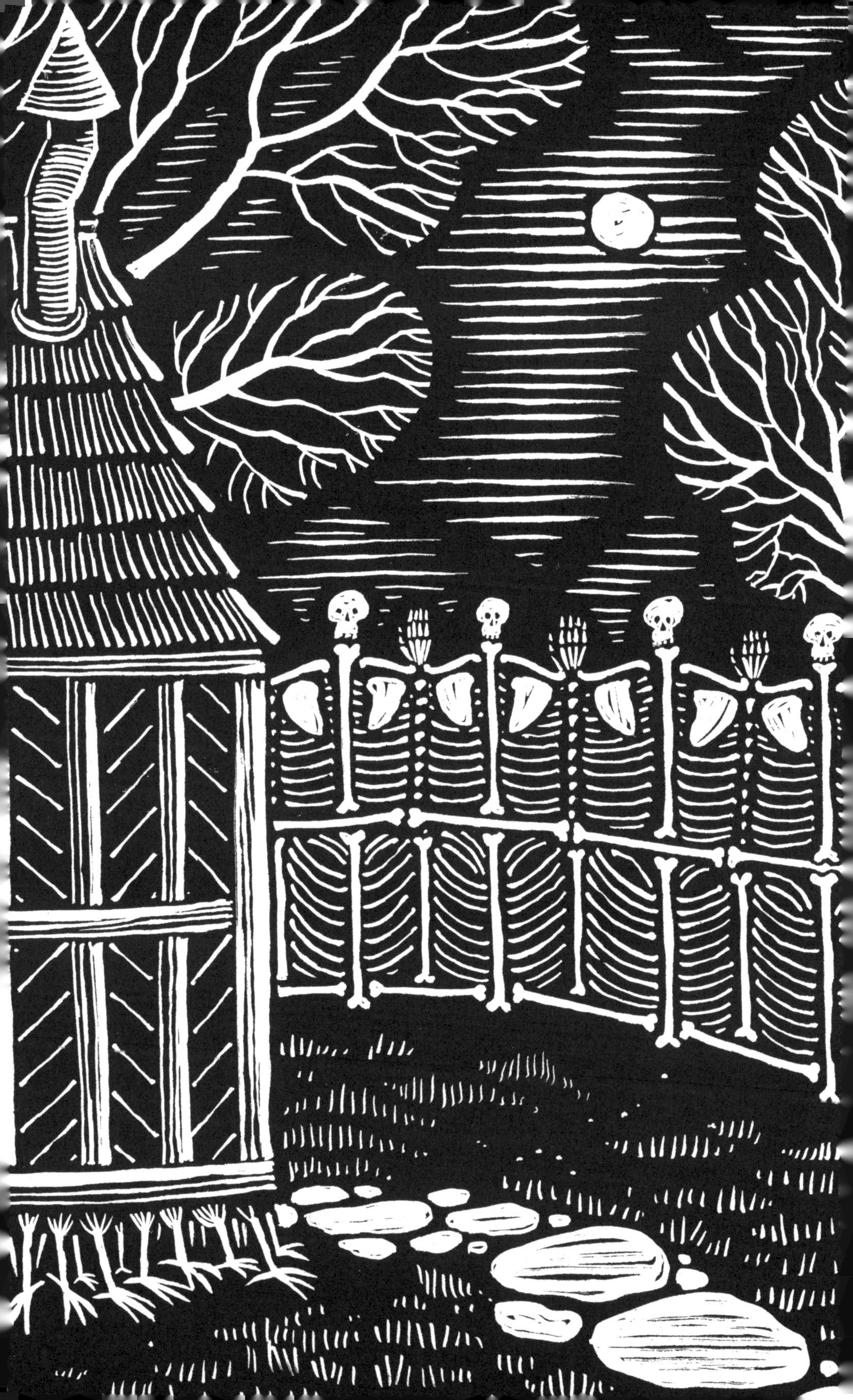

CHAPTER FOUR

fence appeared to be woven out of human ribcages, linked together like chains. It was topped with human skulls facing away from the forest, towards the hut, scores of them running round the fence that embowered the hut. There was a single gate, which was shut. The gate was made from the bones of human hands, somehow solidified so that they looked like webs. The hinges were the bones of human feet and the lock was a human jaw, pocked by teeth that had been filed to razor-sharp points. It was so fearsome a sight that Vasilissa crossed herself, recoiled and clutched at her heart.

But just as she did so, the sound of a horse's hoofbeats thundered towards her once again. This time she spun round to see a horse as black as tar, its rider dressed in similar midnight tones. The horse galloped past and then leapt an unnatural distance, from the thick of the forest by the glade, passing over the grass in the clearing. While it was in the air, its form stretched in mid-leap and the bone gate swung open for it so that it landed inside the fence – only for the bone gate to snap shut, like a bear trap, behind it. As soon as it did the day slipped away, sinking into the forest like white ink into fissures in the earth, and to Vasilissa's confusion, it was night once more.

But it did not appear to be night around the hut. Oh, no, for as soon as darkness rose, light oozed out of the eye sockets of the skulls all around the fence and bathed the hut in a semblance of daylight. Thus the hut and its embowered glade were like an island of unnatural light in an ocean of darkness. As Vasilissa looked upon it she felt such profound terror that she could not bring herself to move. Which was the more frightening proposition: the tar-black forest, or the sickly lit hut on hen's legs?

Before Vasilissa could decide, the world chose for her. The forest, once eerily silent, began to creak, then to groan, then to moan, as if the very trees, underbrush and soil suffered. The creaking of the trees gave way to a cracking, splintering sound as an avenue of them bent apart to open a clear path through their canopies, splitting and breaking in order to do so, bearing their anguish willingly, for they offered an aerial path for Baba Yaga herself. There she was, my child, riding towards the clearing inside a giant iron mortar, steering it with an equally colossal iron pestle, which she used as a boatman would a stick. With her other hand, she swept the air behind her with a wooden broomstick that bristled with bunched twigs, the tips of which ended in starlight.

Her mortar transport stopped short before the bone gate. It floated there, just above the grass of the glade, bobbing as if the air contained waves like the sea. And she spoke.

'Little hut, little hut, stand as thy mother built thee. Turn thy back against the forest and now face me.'

As Baba Yaga uttered this incantation, Vasilissa saw the hut's hundreds of legs move, shift and shuffle, so that the structure rotated completely around, revealing a doorway she had not seen before. A fire burned inside the hut, beckoning warmly to Baba Yaga. But Baba Yaga did not go in.

'What's this I smell?' she asked aloud. 'Meat! Who's there?' And then she stared straight at, or perhaps it was through, the tree behind which Vasilissa hid. The girl knew that there was no point in running or hiding any longer. She instinctively clutched at the wooden doll in her dress and felt a modicum of comfort in feeling it there, though she had no food nor drink with which to animate it again now. So out she stepped from behind the beech tree and placed her foot within the glade. Once within, she bowed and said, with all humility, 'It is only I, Vasilissa, grandmother. My stepsisters sent me to you to borrow fire.'

'Hmm,' said Baba Yaga, fingering a hairy wart that clung to her half-bearded chin. 'I know them. If I give you fire, little girl, then you must stay with me long enough to pay for it. If you do not work for me during this time, then you will become my supper.'

Not waiting for an answer, Baba Yaga spun around and faced her bone gate. 'You, my solid locks, unbolt; my stout gate, snap open!' The bone gate did as it was told. Vasilissa followed Baba Yaga as she floated inches above the grass in her mortar and entered the gate, which clacked shut behind her.

CHAPTER FOUR

The ancient witch hopped out of her floating mortar with an agility that surprised Vasilissa. It was only then that the girl got a good look at her. Baba Yaga was shorter even than Vasilissa, but her features were all oversized. Her breasts were huge but limp, like wet loaves of bread, sagging down over her belly. Her nose was enormous, so oversized that Vasilissa had the impression she might fall over. Her chin, too, was like the base of a crescent moon, tufted with fur like a mangy dog, and with a wart that sprouted several long, feline whiskers. Her eyes shone as if lamp-lit. She had barely any hair upon her head, far more on her chin, but what strips remained were matted down by a black bandana. Giant golden hoops hung from her ears and weighed them down, and her gnarled hands, swollen of knuckle, were studded with golden rings. She wore a white halter above a green skirt trimmed in gold thread. Her bare legs were mapped with blue veins and her feet clad in wooden clogs with pointed toes.

Out of the mortar, which then parked itself in a corner of the hut, Baba Yaga sat atop a brown-tiled stove in which a fire burned green. Because she was so short, and the stove rather large, her veiny legs hung in the air. She swung them in a childlike manner as she looked Vasilissa over with curiosity, or possibly hunger.

The hut appeared far larger from the inside than from without. It was ringed with skull lamps fixed to the walls, their tops sliced off and fire flickering through the eyes and out of the clipped heads. An octagonal wooden table sat before the tiled stove, and to left and right of this central section the hut, which from the outside had looked modest and entirely round, seemed to stretch into long corridors, as far back as Vasilissa could see. They were jumbled with stacks and cascades of all manner of odd objects, most of which Vasilissa preferred not to examine too closely.

'Let us see if you can serve, my dear,' Baba Yaga said. 'Place upon my table all that is in the stove, for I hunger.'

Vasilissa lowered her eyes, nodded and did as she was told. She first picked up a bit of tinder from a pile near the opening to the tiled stove and lit it in one of the green-tipped flames that flickered in an open-topped skull lamp. She then used it to light a candle that stood in the middle of the octagonal table. Then she approached the stove and looked inside. There were three iron platters, each filled with a roasted ox. How the oxen had been placed inside the relatively small opening to the stove, she could not say, nor how she might pull them out. But when she hooked a platter with a bent poker and pulled it towards her, out it slid. The succulent meat was slicked with grease and made her tummy rumble. Three whole roast oxen was quite a meal.

Baba Yaga nodded, and the iron platters floated from the lip of the tiled stove over to the table where she now sat, having hopped down from the top of the stove. She indicated to Vasilissa where her pantry stood, and from it the girl brought a flagon of kvass, a pot of honey and a bottle of black wine. Vasilissa watched the ancient witch eat, more like a shark than a person, tearing off great hunks of ox and swallowing it without chewing. In no time, the three carcasses were naught but bone. Baba Yaga cracked one of the ribs and used it as a toothpick. Having eaten and drunk her fill, she snapped her fingers and a small wooden bowl of cabbage broth appeared to feed Vasilissa.

Baba Yaga, satiated, leapt back to the top of the tiled stove and lay there to sleep upon the tiles, warmed by the fire within. She yawned, revealing a maw of shark-like teeth. Each was a perfect bladed triangle, as if she sharpened them each morning with an iron file.

'Listen to me, little girl, and do precisely what I say. Tomorrow, when I pestle off into the forest, you shall clean my yard, sweep the hut floors and prepare my supper. Then take a quarter measure of wheat from my pantry and remove from it every black grain and each wild pea within. If you do not do precisely what I say, then you shall be my supper.'

In no time, the witch was snoring. Vasilissa waited until she was certain Baba Yaga slept soundly. Then she stole away to a dark corner, removed the wooden doll from her hidden pocket and placed a bite of cabbage and a drop of black wine before it. Before she could utter the words of her incantation, she burst into tears, then bit her lip until it bled, to silence herself so as not to wake the ancient witch.

'Take this meal, my little doll. A bite to eat and a drop to drink and hear of me my sorrow. I am in the house of Baba Yaga and the bone gate is locked and I am so afraid. If I do not fulfil her tasks, she will eat me. What am I to do?'

The little doll's eyes flickered on, like dancing candle flames. It swallowed the cabbage and black wine and replied, 'Do not weep, Vasilissa. I will assist you. Say your prayers and sleep deeply. Sorrow stalks by night but flees the morning light.' The girl nodded and did as she was told, tucking the doll away in her dress, before lying down in a pile of straw before the tiled stove...but not too close to it.

The next thing she knew, she awoke with Baba Yaga leaning over her, her pendulous breasts hanging down above Vasilissa's head.

'How did you do it?'

'Do what, grandmother?' Vasilissa was not quite awake yet.

'Everything I asked. You cleaned my yard, swept the hut floors and prepared my supper. Then you took a quarter measure of wheat from my pantry and removed from it every black grain and each wild pea within. How?'

Vasilissa wasn't sure what to say, so she told the truth. 'With my mother's blessing, grandmother.'

'Blessing?' Baba Yaga spat with disgust. 'Oh no, my dear, that won't do at all. We can't have anyone blessed with blessings here. You must leave straight away.'

Not wishing to wait and see if the witch would change her mind, Vasilissa quickly stood, straightened her dress and made her way to the door.

'Not so fast,' Baba Yaga said sharply. Vasilissa froze. 'You did all I asked,' she continued, 'so you shall have your fire.'

The witch took one of the skulls from the wall, green fire burning through its eye sockets and out of its boneless top. She handed it to

Vasilissa, saying, 'This will provide all the fire your stepmother and stepsisters could want.'

Vasilissa thanked her. She took the skull in her hands. It did not feel hot, though the green flame flickered within it. And off Vasilissa ran, out of the hut on its chicken legs, out through the ribcage fence and into the forest.

She walked until darkness fell, barely finding her way. A black horse and horseman thundered past her as she moved through a glen, and then it was night. The skull in her hands continued to burn with its green flame, but now beams of light shot forth from the eye sockets, illuminating the forest path like a lantern. Not only this, but the beams showed her the most direct route back to the house of her stepmother and stepsisters.

'Do not worry, Vasilissa,' the skull told her through the snapping of its jawbone. Its green fire flashed more hungrily. 'I'll show you the way, and give your stepmother and stepsisters all the fire they think they want.'

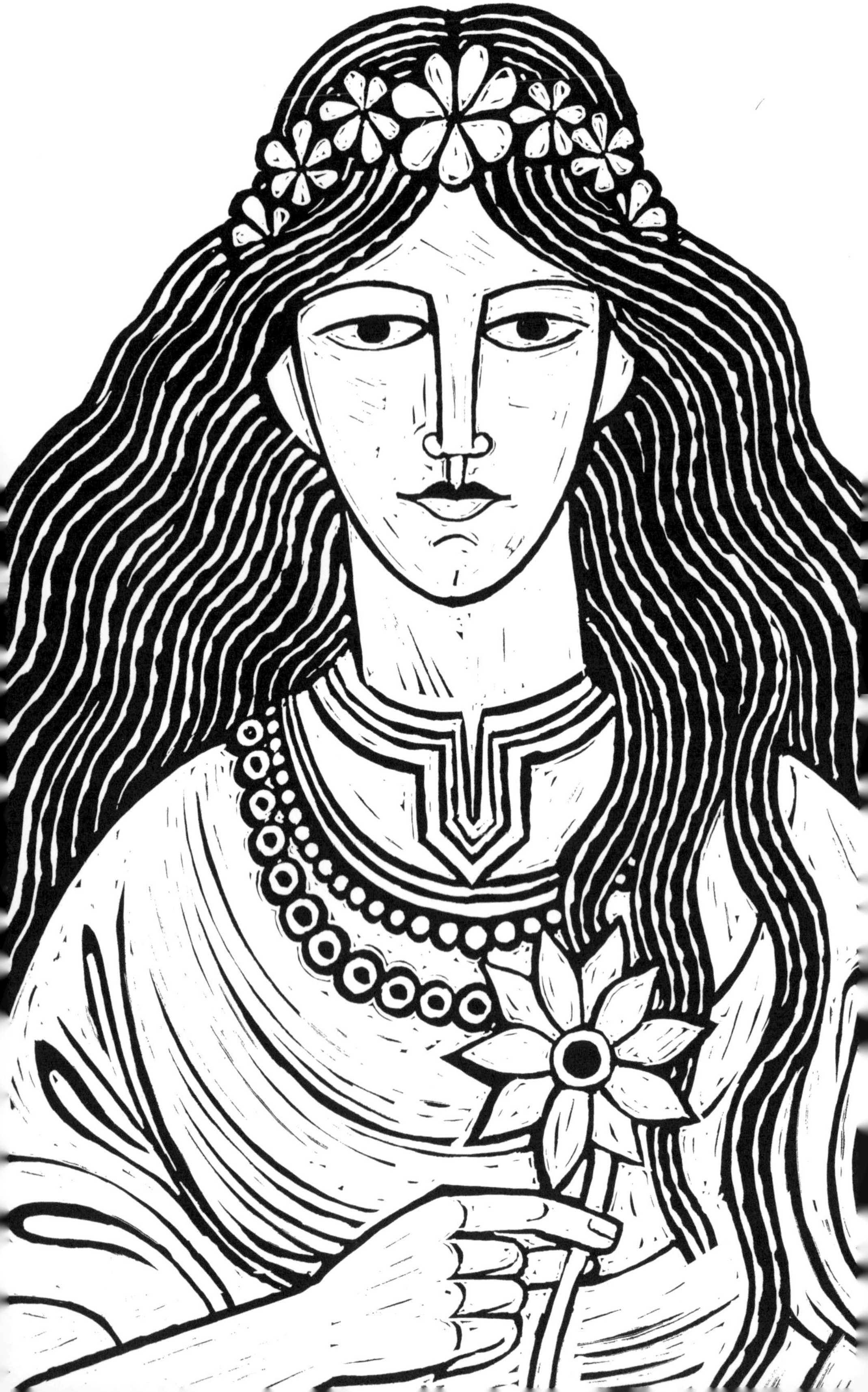

THREE VERSIONS OF THE GREAT GODDESS

Old European cultures with historical links to Africa and Asia were marked, according to some scholars, by female goddess cults. The absence of statues of men from this era and the relative prevalence of female figures, usually with heavily emphasized sexual characteristics, has been read as evidence of the worship of female deities – or of females in general, venerated for their reproductive capabilities ahead of their male counterparts. Some scholars believe that there was one focal deity in prehistoric Europe, and it was female: an embodiment of Mother Earth or Gaia, often referred to as the Great Goddess.

Things changed at the end of the Neolithic period, around 5000 BCE, when Indo-European peoples migrated to the subcontinent that would later become known as Europe. The Neolithic had brought about agricultural revolution, social division, the formation of cities, food reserves, documentation, the control of reproduction and patriarchy surrounding it, as well as collective protection and war. Indo-Europeans consequently worshipped manly gods of war and frightening natural phenomena. The Great Goddess became less important, the sole goddess among a throng of macho gods. But in many ancient cultures, the Great Goddess multiplied and aspects of her became associated with different female godly or semi-godly figures. In Slavic mythology, the Great Goddess remains in the form of three legendary goddesses: Mokoš; the witch goddess Baba Yaga; and Petka or Paraskevi, a Christianized version.

The Lithuanian archaeologist Marija Gimbutas has proposed that the Great Goddess of the Old European religion, the belief system of pre-5000 BCE (of which we know precious little), survived in a variety of forms – even in Christianity in the much-altered form of the Virgin Mary, the only truly venerated female in Christianity.[42] At some point during the push and pull of invasions and exchanges of cultural beliefs over the course of several millennia, the Slavic people adapted the Great Goddess into three variants, each bearing attributes of the original. The Old European Great Goddess was 'synthetic' because she controlled both nature (water, the sun and the moon) and things naturally made or created: life and death, fertility, food, clothing, health and art. She became both multiplied and divided: her attributes were handed out to various lesser female deities and demonic beings (one for birth, one for art, one for health), arranged in a hierarchy. One goddess became many, but each had more specific powers and they could be either benevolent or evil. The ambiguous character of the Great Goddess and her many successors can be questioned: if she is both good and evil, and spreads her power to both sexes, it is certainly a reflection of her older, primary and omnipotent position among the deities.

Early sources on the Slavic pantheon mention Mokoš as the only goddess.[43] Other gods, above all gods of the clear skies and thunder, are supreme in the Indo-European belief, while the Great Goddess rules over nature and social matters, many of them to do with practices, traditions and professions: sheep-shearing, weaving and laundry, for example. The supreme (male) gods deal with incidental and dangerous phenomena; the Great Goddess with everyday life and with chores and activities largely associated with women. It could be argued that the sphere of her activity among humans is more useful, positive and necessary for survival than the occasional volcanic eruptions, lightning strikes and earthquakes for which the male gods are responsible. In any case, we can develop Gimbutas's basic idea that the shifting status of the

Great Goddess reflected the changing social and cultural position of women.

MOKOŠ

Mokoš may be the closest to an intact embodiment of the Great Goddess, but she has some surprising features.[44] For example, in Slavic cultures, she appears as a figure with chicken legs. Mokoš controls fertility, birth and death. Chicken legs indicate the transfer of souls: small, sprightly animals were often noted as the carriers of souls from the world of the living to that of the dead. These are theriomorphic (possessing an animal form), not anthropomorphic (human in form) deities, whose appearance reflects their totemic function – similar to how the perfectly shaped feet of Hermes, the Greek god whose function is to accompany souls to another world, are decorated with small wings. Mokoš is usually depicted with a large head and long arms, symbolically indicating her different functions.

Mokoš's presence throughout the Slavic world is seen in many toponyms, which also confirms her venerable age. Her functions, particularly the most powerful – giving and taking life – reflect her contrasting position in relation to the supreme (male) god, Perun. Mokoš is earth, mud, water, while Perun is associated with the sky and mountains. Mokoš manages the daily chores, which among humans were mostly done by women: shearing sheep, spinning wool, weaving, washing clothes. She regulates the basic elements (water, fire, earth) and the production of food, clothing and living conditions. This regulation also includes punishment, through the denial or complication of whatever is being regulated – she can tangle one's weaving or make it fray, cause a fire to spread out from a hearth, cause disease among livestock.

At first glance, her functions might not seem to be logically connected – what do earth and mud have to do with birth or sheep-shearing? But earth and mud are linked to fertility. Many Slavic belief systems associate the Earth with the female body, and it is traditional (and still widely believed) that the soil must not be dug, tilled or overturned until 25 March each year, because it is 'pregnant'. In the climatic zones inhabited by Slavs, the thaw comes reliably only after late March, accompanied by spring rains that ensure the fertility of the soil. Water is linked to the wool-making process and to laundering. Mokoš establishes the rules related to these processes, particularly when it comes to the calendar: at what time, on what day, in what season and in what way domestic and agricultural activities must be done. What she controls has always been primarily 'women's work', but men must also know these rules because they too can be punished for disobeying, sometimes indirectly, at the will of the women who enforce the rules at home. If a woman disobeys the rules laid out by Mokoš, she might wake to find her weaving undone or in a tangle.

Mokoš's presence may be felt in many stories from other pantheons. For instance, in the *Odyssey* we find Penelope, wife of the long-absent Odysseus, weaving a burial shroud for her father-in-law. She is determined not to accept a new husband from among the throng of suitors that court her, so she states that she will only do so once the shroud is complete; then, so as not to complete it, she weaves during the day and unravels part of her work each night. Is this tactic purely Penelope's invention, or the legacy of a more ancient taboo?

BABA YAGA

Perhaps the best-known figure to be widely associated with Slavic legend in the popular imagination is Baba Yaga, another of the goddesses who emerged after the Great Goddess was fragmented and then adopted into the Indo-European cycle of myths. Baba Yaga is often imagined as a witch, but should really be considered a minor goddess with attributes of her ancestor, the Great Goddess.

Baba Yaga is usually portrayed as an old, ugly woman with long arms and bony legs, flying through the air in a giant mortar propelled by an equally oversized pestle.[45] She lives deep in the woods, in a hut

THREE VERSIONS OF THE GREAT GODDESS

elevated on chicken legs. These two features – the hut on chicken legs, and flight not on a broom but with a mortar and pestle – are her most arresting visual characteristics. She does carry a broom, but with it she sweeps away the traces of her nocturnal flights. She has a long, beak-like nose. She is sometimes described as having one leg that is only bone and pendulous, limp breasts that she can rest on a stovetop or hang over a pole, like drying laundry.

She prefers to move at night. Her interaction with humans is unpredictable and varies from story to story: sometimes she is evil, but sometimes she gives gifts to girls and young women and spends time with them. Vasilissa, a wise girl, receives help from Baba Yaga, as depicted in the legend we retell here (only in part, as the original is very long). Baba Yaga is associated with many soul-bearing animals, including chickens and serpents. She can control the weather and summon storms. Like other Slavic goddesses, she is equally connected to the sun and the moon. She is also well acquainted with plants and their properties, capable of making potions for different occasions. Some myths present her as a cannibal and her hut is sometimes described as being surrounded by human skulls. She is associated with the goddesses of personal destiny and the duration of human life.

The word *baba* in different Slavic languages has very different meanings. It can mean 'grandmother' (the most common usage in Russian), or 'wife', or 'babe'. It can also be used as a derogatory term for a cowardly, effeminate man – or it can mean a midwife. In southern Slavic languages it literally means 'hag', a repulsive, witchy old woman, or serves as a derogatory slang alternative to 'woman'.

Baba is incorporated into the names of several female Slavic demons. Baba Sreda (Grandmother Wednesday) protects women while they weave and forbids them to weave on Wednesdays; Bannaja Baba is a female demon who lives in Russian steam baths. In Ukraine, Žitna Baba is a spirit of grain fields. Dika Baba is the Wild Lady, who seduces young men. Fortune-tellers, traditional healers and witches are also referred to as *baba*. Even the moon is sometimes called

Baba Gale (Grandmother Moonshine). If there's bad weather, like hail, some say that it has come out of Baba's smock. And in Poland, during a sun shower, children will chant a version of 'It's raining/It's pouring/The old man is snoring' with the words 'Rain is falling/Sun is shining/Baba Yaga's butter is churning.'

Baba Yaga is also sometimes thought of as the Slavic goddess of death, or the goddess of all birds. The folklorist Vladimir Propp describes her as the goddess of all forest fauna, of the dead and of initiations. Her distinctive features and myriad colourful attributes have made her an appealing literary figure across many Slavic cultures. Certainly one of the most original versions is the novelist Dubravka Ugrešić's *Baba Yaga Laid an Egg* (2007),[46] in which alliances are made between women of different generations in an ironic context and with a lot of humour. The book concludes with a nearly 100-page essay entitled 'Baba Yaga for Beginners' in which the reader finds resonances between the story itself – which does not contain a character matching the classic description of Baba Yaga – and the goddess of myth.

PETKA

The most striking example of a pagan goddess merged with elements of Christian tradition (what Marija Gimbutas calls 'double faith') is embodied by Petka, also called Paraskeva, Paraskevi or Pjatnica – a figure who appears in all Slavic and other Balkan cultures. The process underlying her changing functions and names is complex and multifaceted. It begins with the Greek translation of the name for the Hebrew day before the Sabbath, the day of preparation, in biblical Greek: *paraskeue* or *paraskevi*, 'preparation'. That becomes a personal name, the name of a Christian saint – two of them, in fact – in apocryphal texts. The meaning of this name is connected to the meaning of Friday, the day of Christ's death.

In Slavic cultures, the name of the day is translated into numerical-onomastic form, where days are also named by numbers – unlike Romantic and Germanic cultures, where days are marked by the

THREE VERSIONS OF THE GREAT GODDESS

names of gods. The fifth day is named after the goddess of love and fertility, *vendredi* in French or *venerdi* in Italian (both from the Latin *Dies Veneris*), while in German it is *Freitag* and in English Friday, both relating to the Germanic goddess Freya.[47] Among the Greeks and the Slavs, this fifth day of the week was called *Paraskeva* (Greek) or *Petka* (various Slavic languages).

Under this name, the former goddess known as Saint Petka gained a very special place in the Slavic pantheon: the position of female protector and punisher. Her role among the southern Slavs and their non-Slavic neighbours expanded. Many place names and first names testify to her presence; she has traditionally been respected by the Roma people, and often by Muslim women in the Balkans. According to Vuk Karadžić, Petka protects women, especially when they are sick and during childbirth, and she punishes violent husbands.[48] She leads women to find medicinal plants, and enforces various rules: for instance, if a woman washes her husband's shirt on a Thursday, the husband will get sick on Friday.

In the Slavic pantheon Petka appears immediately to the right of the supreme saint/god Saint Elijah, accompanied by her daughter Nedelja (the word for Sunday). Other days were also given the names of deities, such as Wednesday (*Sreda*, 'the day in the middle'), in a reverse procedure, as well as a whole package of appropriate taboos about what not to do on that day. Children born on Wednesday are healthy and happy; projects should start on that day; travel can start, too, and sick people can ask Saint Sreda for help. A child born on Saturday can see vampires; Tuesday is a bad day; and so on. It is not known who the father of Nedelja is, or how Petka became a mother. The pairing of mother and daughter features in various ancient beliefs, but there is a particular parallel here with Demeter and her daughter Cora or Persephone. Both Demeter and Petka take care of fertility, housework and women's affairs, and set many taboos related to them (what *not* to do is more often cited than what to do). In both cases, the father is unknown or unimportant.

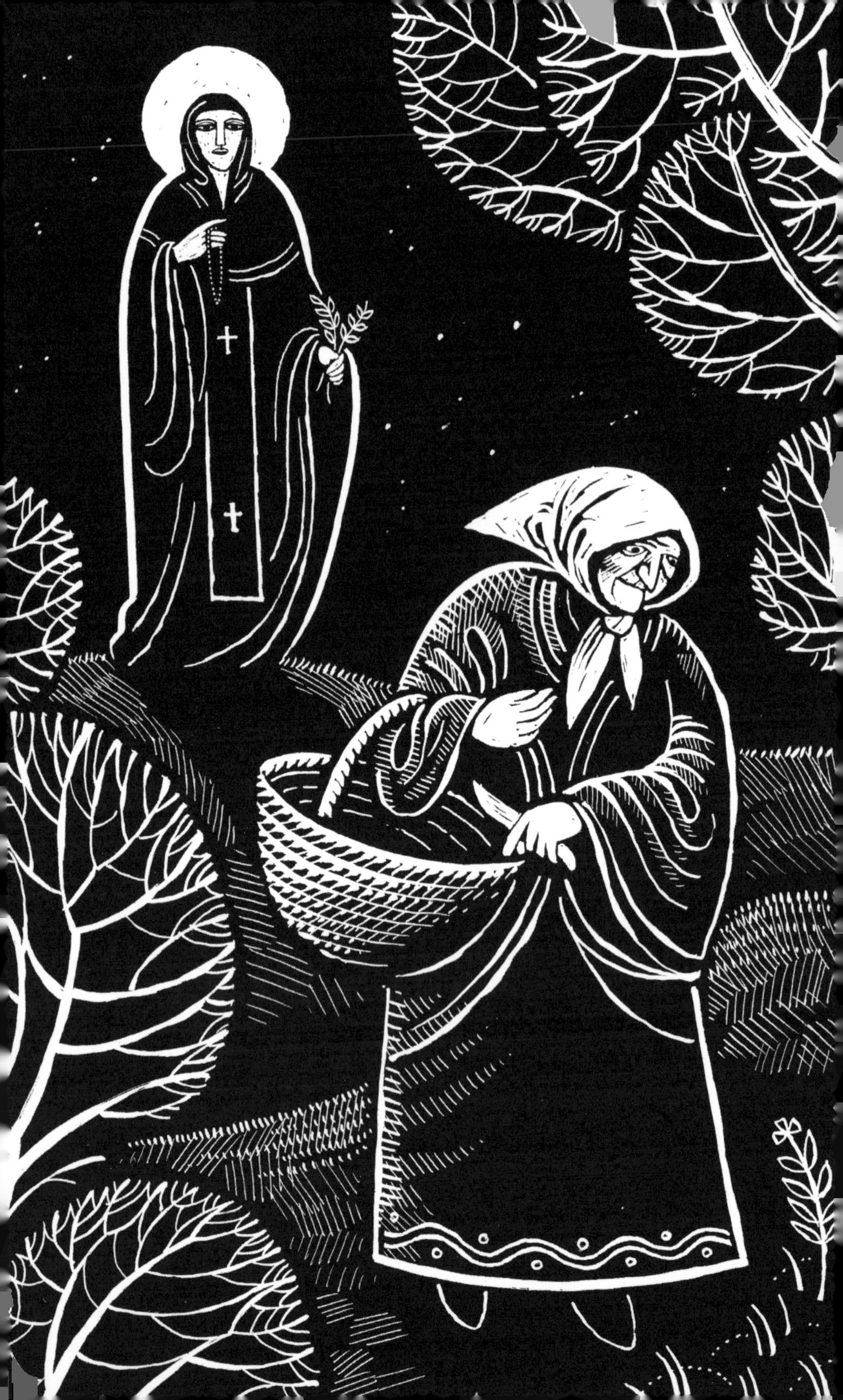

THREE VERSIONS OF THE GREAT GODDESS

The Battle of Kosovo in 1389 led to the transfer of the cult of Petka to the western Balkans. After the battle, in which the principality of Central Serbia was defeated, its leader Lazar was replaced by his widow Milica, who became a nun. She then made peace with the Turkish ruler Bajazit, to whom she gave her daughter in marriage. Milica ruled the principality for thirteen years until her son Stefan came of age. During her reign, she shared power with another nun – Jefimija, the earliest known female Serbian poet, who was also the widow of a ruler killed in battle against the Turks.

These two remarkable women established the cult of Lazar through their texts of praise, but they also believed that women – especially since a significant part of the male population had died in Kosovo – should be given a specific cult that would help them and strengthen their faith. In 1393, the two female rulers travelled to Trnovo (today's Bulgaria); there they managed to acquire the holy remains of a saint named Petka, and subsequently brought them to Serbia.[49] Saint Petka in this case was an 11th-century girl named Paraskeva, from Epivates near modern Istanbul, who had experienced a revelation that she should give away her family's wealth to the poor, travel to the Holy Land and settle in a convent near the River Jordan. When she was twenty-five an angel had appeared and told her to return to her homeland, where she died two years later. This historical figure related to Christianity was merged with the pagan goddess Petka, their attributes overlapping.

The cult of Petka quickly spread to all neighbouring areas. She became the most popular saint in the Balkans, and a huge number of churches were dedicated to her. Her cult is very much alive in the Balkans even today – witness the small church of St Petka under the medieval walls of Belgrade, with its interior walls covered in votive objects. As recently as 1947, when a drought struck Moldavia, relics associated with Petka were processed through the affected region in order to banish the drought.

A visitor today to Epidaurus in Greece, an ancient health complex with a well-preserved amphitheatre, can see a museum of votive reliefs depicting legs, eyes, children, hands – whatever has been healed on the site through rituals and sacrifice to the god of healing, Asclepios, and his daughter Hygiea. Churches in the surrounding villages and elsewhere in Greece are bedecked with zinc plates bearing representations of healed parts, all displayed around the icon of the saint.

The original Great Goddess of all nature and society, who left the sky and elements of the weather to her male co-deities, had to withdraw to the margins of society as a consequence of profound cultural change. However, powerful niches were created here and there, to be preserved for her and what she represented. These were not part of the patriarchy's interests and were sometimes regarded as taboo. Among other things, the dominion of the Great Goddess and, through her, of all women, covered death and grave cults – men traditionally avoided contact with dead bodies, which were considered unclean, just as the female body was thought of as 'unclean' during menstruation or childbirth. In many societies, not only Slavic, it is still women who most often take charge of tending to a dead body, and much social power is hidden in this process.

Other such niches included healing and medicine, witchcraft, the raising of children, oral literature, music and the performance of rituals. Within these areas women can sometimes access power, acquire knowledge, imagine and strategize. Patriarchy still encourages women into these niches and yet, within them, women continue to find their own ways of exerting power: the power of the Great Goddess.

The 'double faith' merging of the Great Goddess with a Christian saint allowed elements of the prehistoric pagan spirit to live on, and even to thrive, during the Christian era and into the present. Its history makes for a fascinating tapestry woven of encounters and mergers between great religions, cults, and accompanying rituals and techniques, of which shamanism (discussed in a later chapter) is especially important in Slavic cultures. Shamanism, with its techniques for communicating between the world of the living and the world of the dead, helps to support the survival of old rituals.

And the next time you see a chicken scurrying across your path, now you'll know that she just might be ferrying a soul into the afterlife.

5

ILYA MUROMETS

◆

PERUN, SUPREME GOD

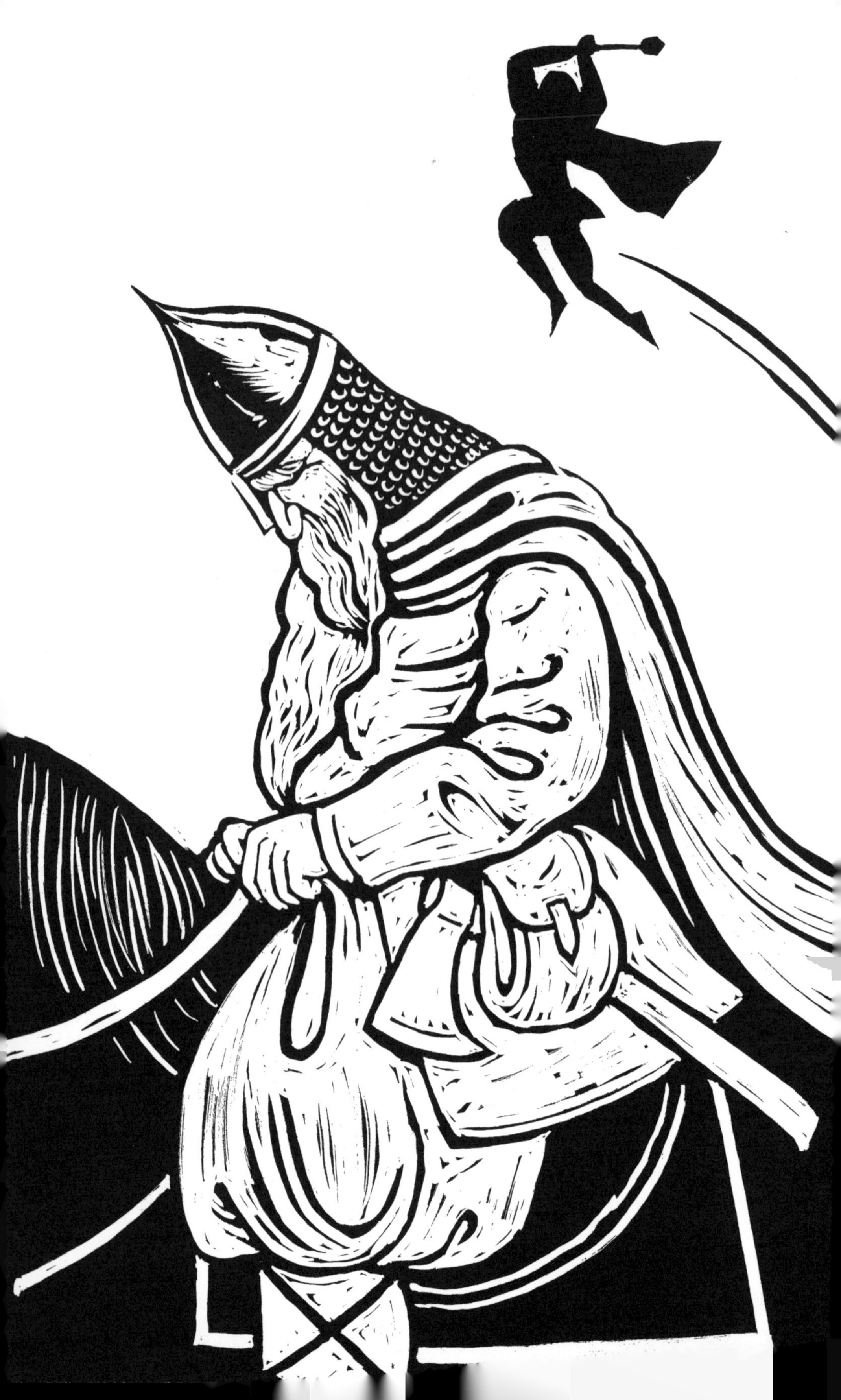

ILYA MUROMETS

In a village near Murom at the time of the Kyivan Rus, when the mighty Slavic lords stood unified against foreign foes – so unlike today, I am sad to say – there lived a youth named Ilya. Since he came from near Murom, they called him Ilya Muromets.

He was born with legs that were unable to support his weight, so he learned to crawl by bearing himself along with only his arms, which grew strong like oaks. His childhood was spent perched upon a large tiled stove, its hearth the centre of his family's humble home. Every morning and just before bed, his mother would load it with wood to keep the fire within glowing at all times. In it, she'd bake black bread and make modest meals to feed the family. And upon it Ilya would sit, warmed by the heat that soaked through the clay tiles.

It was thus for the first three decades of Ilya's life. He grew into a man upon that stove, venturing only as far as he could go using his powerful arms, before returning once more to his place upon the stove. There was little else for him to do – until, that is, he reached the age at which Christ had died and been resurrected.

You see, it happened that one day a pair of pilgrims passed Ilya's home. His parents and siblings were out, so when the pilgrims, parched with thirst from their long travels to kiss saintly relics, called out to ask for a drink of water, only Ilya was there to reply.

'You are welcome, sirs, but you'll have to serve yourselves. My legs have never borne my weight.'

CHAPTER FIVE

The pilgrims entered the house and saw Ilya sitting in his usual spot. They could see that his legs, draped over the edge of the stove, were not strong, but they also saw his good heart – the kind and compassionate heart of a child in the body of, at least above the belt, a mighty man.

'You were born thus?' one of them asked, as they served themselves wooden ladles of water from a wooden bucket.

'So God made me,' Ilya replied. 'And so I must be content with God's plan.'

One pilgrim looked at the other with a gleam in his eye.

'And what if God has other plans for you?' he asked, with a more knowing tone than one might have expected in such an interaction.

'God smiles on those who offer charity to wandering pilgrims, doesn't he, Peter?' replied the other.

The pilgrims dipped the wooden ladle into the water once more and carried it over to Ilya.

'Drink of this, my son,' said one, tipping the ladle towards Ilya's lips.

Ilya drank and thanked them. No sooner had the words of thanks sounded than he felt a change come over him. Energy began to flow into his legs, flexing into muscles that had, mere moments before, been absent from his limbs. Ilya was carried forward by the newfound mass of his legs. Without thinking, he pushed himself off the tiled stove and landed, fully supporting his weight, upon his own legs.

'Saints be praised!' he shouted in surprise and delight. 'I can walk!'

'We saw that there was something special about you, Ilya Muromets,' said one of the pilgrims.

'How do you know my name?' Ilya replied, while still wondering at those legs of his.

'You are destined for great things. We have come from the court of Prince Vladimir. He will need your help. You must go forth and become a *bogatyr*, a knight-errant, a defender of the defenceless. We offer you but one word of warning: do not challenge in combat

Vladimir's current bogatyr, Svyatogor. The world will need you both. Take up your father's mace and horse, for you will find that the sip of water you've just taken not only gave your legs strength but also taught you to ride and to fight.'

'However can I thank you?' Ilya asked humbly.

'Fulfil,' said both pilgrims, waving goodbye.

And so Ilya Muromets set out to become a knight-errant. He truly did find that he could ride, though he'd never been on a horse before. His father's mace felt nimble in his hand, an extension of his fortress arms. He galloped and duelled birch trees in the forest, sprinted and leapt, testing and enjoying his newfound abilities.

On the road towards the court of Prince Vladimir, Ilya suddenly came upon a giant asleep upon a giant horse.

This giant, thought Ilya, must surely be menacing the countryside – for in the stories he'd been told growing up, giants always menaced. If I'm to be a bogatyr, he thought, I must defend the realm against such monsters. And so he rode right up to the giant, who dozed and snored thunderously upon his sleeping black horse.

To reach the giant, Ilya had to stand upon the saddle of his own horse and leap upwards. And so he did, smashing the giant's giant helmet with his mace. The helmet resounded as if Ilya had struck a church bell, but the giant slept on.

Again Ilya rode his horse around, climbed up onto the saddle, then leapt up as he passed, smashing his mace against the giant's head. Once again the helmet tolled like a church bell but the giant did not appear to be harmed, nor did he even wake.

When Ilya did this a third time, the giant reacted, but not as one might expect. Still asleep, he picked up Ilya and tucked him into his pocket.

There Ilya remained. It was more comfortable than you might expect, and after a time he fell asleep. When he woke, the giant, too, had woken. Ilya scrambled out of his pocket, slid down the giant's hip and turned to face him.

CHAPTER FIVE

The giant wore a much-dented battle helmet. He had a long white beard, and kindly giant eyes beneath a canopy of white eyebrows.

'I am Svyatogor, bogatyr of Prince Vladimir.'

'I am Ilya Muromets, and I must apologize to you, for I was told that, whatever I do, I must not challenge you. And yet, not knowing who you were, I've done the one thing that was forbidden me.'

'It's just as well,' Svyatogor replied, his voice like a distant earthquake. 'I am old and no longer able to defend the kingdom alone. My dear, blind father once told me that a legless man would take my place. I never believed him until now.'

'So you know of me?'

'And other things,' Svyatogor replied, chuckling. 'I knew that my time was approaching to pass from this world when I could no longer lift my magic bag, and when the world could no longer lift me.'

'What do you mean?' Ilya wondered.

Svyatogor pointed to a small bag made of burlap, a bag that was more appropriately sized for Ilya. It looked like a thimble in Svyatogor's hand.

'When I try to lift my magic bag, the earth gives way and I sink into it. My weight combined with that of the bag is too great. Whoever can carry it without sinking into the earth shall inherit it and go on to replace me as the defender of the realm. Go on, then...'

Ilya nodded and approached the burlap bag. He lifted it with ease, for it appeared to be empty. And he did not sink into the earth.

Svyatogor smiled. 'So it *is* you. So be it. Let us travel together towards Prince Vladimir's court. There is one more test to pass.'

And so Svyatogor the giant and his comparatively little friend, Ilya Muromets, journeyed together and through several adventures, until they came to a grey stone quarry, thick with mist. As the mist parted around them they saw a colossal stone coffin lying in the midst of the quarry, carved directly into the stone of the mountain, with a stone lid lying beside it.

Both Svyatogor and Ilya knew immediately who it was for, but by now Ilya could hardly bear the thought of being without his friend. So Ilya lay down in the coffin first.

Once inside, he wept, for it was far too large for him. Svyatogor smiled and nodded, calmly helping Ilya out of the coffin with his oversized hand. He then climbed in, and it was a perfect fit. The stone lid began to close, and he closed his eyes along with it.

Svyatogor had been, until this point, at perfect peace with his fate. But at the last moment his eyes flashed open, for he suddenly realized that he had not yet passed to Ilya his power.

'Ilya, you must take this from me, to defend...' As Svyatogor spoke, a white frost emerged from his mouth and passed into Ilya's. But the lid slammed shut before it had quite finished. Some of the giant's power had passed over, but not all.

Ilya wept for the passing of his friend. In his despair, he punched a boulder that sat in the quarry. The boulder shattered under the force of his bare fist, as if it were made of dry leaves. This surprised him so much that it shook him from his mourning. He sought another boulder and found that he was able to pick it up with one hand, throw it into the air and catch it upon a single finger.

Seeing what power had been passed to him, Ilya determined to fulfil his destiny and replace Svyatogor as the bogatyr of Kyiv. He would offer his services to Prince Vladimir the Fair Sun (who would one day become the future Saint Vladimir, though no one knew it then). Even Ilya himself would eventually become a saint, though many adventures awaited him first. He would free Kyiv from the bloated monster, Idolishche Poganoye, and he would single-handedly repel the invading Polovtsi from the walls of Chernigov, lifting the siege. Once, he would lose his mace – but when that happened, he still fought off a cohort of enemies armed only with his own boot.

CHAPTER FIVE

One day, passing through Bryansk Forest, Ilya came upon a glade where all the grasses and meadows had become entangled, the azure flowers had lost their petals, the dark trees bent down towards the earth, and a number of people lay dead on the ground. They had been felled by the magic whistle of a forest monster known as Nightingale the Robber. Nightingale would perch in a tree and either stun travellers with his whistle, should he blow into it but lightly, or slay them with a full breath.

Ilya withstood the whistle when it came, although it stripped half the forest of its leaves and scorched the grasses. Then it was Nightingale's turn to be stunned, for never before had his whistle failed him. Ilya shot him from his tree, landing arrows in his eye and temple. Nightingale fell from the branch, wounded but still living.

Ilya then dragged him to the court of Prince Vladimir, who was interested in the whistle and asked to hear it. Nightingale replied that he was too wounded to demonstrate its power, but if the prince really wanted to hear it, he could be healed with a flask of wine.

The curious (if not, at this point in his career, overly bright) prince called for wine. Nightingale drank it down in a single gulp and was healed. He then blew into his whistle. Immediately all of Vladimir's palaces were destroyed, and half the people within them killed. At this, Ilya shook his head, lifted Nightingale up, took him to a field outside Kyiv and cut off his head.

Ilya's relationship with Prince Vladimir was not always rosy. On one occasion, when the prince had failed to invite him to a party, Ilya had a tantrum and knocked down all the church steeples in Kyiv. Alarmed by this behaviour, the prince sent an invitation to Ilya, who was delighted to attend the party after all and was deemed the most charming of all the guests.

Despite occasional moments like this, Ilya remained chief bogatyr for the rest of his days, defending Kyiv against all its enemies – including the fearsome Kalin, khan of the Tatars and master of the Golden Horde. It is said that even now, a millennium later, the spirit of Ilya Muromets remains to defend Kyiv against foreign enemies...even fellow Slavs, should a new khan send brethren into irrational battle against brethren.

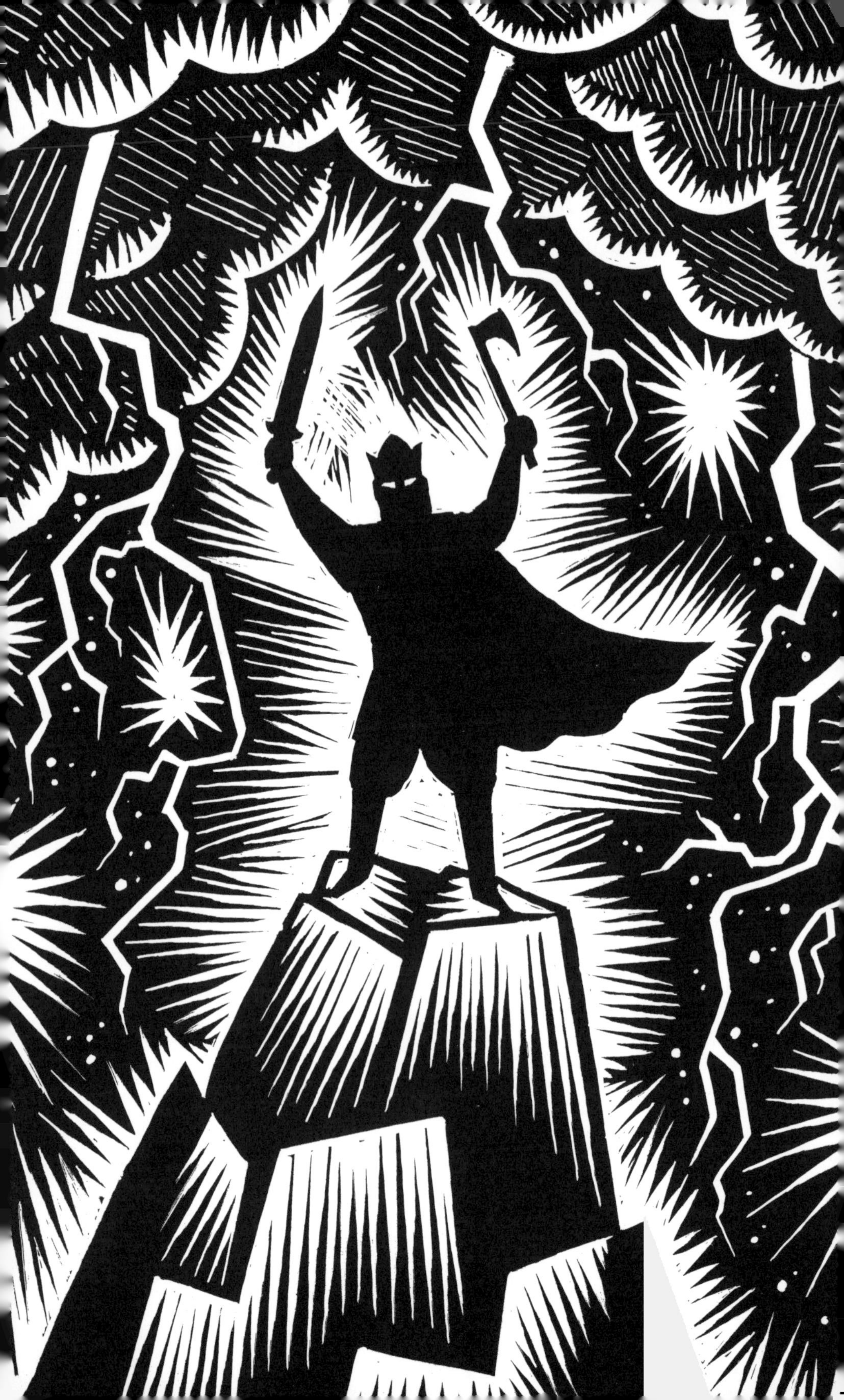

PERUN, SUPREME GOD

There are gods of specific realms and practices, and then there are universal gods: catch-all figures cobbled together from various traditions and imbued with a cornucopia of powers. The supreme god of most if not all historic Slavs, from the Baltic region to Russia to the Balkans, was Perun.

Perun probably belongs to the Indo-European mythos. It's a little too simplistic to equate him to Zeus/Jupiter, although he is the god of thunder and lightning as well as the supreme god, ruling all others. He is also the god of mountain peaks, justice, ruling power, war: manly things. But that is not all, for he is the god of fertility too. There's a manly component to that, of course, but in most pantheons fertility is framed as a female attribute. Perun's struggles with other gods for supremacy are described in innumerable myths, and it has also been a struggle to establish the historical view of his role among scholars of Slavic culture.

For a long time, Perun was thought to have been a late addition to the pantheon, included only as a response to Christianity. There was indeed a younger generation of deities added during the Christian era, like Saint Petka, so this seemed plausible. Scholars also considered it problematic that Perun's functions were so numerous – surely they could not all be connected with only one god? It seemed suspicious, too, that he was known only to Baltic and Russian peoples, or so it was thought at one time. These doubts about Perun pervaded the scholarship of Slavic mythology.

The Italian Slavist Evel Gasparini argues that Perun has no direct connection with humans – hence his seeming inactivity in myths – but instead governs them from a distance, through other deities.[50]

CHAPTER FIVE

He's the general, and other gods are the ones carrying out his plans. Or he might be evidence of Slavic monotheism – Perun is the only true god and others are holy figures, like saints, acting out his wishes. Gasparini tries to prove this hypothesis by connecting the notion of Slavic monotheism to the Finno-Ugric and Iranian religious systems. It has also been suggested that Perun was a borrowed deity, taken by Slavs from Norse mythology – that Perun was originally Thor.

Perun's ubiquity is reflected in the fact that his name has historically been found throughout the Balkans, confirming his presence among all Slavs. The scholar Veselin Čajkanović believed that the southern Slavic name Pera was not adapted from the Christian name Petar (Peter), as sometimes assumed, but that it originated from Perun and was therefore much older.[51]

Russian researchers of the 20th century came up with a triangle connecting the three oldest deities of the Slavs: Perun, Mokoš and Veles – a heroic triad. Mokoš, Perun's wife (Heaven/Earth), cheated on her husband with Veles (darkness/fire), for which she was punished.[52] No single surviving myth conveys this story, but it aligns with the binary oppositions that scientists needed in order to organize and classify beliefs. For V. N. Toporov this is the 'main' myth, featuring as it does a heavenly wedding and a fight with the forces of darkness.[53] Aspects of it are reflected in 'humanized' Slavic epics and other forms of oral literature such as Russian *bylinas*, or epic tales, which transpose the myths of the three main deities onto (super)human heroes battling monsters – many of which are allegories for invading armies like the Tatars.

The Slovenian god Kresnik, a god of fire, is one of many well-known variants of Perun, supporting the theory of a 'main' myth that served as the basis for numerous others. After scholarly debates over two centuries, the prevailing opinion emerged that Perun was the supreme god – perhaps the only truly ancient god, who had become anthropomorphic in his later versions.

Perun manages the most powerful natural phenomena: the strongest sound (thunder), the strongest impact (earthquakes) and the

PERUN, SUPREME GOD

strongest light (lightning) – something instantaneous, fast, unexpected and extremely dangerous, capable of bringing about fundamental change and destruction on Earth. But it is accompanied by other natural phenomena: rain, wind, clouds, fire, clear skies, sun. That is why the list of Perun's competencies is so long and varied, as well as the list of male deities who compete with him in certain areas: Svarog/Svarožič, Svetovid, Dažbog/Dajbog/Daba, Porovit and Jarovit represent the seasons, different jobs, different gifts for mortals, different functions performed by the supreme god at the same time. The question remains as to whether these deities are all ultimately descendants of the supreme god. Some of them seem to have been as important to certain Slavic groups as Perun himself: Dažbog is one of these. His name means 'giving', one of the most important qualities of the supreme god.

There is, among all these figures, a common image of the supreme male deity. He is a middle-aged, bearded man equipped for war, armed with a hammer, axe or arrow, often on horseback. All of these attributes could be described as Indo-European signs of male power. Perun is also described as having a silver head and a golden moustache. Curiously, he does not have a significant sexual life in myths – at least, nothing to compare with that of Zeus, who rarely missed an opportunity to strike up an affair with any female (or, for that matter, male) deity, human, monster or animal.

In Christian syncretism, Perun is equated with Saint Elias (mixed with the Old Testament prophet Elijah) and Saint Peter. In the former context he changes his horse for a horse-drawn carriage with which, just like ancient Helios, he follows the sun's path in the sky every day. This has been linked to Elijah rising into Heaven, as described in 2 Kings Chapter 2, Verse 11: 'Behold, there appeared a chariot of fire, and horses of fire...and Elijah went up by a whirlwind into heaven.'[54]

The power of Perun to regulate social relations, ruling and judging fairly, is described in the earliest written documents on the Slavic

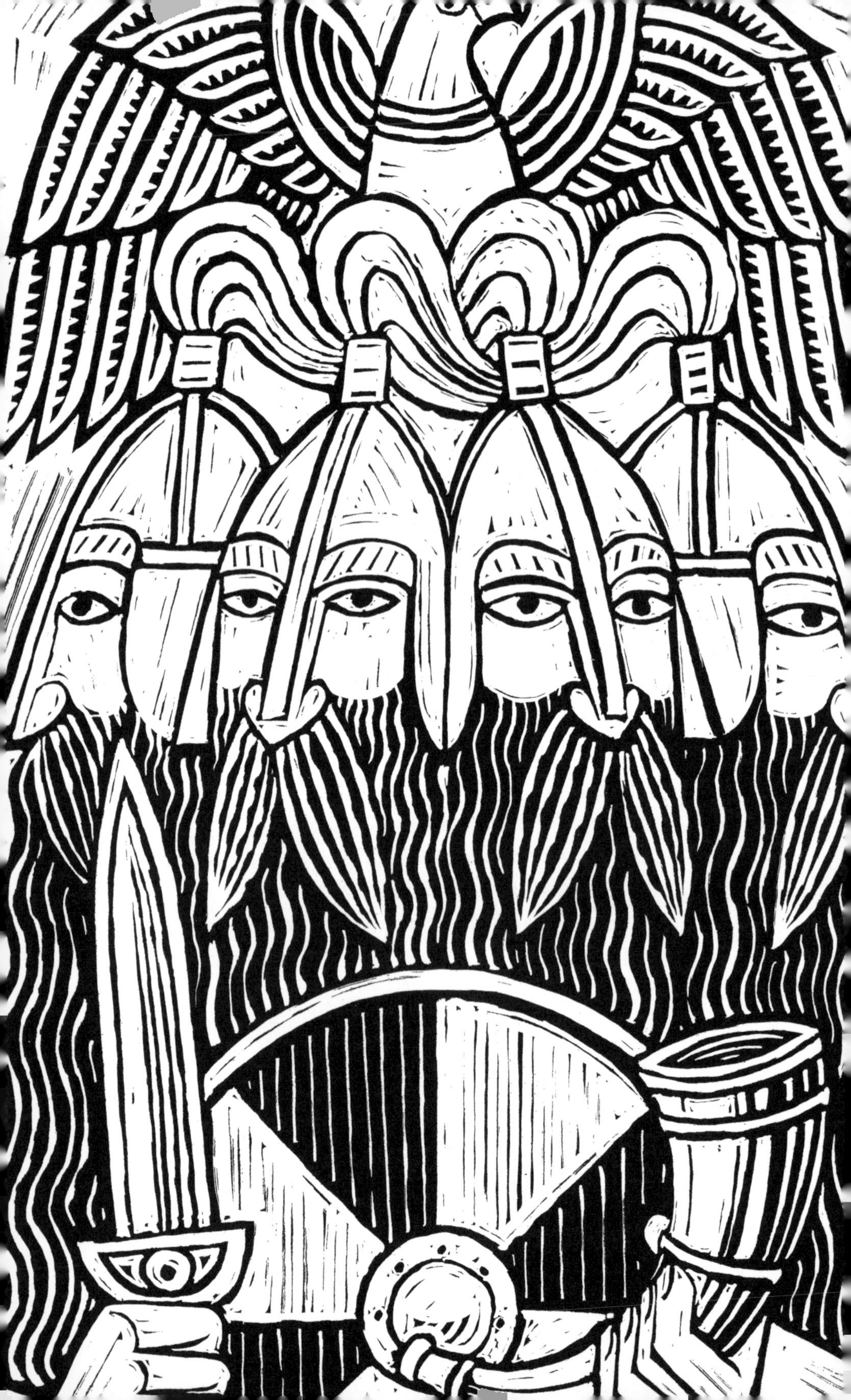

pantheon: three peace treaties from the 10th century CE (two of them armistices with the Byzantine Greeks) cite Perun as a guarantor of fulfilling the agreed-upon conditions. These prerogatives were also valid in the Russian cults of Novgorod and Kyiv. Prince (later Saint) Vladimir nominated his relative, Dobrynya, to the Slavic pantheon (with a holy place and cult figures) in 980, but just a few years later he converted to Christianity and demolished his pagan monuments, in part due to an uprising of the pro-Christian citizens of Novgorod.[55]

Perun the thunderbolt-bearer usually resides on mountain tops, on clouds or elsewhere in the sky. His tree is an oak (as is that of Odin, supreme god of the Norse pantheon) and his flower is the iris – *Iris Germanica*. In Bulgarian and Serbo-Croatian, the name of this flower is *perunika*. In Serbo-Croatian there is also a variant name: *bogiša* or 'god's flower'. Iris is used as a remedy for a number of diseases. Traditionally, when the holiday of Saint Petar Bogišar was celebrated in Dubrovnik, consecrated iris flowers were given away in churches and brought into houses as protection from lightning strikes. The iris was also said to protect vineyards from lightning.[56]

The Montenegrin prince-bishop and poet Petar Petrović Njegoš wanted to name an official state coin the *perun*, although he died before this project could be realized. With his numerous competencies, Perun was the preferred deity of many rulers and princes, and therefore of war and military skills. Consequently we find the continuity of Perun precisely in that social group, in the warrior class.

Ilya Muromets, the Russo-Ukrainian hero whose legend we retell here, was sometimes called 'Perun', and was later canonized as a Christian saint. He was one of the legendary bogatyrs, knights-errant in Russian bylinas, who were said to have superhuman abilities and who fought for real, historical princes; Ilya was essentially the guardian of Prince Vladimir of Kyiv.

If we take a step back and consider Perun's characteristics – fighting ability, striking power, loneliness at the top, authority and the ability to dispense justice, but also stubbornness – we can see connections with many other mythical and legendary figures, not all of whom are associated with a particular location. Such characters are often nomadic, living in the mountains. They may have been unfairly barred from a position of unequivocal authority, which they must fight to regain. They usually do not have a partner, but if they do, they are ready to severely punish her infidelity. They fight individual human enemies as well as monsters, dragons and entire armies, vanquishing them.

Figures like this can be found in all Slavic cultures. While Ilya Muromets is the most famous Russo-Ukrainian example, in the Balkans we find the folk hero Marko Kraljević: fearless, energetic, aggressive and merciless to his enemies, he prefers to stay alone in the mountains in the company of his horse. Ilya is likewise childish at times: quick to anger, but equally quick to forget and recover his good spirits.

The prominence in Slavic culture of mythic heroes like this helped to shape the public perception of, and even the actual behaviour of, real-life rulers. The imaginary attributes ascribed to the 20th-century Yugoslav president Tito (Josip Broz) reflect this phenomenon. His military successes against the Nazis, mainly in the mountainous parts of Yugoslavia, his ruling style, his political achievements and global reputation were reflected in his authoritarian rule of Yugoslavia. He projected an implied immortality (keeping his role for life), lived an almost royal luxurious lifestyle despite ruling a socialist country without an aristocracy, and exerted complete political control – in a sense, he was the 'supreme god' of Yugoslavia. After his death, the country disintegrated into a destructive war accompanied by social decline affecting the majority of the population. This led unexpectedly to a cult of Tito within post-Yugoslav countries, a 'Yugo-nostalgia' for the 'good old days' that fed back into the utopian legend of a better past.

PERUN'S FRIENDS AND FOES

Most myths about Perun imply that he came to the position of supreme god after a long struggle to take power. Many gods are beneath him, serving different functions that complement the cult circle of various

PERUN, SUPREME GOD

Slavic cultures. The characters of these gods, like that of Perun, seem fluid, but it is unclear how safely we can draw conclusions about them given the complicated history of cults and changing beliefs as well as broader changes to the culture and social structure of Slavic peoples. Scholars have attempted it, but it's a tricky business, nowhere near as straightforward as studies of some other pre-Christian religions. Studying the Slavic religion can feel like grasping at wind-blown leaves. There are clues here and there but they are few and far between, and much inference is required.

In their modern reconstruction of the religious system, V. V. Ivanov and V. N. Toporov determined which gods belonged to the main circle by considering the earliest Russian sources alongside the best available archaeological evidence and documentation.[57] The next down the ladder after Perun, part of the trifecta of male deities, is Veles (sometimes called Volos), the god-shepherd of cattle and sheep and also of wealth. He is most heavily represented in Russia, but in some Slavic cultures Veles also becomes the god of the underworld, shifting his position from literal shepherd to shepherd of souls. Perun and Veles reflect social conflict: Perun represents the military and social power of the princes, whereas Veles is presented as the god of all Russians, the owner and distributor of gold.

Stribog is identified as the grandfather of the winds, while Dažbog or Dajbog/Daba is a god of the sun and a son of Svarog – who is also connected to the sun. Both Stribog and Dažbog are atmospheric deities (the suffix *bog* means 'god' in most Slavic languages). Among southern Slavs, Dažbog becomes the leading god, a lame shepherd regarded as a 'giver'. When Christianity was adopted he became the Devil, and some of the pagan stories associated with him were reworked into tales of the Devil's activities. The lame Devil (*Hromi Daba*), however, also has good qualities in those cultures: for instance, he teaches people skills, like blacksmithing. His lameness is parallel to the lameness of the wolf leader. This characteristic has persisted into modern pop culture: when Disney comics were translated for a

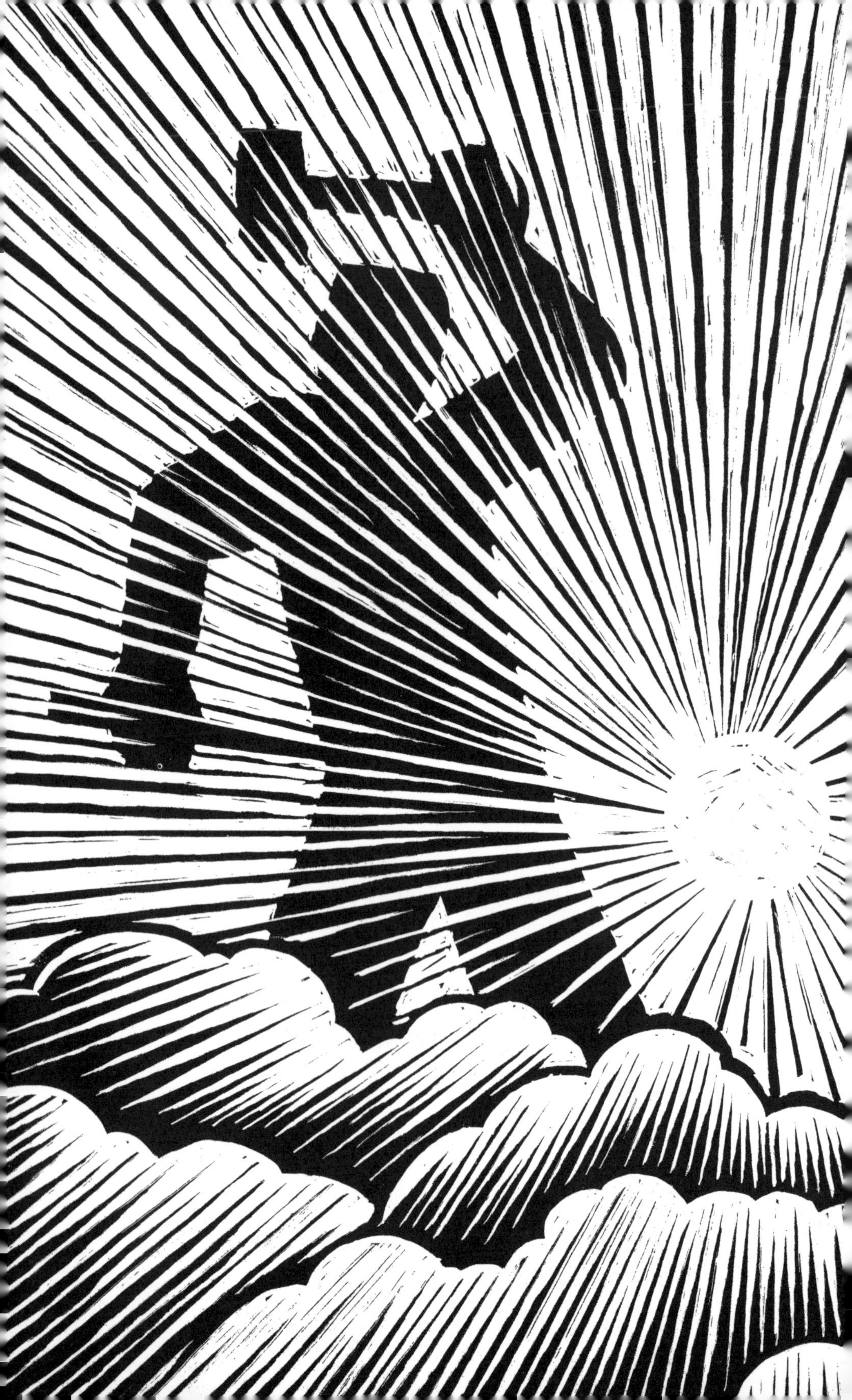

children's magazine in Belgrade in the late 1930s, the character Peg Leg Pete, nemesis of Mickey Mouse, was dubbed Hromi Daba.

There are some other Slavic gods who are specifically referenced in historical contexts, but about whom details are scarce. Svarog is a sun deity too, but it is unclear what he presides over. Hors is another whose domain is unknown. Semargl, or Sim and R'gl (sometimes presented as a single entity, sometimes as a pair) have non-distinctive specifications. Their names may come from 'seven heads' – as previously noted, polycephaly is a common characteristic of Slavic gods. Svetovid has four heads, Triglav has three, Porevit five.

The pantheon of north-western, therefore Baltic Slavs helped Ivanov and Toporov to better understand the Russian pantheon and identify some common features and differences. There, four-headed Svetovid is the supreme god, a warrior on a white horse bearing a sword and accompanied by an eagle. His multiple heads serve him well in battle. Triglav is a three-headed god on a black horse; his functions are less clear, but the highest mountain in Slovenia is named after him. Svarožič (a nickname of Svarog/Radgost) is a god of war with a talking horse that can predict the future. Jarovit too appears as a god of war: in his temple he guards an untouchable golden shield, which is carried before an army in war. Rujevit is yet another god of war: he wears seven faces and wields seven swords. The scholar Marija Gimbutas posits that Jarovit, Porevit and Rujevit could be the gods of the seasons. Pripegala has been described as a Dionysian figure, associated with wine and parties, but little more is known about him. Many Slavic cultures also feature the duo Črnobog and Belobog, whose names translate as Black God and White God – part of a wider theme of deities appearing as pairs in conflict.

It is possible that the fluid relationships between Perun's fellow gods, and the ambiguity of their prerogatives, reflect the social dynamics of the Slavic world. Beliefs would have been shaped by the priorities of the ruling classes, with leader gods often represented as dealing with the same issues handled by real-world rulers while everyday deities focused on matters of interest to the lower classes. But if this line-up of gods is notable for its imprecision and uncertainty, there are clear practical reasons for that too. So little archaeological material survives that we must rely on written sources, and these are largely Christian. Byzantine, Russian, Latin: all of them weaving their own misunderstandings, misinterpretations and flights of imagination into the historical narrative.

6

THE WATERMAN
◆
CREATURES OF THE DEEP

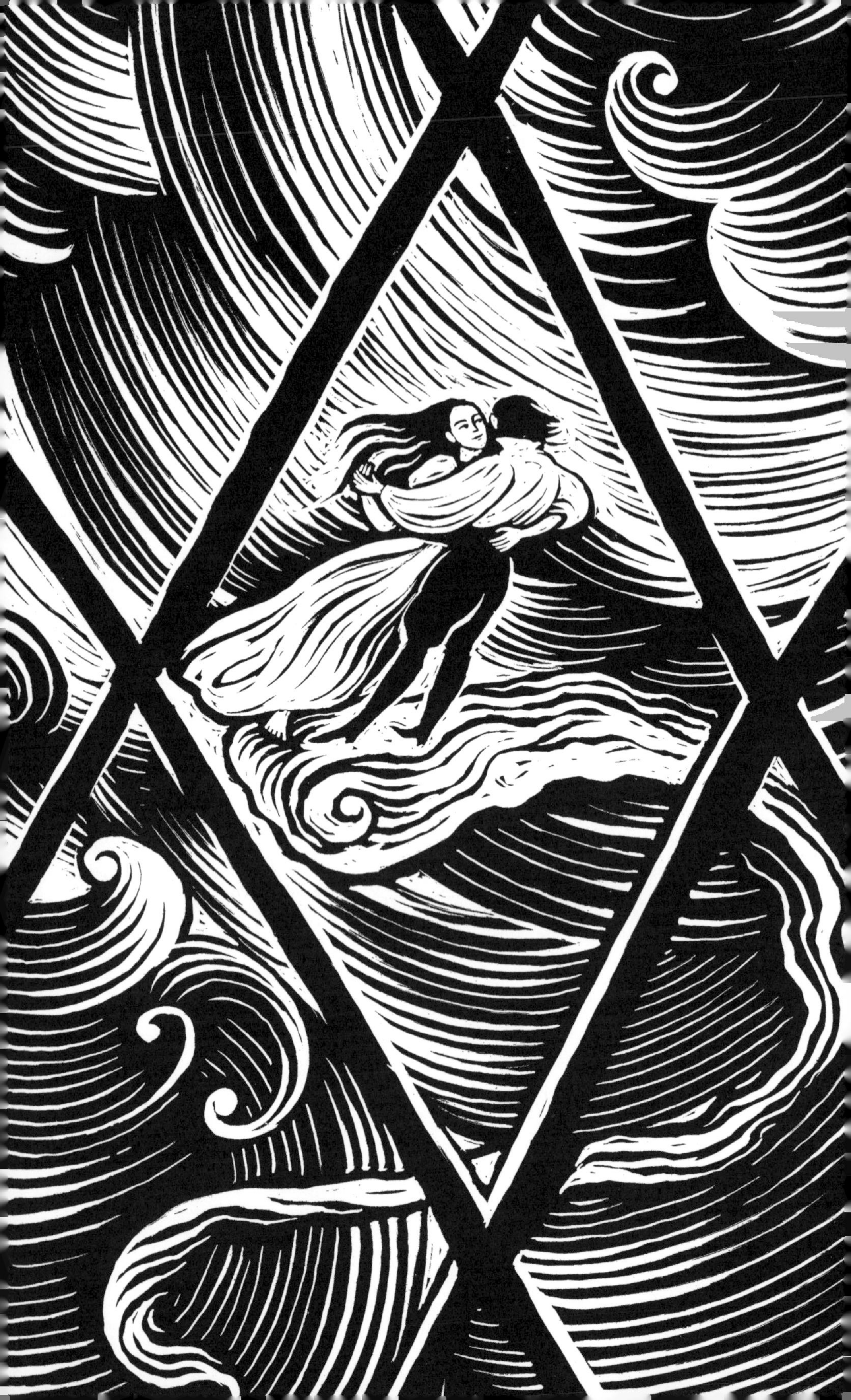

THE WATERMAN

Urška was the most beautiful maiden in Ljubljana. She could seduce anybody, but she preferred not to let anybody near her. Conquering hearts was what pleased her most, more than it did any man. She was cunning and knew how to please parents and old ladies. The women and girls in her circle were often driven to secret tears because Urška stole the hearts of young men, whether their sympathies were hidden or overt. And none of these young men could conquer Urška's heart, nor even steal a kiss, much less convince her to marry. No riches could impress her, no nobility stoke her interest; no lands could attract her attention. She loved to move others and remained unmoved herself.

What dwelt within the mind of this maiden? What was her secret desire? What did she really want? Well, she wanted the entire city of Ljubljana, and she had it, at her feet. The whole city adored her.

Until...

◈

One day, Urška stood gazing down the serpentine length of the Ljubljanica River when she was suddenly seized by a force she'd never before felt. She had an unfulfilled wish. She wanted to go further, to see more.

Not long after this, her father, a wealthy merchant, took Urška and her mother for a carriage ride near Zalog, where the Ljubljanica flows into the mighty Sava River. It was a wonderful day, bright and blue. Their white horses had flowers and ribbons in their manes, which whipped in the breeze. Their driver sang sweet love songs as he urged the horses forward. Urška's mother was pale but beautiful beneath her lace umbrella. Her diamond earrings sparkled and her golden locks, streaked with white, escaped like tentacles from her hat. Urška wore an embroidered blue dress and a tiny bonnet. Her white

CHAPTER SIX

skin was like marble in the sun and the light shifted the hue of her tightly braided hair from chestnut to honey. Her father was happy, humming along to the driver's song, recalling the village of his youth.

As they approached the V-shaped point at which the two rivers met, the shore grew steep and was carpeted in huge yellow daffodils. Narcissi, as the locals called them. It seemed that the grand river melted away into the sunlight, the waters merged with the flowers, and everything urged Urška to go south, to lose herself in this moving light and to escape everything: the city, the adoration, the desiring gazes, the less gifted friends. She felt again that new sensation, deep within her body. She wanted to get away from her world.

They stopped at a guesthouse on the way home. Father drank beer with the driver, Mother sipped her coffee, silent and smiling. It seemed to Urška that they had something she lacked. Peaceful intimacy, tangible moments of happiness and freedom. She felt humbled and almost guilty. If some young man had approached her at that moment, she might have been touched and ready to look on him with sincere sympathy. But there was no one there.

When they returned to the city, Urška was a different girl. This change was not visible from outside – she remained as unreachable as ever. But inside, she had lost her desire to be admired, to leave young men charmed and hopeless.

At the height of that summer there were Sunday afternoon dances on the banks of the Ljubljanica, on a wooden platform overlooking the river near to the Old Plaza. Her parents took Urška to the dance as usual. They left her perched on a bench at the edge of the platform with the other girls while they took their place outside the guesthouse nearby, a few steps from where the dancing would commence. A small band featuring a violin, cymbals and trumpet played beneath a linden tree. On the other side of the platform were benches where the young men sat.

Gazes were exchanged. A young man would, if encouraged, cross the platform and approach a girl, asking for a dance. Not a soul dared approach Urška, so certain were they that she would decline. Yet Urška had never looked so beautiful: her bright blue eyes reflected both the sun and the Ljubljanica, and her chestnut-honey locks fell freely down her back, held by a comb studded with green glass beads the colour of the river's depths. She wore a light green mousseline gown tied with a green satin belt. A collar of white Richelieu lace hugged her tender neck, and her tiny feet were dipped into green suede shoes. Yes, she was the envy of every girl in Ljubljana. Those shoes were a gift from her father, who'd bought them in Vienna. Then her mother had ordered the gown to match. The colour of envy. And of the river.

No, the queen of Ljubljana did not send a sign to any of the young men on the bench across from her. She still did not dance. Even as the eyelid of the sun closed behind the trees and the houses on the other bank, she did not dance.

Then she saw him.

Had he been there all along? He was seated on the bench among the other young men, watching her with a smile. A glass of wine was on the table before him, while the other men drank beer. He wore a white shirt and green vest, which he removed and hung on the back of the bench. His muscular legs were wrapped in black trousers and fine, soft boots. He had brown hair that flowed loose and long. The corners of his eyes were creased: he must be a little older than the other young men. And those green eyes – when his gaze touched her, Urška felt the urge to shudder, though the day was hot. But her nature made her merely shake her hair and offer up a half smile. He smiled back.

Then he turned to the band, which had paused for refreshment. He did not stand up nor did he utter a word to them. And yet they started to play. All heads turned, all attention was captured, as the band started a new dance coming from Vienna, a waltz. That very morning at church, the priest had mentioned this new invention of the Devil, this immoral and impudent dance from Vienna, a dance which prompted, nay required, a male and female body to press far too close to one another, provoking sinful thoughts and corrupting the souls of decent folk. Even those who merely watched the dance were equally exposed to sinful ideas.

The girls on their bench started to giggle. Urška's mother suddenly felt the heat and began to fan herself faster and faster.

Then the green-eyed man came to ask Urška for a dance.

He was tall, perfectly built and moved with a panther's elegance. He bowed, asked for a dance and then for her hand. He kissed Urška's hand and, when she stood, he put his own hand around her waist. He smelled of fresh water and waterlilies. Urška thought for a moment that his eyes shifted to a darker shade of green. But of course they couldn't, could they?

He took a deep breath, touching her hair with his lips. She smelled of blue hyacinth, roses and cherries. He told her that he'd come a long way, from where the Sava and Danube meet, in Belgrade, just to see her after hearing of her beauty. Would she like to see his part of the world?

Without realizing that she was speaking, Urška replied that she would like nothing better.

They waltzed in expanding parabolas, slowly then swiftly, as the music demanded. The platform was their own: nobody else dared to dance the waltz. As they spun, their bodies almost merging, Urška had the impression that she was not touching the ground, but rather flying in his arms.

If only this feeling could last forever, she thought as she closed her eyes.

The music sped faster. The sun was now a closed eye behind the trees and houses, only a bruise-coloured glow remaining in the sky. Clouds oozed in from the north and the skies darkened. The dancing pair spun ever faster, his grip around her waist ever stronger.

'I will lose my shoes,' she said to him.

'You will not need them,' he replied.

His voice was soft. It swam into her ears, his words calming, and yet the dance and the closeness of their bodies burned. A strong wind came up, strong enough to raise waves on the Ljubljanica, which was now as grey as the skies. As were his eyes, Urška saw. A peal of thunder made the guests at the dance scream, and people ran for cover under the veranda of the guesthouse before the skies could open. All but the band who, as if nothing had happened, continued to play, ever faster and with more passion. Thunder rolled to the earth and lightning brightened the skies, rain hammering down as if joined to the rhythm of the dance.

'Will you come with me?' he asked.

She nodded, hiding her face in his chest.

'Nobody will ever love you as I do,' he said.

Now they whirled around without touching the ground. Urška was certain that this was the life she wanted: no houses, no parents, no ordinary young men, no church, no marriage, no friends with their petty talk, no corsets, no shoes…Just the deep water of his eyes, and the whirling, and his arms.

They were seen waltzing with the elements for a while. All the guests, huddled under the veranda and staring out through the warped glass windows of the guesthouse, bore witness. They would later swear, hands on hearts, that the two young people danced in the rain-kissed air itself, above the wooden platform, like a pair of leaves clinging together in the face of the wind. Then they descended, never stopping their dance for a moment. They made a few turns on the shore of the river and then disappeared into the water.

The storm stopped. The band stopped playing. And all that remained of Urška was a pair of green suede shoes upon the riverbank.

The story goes that Urška was taken by the Waterman, a slimy, green-skinned creature, half lizard, half fish, who lived in the deep green water of the river, and that this was her just punishment for being too smart and conceited. But some people, perhaps wiser, say that the handsome Waterman took her to Belgrade and taught her about waters and seas and life within them; and then, eventually, they went to the shores of Georgia on the Black Sea, where he was king of the dragons and the sun worshippers. And there they lived a happy, immortal life.

Which, if either, is true is for you to decide.

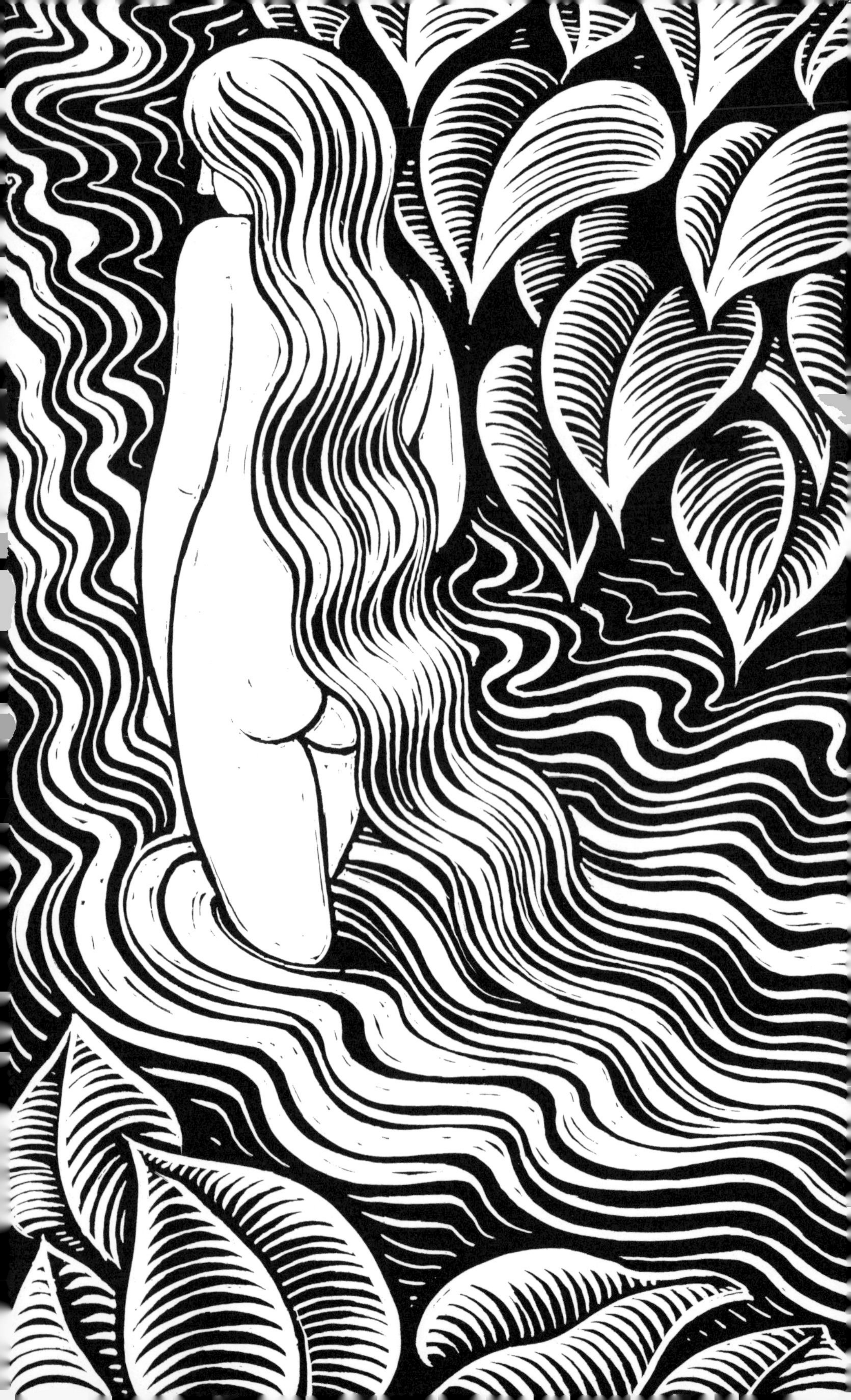

CREATURES OF THE DEEP

If you've ever turned your back to a fountain, closed your eyes and thrown a coin over your shoulder into the water, then you've participated in an ancient Slavic ritual – one that originates in a fear of the dead. The coin is a sacrificial offering to appease the vengeful dead souls who are said to inhabit bodies of water. Some may have been accidentally drowned, others sacrificed; still others may have merely passed away, and their restless souls continue to float.

Slavic legend tends to focus on bodies of fresh water, but it doesn't discriminate when it comes to their size or importance: wells, springs, lakes and rivers all have the capacity to house dead souls and contain prophetic powers. Sacrifices to the waters need not be in the form of coins – Bulgarian fishermen will drown a chicken or a rooster in the Danube River, while Ukrainian fishermen do the same in the Dnieper River. The ancient Slavs would even drown humans as sacrifices.

In exchange for taking life, water offers knowledge through divination. In myths, this can be expressed in the form of aquatic creatures who answer questions. Fish that can speak to humans – often goldfish, pike, carp, eel or catfish – feature frequently. Sometimes they fulfil wishes, genie-like, or predict the future. They may not always be willing to do this, but they will often help a human hero to solve a problem.

Various non-aquatic creatures also feature in Slavic myths around water. Snakes often appear, as do horses, the latter usually as ritual figures of violence or violent sexuality. Horses can also be bringers of water. A spring called Hippocrene, 'horse's spring', on Mount Helicon in Boeotia (modern-day Greece) is said to have been made when the legendary winged horse Pegasus stamped his hoof into the rock. A talking mare sometimes emerges from the water to aid the hero of a Slavic fairy tale.

If the future can't be predicted via talking fish or horses, then the art of divination can be practised by humans in touch with water. Lecanomancy or hydromancy involves 'catching the stars' on the surface of water, usually in a vessel, and examining their reflection in the water.[58] This ritual is sometimes transferred by analogy from water to mirrors. Even today in the Balkans and other Central European Slavic cultures, all mirrors in a home are covered with black cloth after a death in the family. This is so that the soul of the dead person, having crossed over to the other side of the mirror, cannot see the living.[59]

Water can also be a bringer of life. The bunches of eggs that fish and frogs release are associated with fertility. In a Serbian ballad rife with Freudian subtext, a queen of Buda becomes pregnant after eating an eel. Water rituals can be used to predict pregnancy and encourage fertility; some wedding rituals involve visiting wells and 'sacrificing' water by pouring it out.

Any rituals involving pouring water, whether to summon rain or request a favourable outcome, tend to be performed mainly by girls and women. The Balkan 'Dodole' were young girls involved in a pagan Slavic ceremony in which they dressed in robes made of woven green leaves to perform a ritual dance and make the rounds of local houses, singing incantations and pouring water symbolically.[60] They represent Dodola (also called Peperuda or Dodola Perunitsa), a goddess associated with rainclouds who was the lover of Perun.

Some Balkan rituals involve making cakes and then bringing them to running water. Part of the cake is thrown into the water and the rest is taken back home, where it is distributed to children, provided they eat it only inside the house. Smooth, egg-shaped stones can be taken out of a river or stream, then 'washed' in a cloth brought from home; the stones represent the souls of the deceased, and each is named after one of them. Candles are then lit for them all. In other variants, water is splashed when a journey begins or when a dead person is taken out of the house, and graves are occasionally splashed with water. Pouring or splashing water is also used to summon rain in times of drought, and to bring luck. Whenever I left home to take exams at university, my grandmother in Belgrade used to 'pour water'.

Water birds can also have magical properties, particularly in connecting the living with the dead. Swans, cranes and other waterfowl appear not only in traditional fairy tales but also in relatively recent popular culture: Mark Bernes, a Soviet singer, recorded the song 'Zhuravli' (Cranes) in 1969. Based on a text by the Dagestani poet Rasul Gamzatov, it tells of unburied soldiers on the battlefields who turn into white cranes. Bearers of souls, healers – these are the roles of water birds, preserved in the collective memory.

All of this makes sense when we consider that water is the primary material in many mythical contexts. The beginning of the world sees land emerge from water; in Greek mythology, the dead cross the River Styx to reach the land of the shadows.[61] Water provides boundaries and borders to territories. Etiological and cosmological myths of all Slavic cultures include rivers and oceans that surround the world.[62] That is why Slavic myths are so full of watery elements, from sea kings to giant fish to floating cities. Every spring, well, river and lake has its inhabitants, real and mythical.

BANNIKI

Among the anthropomorphic inhabitants of the waters and their immediate surroundings, we find she-demons who protect traditional Russian steam bathhouses. These little structures, called *banya*, take the form of log cabins.[63] They resemble saunas, with a wood-fired stove to provide steam and heat the water, and wooden benches around it. Sometimes women would give birth there, lending them an association with vital force. There are specific rituals associated with bathing in a banya. Hats made of felt are often worn to protect the head from the intense heat, as well as felt mitts – temperatures inside can surpass 90° Celsius, approaching 200° Fahrenheit. A mat is brought to sit on, so one's skin does not come into direct contact with the heated wood. Herbs can be added to the steaming water. Dried wormwood was traditionally hung on the walls and bunches of dried leaves, particularly white birch, called *banny venik*, were used to fan or massage the body, or dipped in water to soothe the skin.

Banya are found in various northern Slavic countries and are popular places of divination in myths thanks to the interaction with a *bannik*, a bathhouse spirit. These are either she-demons or small, impish old men who should be invited to share the hot bath the third time that wood is added to the fire to warm the waters. They can help and heal, but also cause harm: black hens are sacrificed to appease them, and if a would-be bather inadvertently disturbs a bannik while bathing, they will be scalded by boiling water or drowned in the bath. In order not to offend them as pagan beings, no Christian images are allowed in a banya.

A good reason for inviting a bannik to share your bath is that they can predict the future. One version of the tradition involves first stoking the fire that heats the waters a third time, then turning one's back to the water while standing in the doorway. The bannik will softly caress your back if your future is bright, and scratch you with clawed fingers if not.

RUSALKAS

Slavic creatures have lately made their way into pop culture beyond the Slavic world. The folklore-inspired video game *Black Book* allows the player to take on the role of Vasilissa, an apprentice witch who does battle with a bannik. And the hugely popular *Witcher* novels by the Polish author Andrzej Sapkowski – adapted for a video game series as well as a Netflix TV show – are packed with Slavic monsters for the titular character, a mercenary monster-slayer, to battle. Among them is a *rusalka*, a nymph associated with water.

Rusalkas are demonic creatures found in forests, especially among conifers, in fields at night, and around water. In appearance and

CREATURES OF THE DEEP

behaviour they are broadly similar to the nymphs of other ancient cultures. Aquatic rusalkas, capable of living in or out of the water, are presented as near-nude beauties with long hair, sometimes tinted green. Their beauty and song, siren-like, attract men, whom they then drag into the water and drown by tangling them up in their long hair. In rare cases they might take a man underwater and keep him alive, enthroning him as a king of the underwater world. They have the power of foresight and healing, but sexual seduction is what they are most associated with.

Russian researchers have noted that the conceptualization of the rusalka changed significantly during the Romantic period owing to the influence of Western culture. Motifs of guilt and sin, typical of Christianity, appeared where they previously had not. According to more recent myths, rusalkas are created when someone drowns, whether by accident, murder or suicide, especially pregnant unmarried girls, or children. Rusalkas sometimes marry a beloved man who stays on land, but as wives they are unstable, often running away with their child or leaving it for their husband to raise alone.

Rusalkas appear in numerous works of literature, art and music. Pushkin, Gogol, Shevchenko, the Czech composer Anton Dvorak (who wrote an opera called *Rusalka*) and many others reference them.[64] The Slovenian philologist Franz Miklošič believed that the name originated from the ancient Roman summer holiday of Rosalia, when roses and violets were woven into wreaths and set upon the figures of household gods and on the graves of ancestors. Russian customs preserve the hanging of wreaths on the branches of trees by the water and the ritual 'leading' of a girl, representing a rusalka, who wears a wreath adorned with flowers. The rusalka's day is Thursday, especially the Holy Thursday before Easter.

VILAS

Unlike rusalkas, *vilas* (roughly translated as 'fairies') in southern Slavic cultures have not changed much as a consequence of Western influence.[65] They inhabit the same areas as rusalkas, and those near or in the water behave similarly to rusalkas, but they are less overtly sexualized. Rather than being naked they are often lightly dressed in white, and sometimes they have hooves like a goat's rather than feet. They are talented singers and dancers and they don't like to be spied on: they will severely punish a covert observer when they find him, or if he accidentally sees a 'fairy ring' (a group of vilas engaged in a ritual dance). That said, vilas have also been said to cure madness by dancing around a patient, as mental illness was sometimes thought to be caused by a vila entering someone's body – she could then be tempted out of the body in order to join the fairy dance.

Vilas do not take kindly to being outsung, and they'll punish someone who sings better than they do. But they are not evil. They willingly take in lost or abandoned infants and even breastfeed them, conferring special powers and strength upon the child. They can become ritual siblings to humans: the terms for this, *pobratim* and *posestrima*, incorporate the words for brother, *brat*, and sister, *sestra*.[66] This special relationship, based on a kind of oral contract, guarantees that the vila will provide sisterly protection and aid to the other sibling, defending him or her against violence, the law or any other authority. Ritual siblinghood is an Indo-European institution, characteristic of a warrior society in which there has historically been a real need for strong alliances. It is widely present across many Slavic cultures, but is best known in the Balkans.[67]

Vilas symbolize women's freedom and independence, their resistance to partisanship and to rules – especially restrictions on mobility. While most women in Slavic societies historically wore their hair back, often in long braids, vilas wear theirs loose as a symbol of freedom. This symbolism remained strong even in the 20th century. During the Second World War, women in Bosnia ritually unravelled their hair to ensure safe passage for the partisans, Yugoslav guerrillas battling the Nazis. In the vocabulary of ritual, unbound hair represents the pouring of water, flowing down one's back like a waterfall.

Water vilas have special knowledge about medicinal plants, so they can help with diseases and injuries. The healing they provide may take place in a dream experienced while sleeping beside a body of water. Their punishment for anyone they catch spying is to take away the offender's legs or arms, or blind them – conversely, they can also cure blindness. Sometimes it is enough to wash one's eyes with water in which a vila has bathed.

WATERMEN

While dragons are prevalent in most world myth systems, they are few and far between among the Slavs. Where they do appear, they take the form of a male aquatic creature. All Slavic dragons are male and live exclusively in water, only emerging to catch and eat cattle, or sometimes people. The dragon regains strength when he dips his head back into the water.

Although the dragon is largely a syncretic demon, influenced by biblical representations of monsters and the legend of Saint George slaying a dragon, it does partly originate in the water demons of Slavic cultures. A dragon is a guardian of the water, especially of mountains that are supposed to maintain the reserve of water. There are many such myths in Slovenia.

Male watery creatures, unlike seductive rusalkas and vilas, are described as green, slimy, monstrous beings with scales (rather like the *Creature from the Black Lagoon*), but they know how to transform into handsome men to seduce and kidnap a girl. Such is the theme of Slovenian poet France Prešeren's poem 'Povodni Mož', on which the legend that accompanies this chapter is based. In it, a conceited young beauty from the city of Ljubljana, who refuses all suitors, is punished by being kidnapped by the Waterman ('Vodni mož'). This may originally have been Prešeren's revenge fantasy against the object of his unrequited desire, Julija Primic.

Watery creatures have a special relationship with sailors and fishermen. They can sink a boat, but they are also vulnerable to being caught in fishermen's nets. With the entwinement of pagan beliefs and Christianity, the traditional functions of a water creature began to be taken over by Saint Nicholas. According to legend, he was martyred by having an anchor hung from his neck and then being thrown into the ocean. As a consequence he was considered a patron saint of sailors, protecting travellers on seas and rivers. In an old Serbian oral ballad that offers a complex tapestry of Christian, pagan Greek and pagan Slavic beliefs, Saint Nicholas is invited by God to go to the forest and prepare boats to transport souls of the dead across the river to the underworld.

7

FIREBIRD
◆
SLAVIC MAGIC

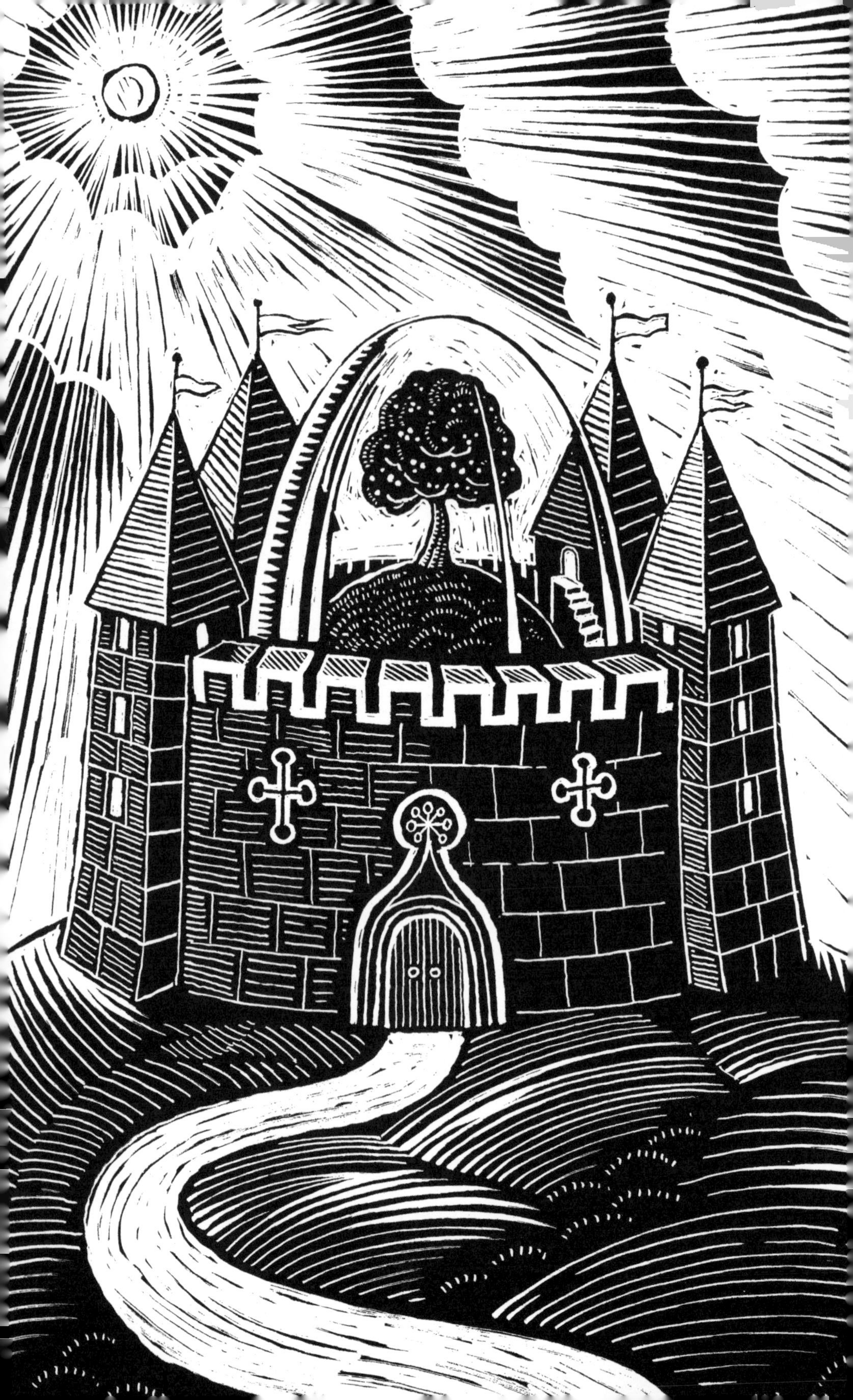

FIREBIRD

And in my dreams I see myself on a wolf's back
Riding along a forested path
To do battle with a sorcerer-tsar
In that land where a princess sits under lock and key,
Pining behind massive walls.
There gardens surround a palace all of glass.
There firebirds sing by night
And peck at golden fruit.
    From Yakov Polonsky, 'A Winter's Journey' (1844)[68]

There once lived a sorcerer-tsar with thirteen adopted daughters and thirteen adopted sons. They all dwelt in a castle – and it was no ordinary castle. The keep was shaped like an egg and made entirely of glass, which the sorcerer-tsar's magic protected against hail and lightning. The glass caught the fire of the sun to keep warm his most prized possession: a tree that bore golden apples.

Golden apples that someone had been stealing.

The sorcerer-tsar set his guards to watch the golden apple tree in the orchard all night, but they found no one. After all, how could someone from outside get into the enchanted glass castle?

Not long afterwards, the youngest of the sorcerer-tsar's children, Prince Ivan Tsarevitch, a clever lad just emerging into manhood, was playing in the orchard when he came upon an enormous feather like nothing he had ever seen before. It glowed and was warm to the touch, and its colour was a mixture of every hue of orange and red with flickers of blue here and there, shimmering and shivering in the gentlest breeze.

CHAPTER SEVEN

He brought the feather to his father, who sat brooding on his throne, playing with a golden egg pendant that he always wore around his neck.

'But this is a feather from a firebird! The firebirds were once my pets, living happily enough, it seemed, in the glass garden. I've not seen them for centuries and I would dearly love to once more feel the burning of their song in my ears. Ivan, if you can find and bring me a firebird, I will reward you and make you my heir.'

Prince Ivan, who had never imagined he had a chance at inheriting the kingdom, what with twelve older brothers in line before him, accepted the challenge and set off on his horse, Alexander. Together they wandered through the forests of the kingdom, but nowhere did Prince Ivan see any sign of the firebird.

One day he was feeling hopeless and spoke, to himself, really, about his plight, as he brushed Alexander's mane.

'It seems I'll never find a firebird,' he said. 'Perhaps I should give up, but I fear that my father will have me thrown into a pot of boiling water if I return empty-handed. He can be grumpy that way...'

'You're not going to become soup,' said someone in reply.

Prince Ivan looked around, surprised.

'Over here. You missed a spot behind my ear.' It was his horse, Alexander.

'I didn't know you could speak,' replied Prince Ivan.

'You'd never held a firebird's feather before,' replied the horse.

'I don't suppose you'd know how I can find the...you know, the entire firebird?' Ivan asked sheepishly.

'I do,' said the horse.

'...And?' encouraged Ivan hopefully.

'Let's share a bag of oats, and I'll tell you.'

Alexander explained that to catch a firebird, Ivan would have to sow an untilled field with kernels of corn. When the light of the full moon hit the corn, it would spark into blue flames that would draw firebirds to them.

And so Prince Ivan did as his horse instructed. He sowed kernels of corn in a field and waited in the shadow of the forest until the full moon rose. Sure enough, the light of the moon struck the corn and the corn reflected back a blue flame. From over the treetops behind Ivan, a shadow swooped and settled down upon the field.

It was an enormous bird, far larger than an eagle, and with feathers that appeared to dance in every tone of red and orange, as if the bird were engulfed in flames that did not harm it. Ivan sprang forward and tackled the bird from behind. They rolled through the field, wrestling as the bird sought to shake him off. The heat from the firebird singed Ivan's clothing, but he held on.

At last the firebird stopped struggling and turned its raptor head to look Ivan straight in the eye.

'This is not the way to win the kingdom,' she said.

'But my father asked that I bring you to him,' Prince Ivan replied, still breathless from the fight and afraid that the bird would slip like mist from his grip. 'If I bring you back he will make me his heir. And if I don't, I fear that he will make me into soup.'

'You might be his heir, but you will never be tsar,' the bird said. 'Your father is Koschei the Deathless. Have you ever wondered why he is called this?'

'Because he hasn't died yet?' Ivan asked.

'Because he cannot die,' said the bird. 'He has already lived for centuries and will live for centuries more. He is not a good man.'

'I sensed that,' said Ivan, 'what with his frequent threats to make me and my siblings into soup.'

'If you let me go, I will help you to inherit the throne. And I will bring you the princess of your dreams.'

This sounded like a better deal to Prince Ivan, and so he released his grip on the firebird. She launched skyward and, for a moment, he feared that he had been tricked. But the firebird turned in the air and swooped back down towards him. Then he feared he had been tricked again and was about to be torn to shreds by her talons.

CHAPTER SEVEN

However, the firebird landed on the ground beside him with one of her own feathers in her beak, which she offered to him. A single tail feather, still radiating heat.

'With this feather, you can call on me to help you once,' she said. 'Up ahead, the path splits into three ways. Choose the proper way and one of my kin will tell you how to capture the kingdom.'

Then the firebird disappeared beyond the clouds.

Prince Ivan tucked the feather into the band of his hat, mounted Alexander and set off in the direction the firebird had indicated. Soon they came to a huge boulder standing at a point where three distinct paths stretched out before them. The stone was carved with ancient letters that Ivan could not read, but which he somehow understood.

'Choose a path,' the stone letters stated. 'The one on the left will lead you to hunger and cold. The one in the middle will lead you to live, but your horse will die. The one on the right will lead you to die, but your horse shall live.'

Prince Ivan looked down at Alexander, to reassure himself that, while the horse could talk, he could not read, and he set off down the middle path.

Not far along the path the woods closed in, blotting out the moonlight, and a howl sent shivers through Ivan's body. Suddenly a giant grey wolf leapt upon them, knocking Ivan off Alexander's back. Ivan leapt up and drew his sword, but too late – Alexander was no more. The great grey wolf, twice the normal size, glared at Ivan with gore-soaked jaws. She looked ready to spring but saw the feather on Ivan's hat and smiled. Not an I'm-going-to-eat-you smile, but a friendly one.

'Hello, Prince Ivan,' purred the wolf. 'I'm your adopted sister, Tsarevna.'

'You are?' he replied, still shaking from the attack. 'You look different from how I remember you.'

'Our so-called father turned me into a wolf, and all our twelve sisters into firebirds, to keep us imprisoned.'

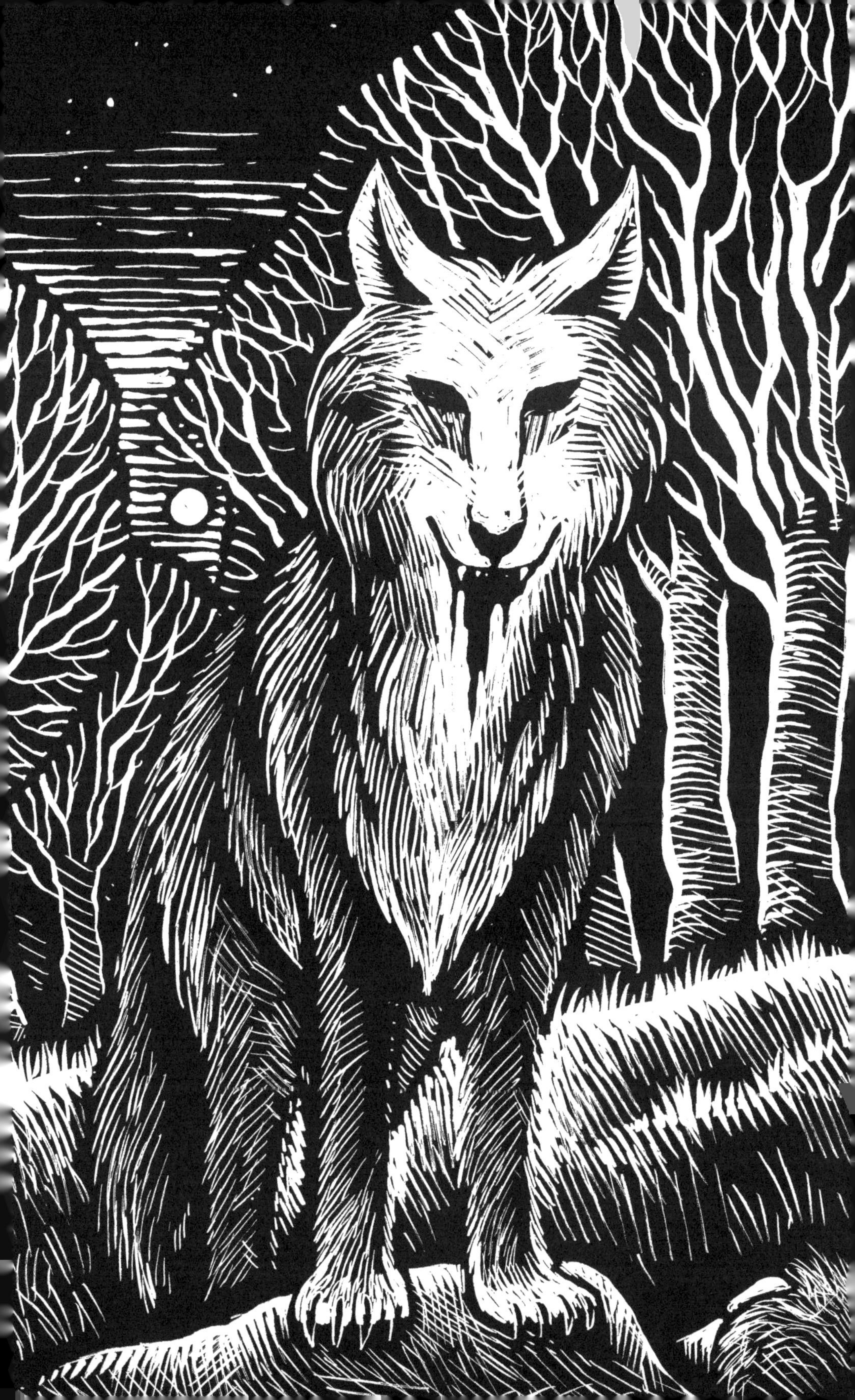

CHAPTER SEVEN

'I'd wondered why I hadn't seen any of you for ages.'

'You can rescue me and our sisters and win the kingdom. Koschei the Deathless has never been a father to us. As you are the youngest of us all, perhaps you do not know, but he stole us from our families, each of us, when he could have no children of his own. Will you help us all? Help me?'

Ivan was moved by her plight and the beauty of her voice. He nodded.

'Then climb on my back and I will tell you how to defeat him.'

Prince Ivan climbed onto the great grey wolf's back and they set off. As he rode, Tsarevna the wolf spoke to him.

'Koschei the Deathless cannot die because his soul is not kept within his body. He has hidden it away, but I have learned where. It is inside the eye of a needle that is hidden inside an egg that is hidden inside a duck that is hidden inside a hare that is hidden inside a chest that is hidden in a hollow log.'

'How did the duck get inside the hare?' Prince Ivan wondered.

'Don't ask stupid questions,' Tsarevna replied.

After a night and a day of riding, when the moonless sky was black and the stars all but invisible in the infinite distance, they stopped at the edge of a pond. In the centre of the pond floated a large woven carpet of the sort made in Persia. Upon this carpet was a large log and together they bobbed gently upon the surface of the water.

'Swim to the carpet,' the wolf whispered. 'Retrieve what is inside the log. I'll try to hold them off.'

'Hold who off?' Prince Ivan asked, but no sooner had he done so than the pond water began to bubble and shift. Into the water Ivan dove, swimming as hard as he could for the carpet and the hollow log upon it. It was a good thing that he was a fine swimmer, for out of the black waters of the pond rose thirteen *vodyanoy*, water spirits that looked like men but had the faces of frogs. They reached out their slimy, green, webbed fingers to seize Ivan, but Tsarevna the wolf tore into them, rending them with her jaws. They shifted their focus onto her and threw themselves upon her, seeking to drag her into the pond and drown her there.

Ivan reached the carpet and managed to pull himself up onto it, but was still just floating in the midst of the pond. He looked over his shoulder, helpless as the *vodyanoy* wrestled Tsarevna the wolf into the black waters. He reached his hand into the hollow log and found a gilded chest inside. He pulled it out and threw open its lid. Within it sat a hare, looking far too small to have swallowed a duck. Ivan quickly shut the lid, before the hare could jump out. He looked up at the sky, wondering what to do. He looked back at Tsarevna the wolf. Then he seized the firebird's feather from his hat and wished with all his might that the firebird might save them.

The feather burst into a flame that did not burn Ivan's hand. But as he wondered at its magical glow, the carpet upon which he stood in the middle of the pond began to stiffen and rise up off the water, into the air. Water dripped like tears from it as it carried Ivan upwards.

'Tsarevna!' he shouted. As if it had heard him, the carpet twisted around beneath his feet and shot towards the great grey wolf, with Ivan upon it. It smashed into the pile of *vodyanoy*, knocking them back from Tsarevna. Prince Ivan helped her onto the carpet, and together they flew away into the sky.

As they flew towards the glass castle, Ivan showed Tsarevna the hare inside the chest.

'We must crack the egg that is inside the duck that is inside the hare,' she said.

'And how can we do that?' Ivan asked hopelessly.

'How on earth is the world run by men?' Tsarevna wondered aloud. She took the hare in her enormous jaws and bit down hard. A crack was heard, loud as a thunderclap, followed by a lightning-fast burst of white light. When Ivan's vision returned, he saw that Tsarevna was no longer a giant wolf but a beautiful young princess, about his own age, wearing a wolfskin to cover her nakedness.

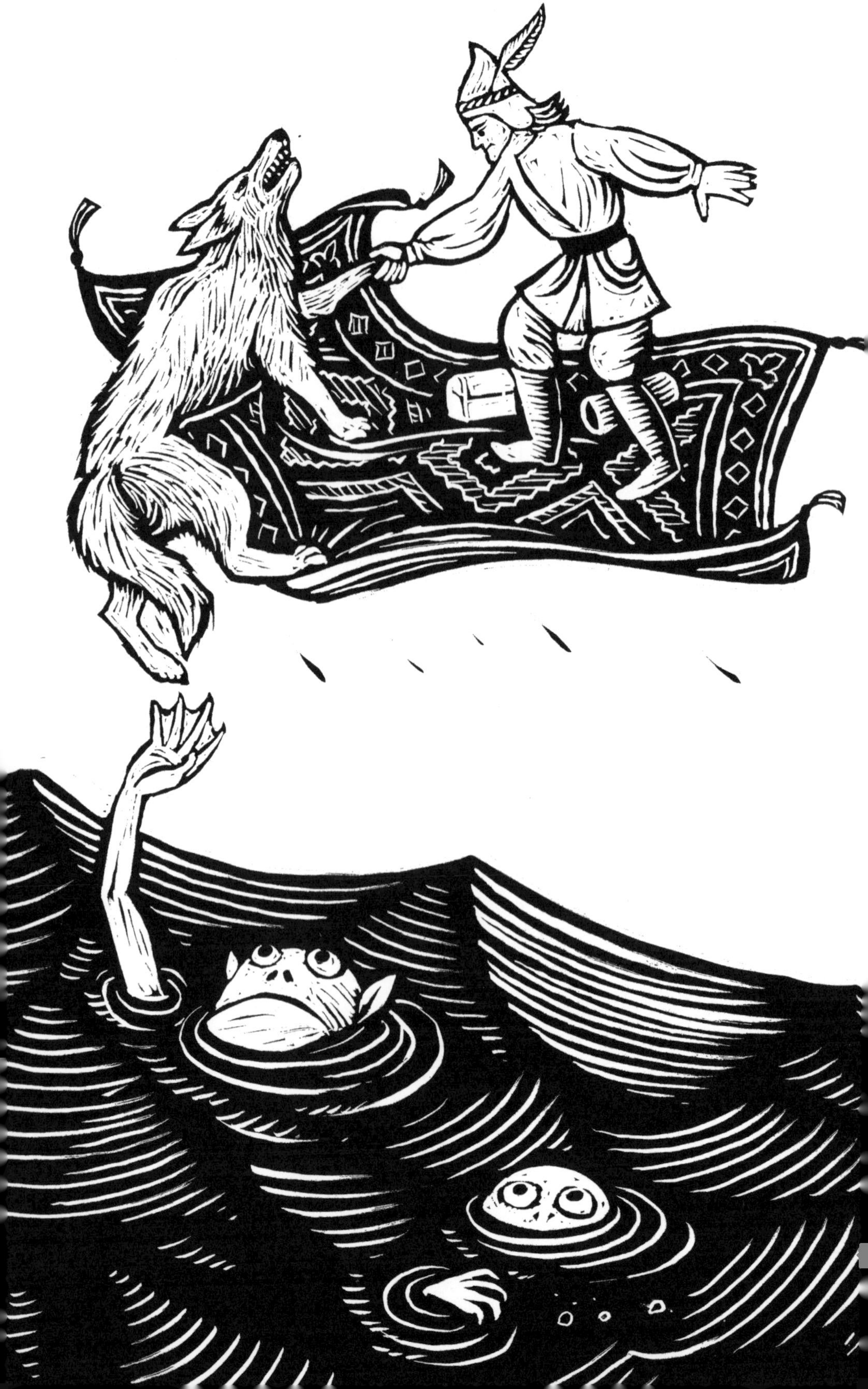

Ivan and Tsarevna held one another as the carpet flew them back to the glass castle. When they arrived, they were not surprised to see that the glass egg which had once stood for the castle's keep was no longer there – and nor was Koschei the Deathless, for now he was Koschei the Dead. It was a more appropriate title.

Prince Ivan and Princess Tsarevna married. Their adopted siblings were human once more. And best of all, no one was ever made into soup again.

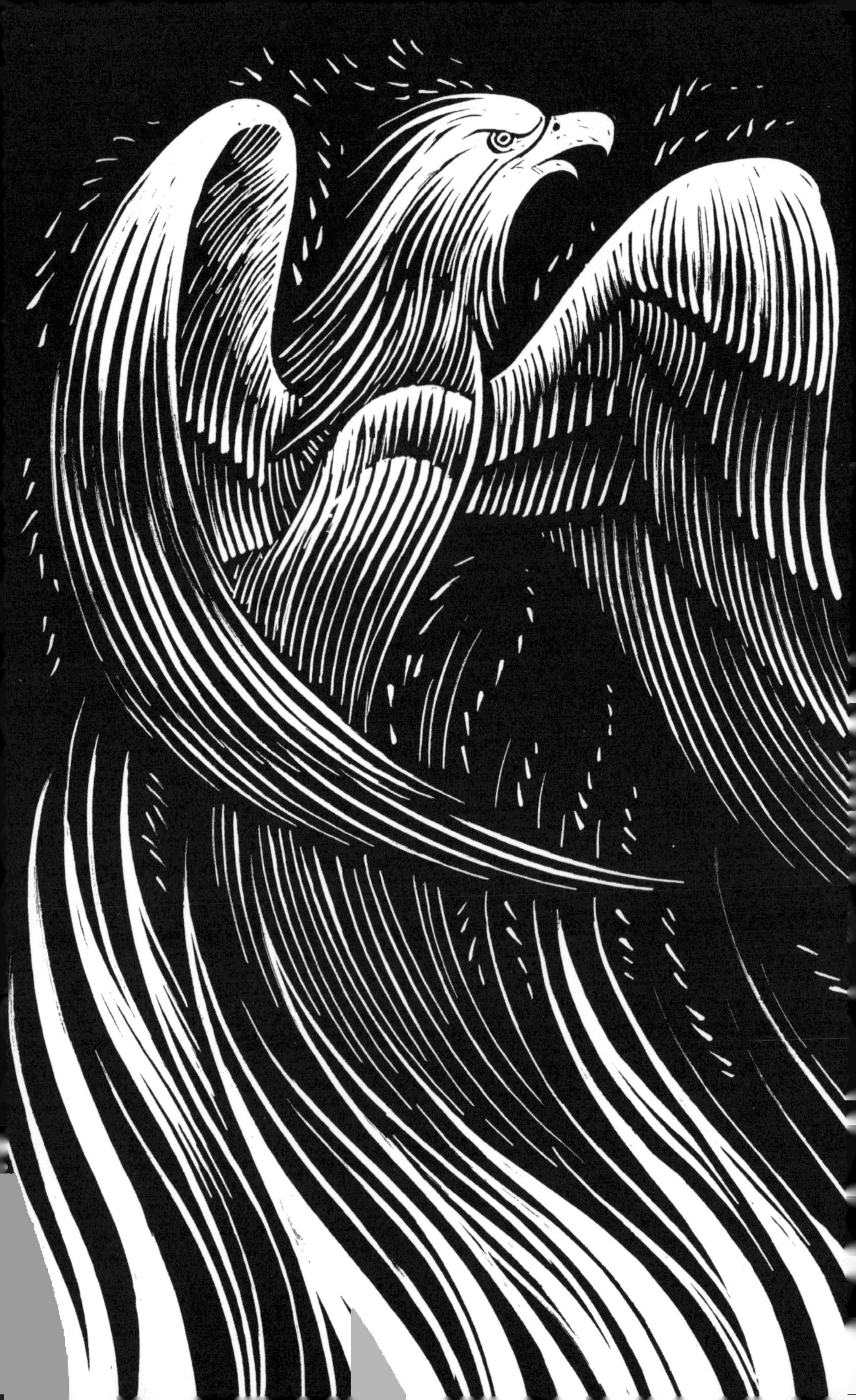

SLAVIC MAGIC

If we want to place magic into a particular social, historical and cultural context within Slavic mythology, there is a fluid but useful term that can assist us: shamanism. Today, this word is often criticized for its associations with colonialism, and it is true that there has often been an element of condescension attached to its use. However, it is still used in anthropology and ethnography and, in the absence of a better alternative, can be helpful.

The origin of 'shaman-hood' (an alternative term) dates back to prehistory. The oldest undoubted material remains of shamanic techniques date to about 30,000 BCE and were found in today's Czech Republic. The broadest definition of the term includes mediation techniques between humans and other, invisible worlds. The presence of these 'invisible worlds' is accepted in most world cultures, whether the worlds are Heaven and Hell as understood in a Christian context, or pagan realms deemed heretical and preposterous. The difference is really only in the details.

Shamanism is present the world over, and was first named in the Russian language in the context of contact with a variety of cultures in locations ranging from northern Europe to Asia. It became known in Europe through reports brought back by travellers in the 17th century. The etymology of the word is still the subject of debate, but a Tungusc origin (a people from Siberia) is most often mentioned. The basic meaning would be 'knowledge', but 'priest' is also implied.

A shaman is an individual with special traits, inherited or learned, who is able to separate his soul from his body through various techniques, both visible and audible. Through such approaches as trances, dreams, dancing, listening to or producing sounds or music and speaking in tongues, a shaman communicates with deities, demons and the souls of the dead. He (historically, a shaman has usually been a 'he') employs assistants in this communication, most often animals – sometimes totems of his ethnic group – with whom he can communicate. As a mediator between the worlds, the shaman confirms the thesis of three other worlds: the divine or celestial world, the human–animal world, and the underground world of souls and various demons. This is one of the key points where pagan shamanism diverges from Christianity; Christians believe in the divine/celestial (Heaven) and the underground world of souls and demons (Hell), but not the human–animal continuum.

In shamanism, the boundaries between these worlds are by no means clearly defined. Separation of the soul from the body is the shaman's most powerful tool, because the soul is stronger than the body in Slavic beliefs. In Serbian epic poetry, the defeated hero, before dying, sometimes begs the victor to marry his sister, because this way his soul will continue to live. Even more convincingly, suicide provides a means for the soul to take revenge in a way that the living cannot achieve. Therefore suicide, in Slavic beliefs, can sometimes be a productive tool, a weapon.

A shaman is a practitioner of magic, and his field is most often medicine – specifically, healing the victims of demons. The shaman must therefore know a great deal about the medicinal and poisonous plants, objects and tools that facilitate communication with demons. Visible indicators of these abilities are often part of a shaman's equipment. These have traditionally included drums and percussion (because ghosts are more sensitive to sound than humans), animal parts (horns, fur, leather, feathers) and magical items such as stones or crystals, sometimes sewn directly into the shaman's skin. But a shaman always remains mortal, albeit with special experience, abilities and knowledge.

The main attraction of shamanism – the ability of humans to connect spiritually to other aspects of the world, and particularly to nature and animals – aligns closely with what are known as New Age beliefs. In Slavic cultures, the shaman represents humanity's openness to all invisible forces, in our world and beyond. In this way a shaman differs from, say, a Catholic priest, whose role is more focused on the preservation of cult frameworks and the transmission of religious narration. That is probably the reason why shamanic actions have left such deep and distinctive traces in Slavic cultures, and why the social position of professional shamans has been preserved for so long.

WEATHER WARRIORS

A *zduhać* is a Balkan variant of a shaman, with distinct traces in non-Slavic Balkan cultures. The term refers to a mortal with the ability to fight natural elements, such as storms. In modern Greek, the word describes territorial demons who protect their villages and surroundings.

The myth about the other variant of the protector from natural disasters, the so-called dragon man, has been preserved in Bulgaria, Serbia, Macedonia, Bosnia, Montenegro and Albania. The difference between a zduhać and a dragon man is that a dragon man fights alone against calamities (which are embodied in a monster called Ala in Serbo-Croatian), as well as for the preservation of crops, fruits and livestock. The zduhać, on the other hand, functions in groups which fight with other groups of zduhać: the winners take the crops and fruits of the vanquished. This has historically been used to explain why some agricultural areas remain barren for a time. Groups of zduhać from Bosnia, Serbia, Dalmatia and especially Montenegro were traditionally believed to fight against zduhać from Albania and Italy.

Some historical figures, even church dignitaries and leaders, were thought to be zduhać, an attribute that brought them fame. There is a well-known story about a famous spirit from Bosnia who received a message from a friend in Buda (part of today's Budapest) who was in trouble. At that moment, the zduhać was at the barber's shop, but his soul flew to Buda, settled the problem and returned to his body, which remained all the while in the barber's chair. Zduhać were highly esteemed in their communities as protectors of fields and cattle, and they were often rich landowners themselves. Shamans of this type are known throughout the Slavic world.

Zduhać and dragon men are people of great physical strength, but with signs that indicate their ability to separate the soul from the body: they are usually pale, sleepy, with tired eyes. Dragon people sometimes have folded wings that are recognizable under their clothes and webbed skin between their fingers. Both zduhać and dragon people sleep for a long time and are difficult to wake. Dragon people fight with oversized farming tools, swords, or sometimes whole oak trees which they pull out of the ground to use as weapons. Zduhać fight with wooden poles, sometimes with short sticks smouldering with flame on both ends. Some zduhać retire before the fight, move to a high position and wait for the Devil, who gives them a hat with which they can fly and fight more fiercely.

Sometimes human veins are torn out of the dead and tied around a zduhać's ankles. They carry with them bowls, brooms and various other items used in rituals involving ghosts. Both dragon people and zduhać know how to fly, with fights often taking place in the air. They are also known for being lovers and seducers: at night they descend through the chimney into the house (the usual path for souls and demons) to visit their mistresses. Their descendants, however, are weak and do not live long.

Zduhać and dragon men routinely engage in battles against other demons dangerous to humans, such as vampires or werewolves. A zduhać, especially in Serbia, can also be an animal: there are stories describing them as rams, huge black birds or roosters. Saint Nicholas has some shamanic or zduhać traits, especially in the Balkans: in one story from Serbia he appears before God all wet and covered in mud, excusing himself with the explanation that he has been fighting winds and thunder to save sailors on a ship at sea.

The character and behaviour of the zduhać and the dragon man precisely correspond to the shamanic model. Neither can be associated

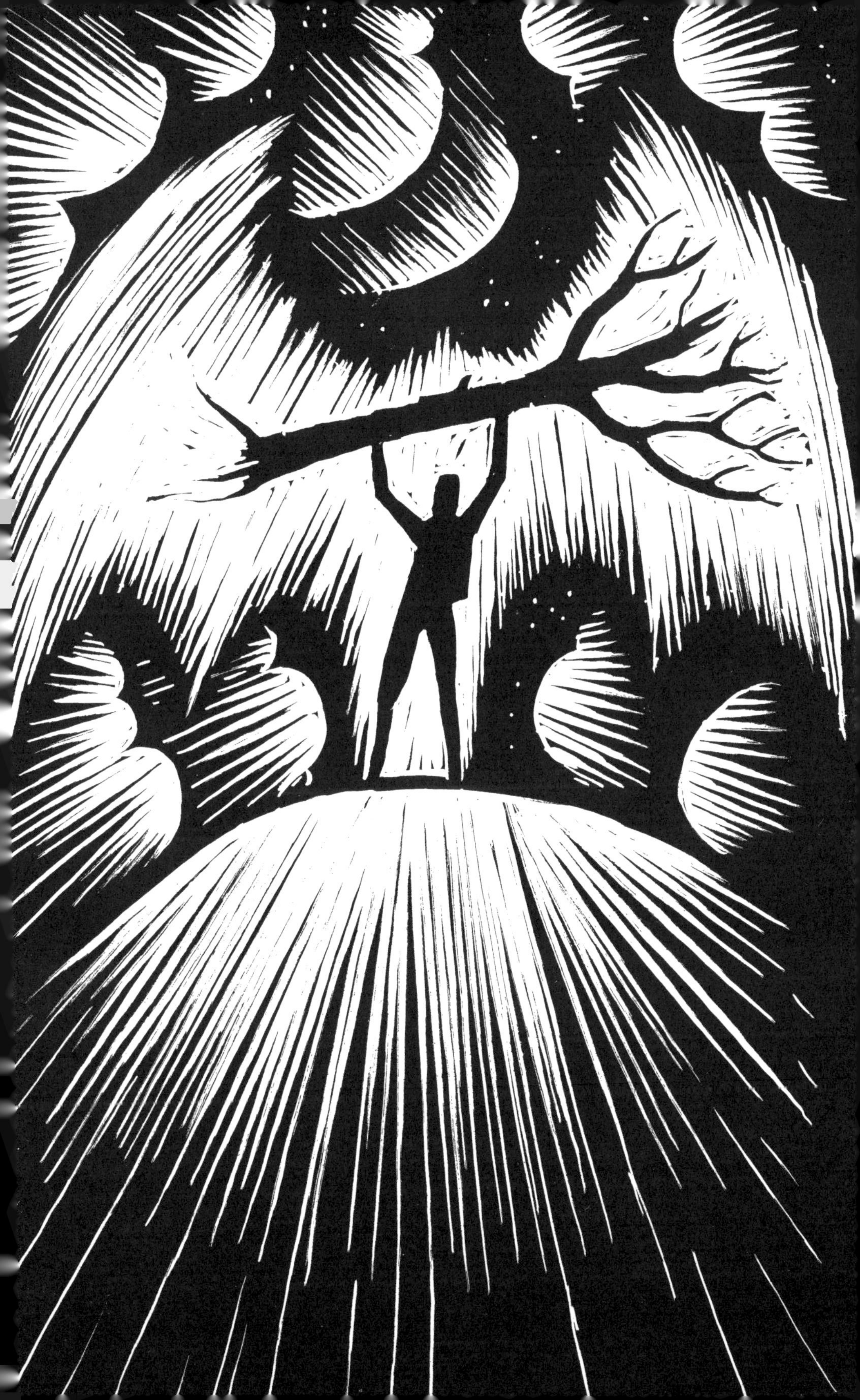

with a specific deity or cult; their role is primarily social, interacting with the people. They are mortal but with superhuman abilities.

WITCHES

Witches (*veštica* in Serbo-Croatian), unlike zduhać and dragon people, represent a diverse group of mortal and immortal beings, although their role is also primarily social. They can be born as witches (like Baba Yaga), perhaps to serve or accompany a female deity; they can become witches after death; or they can learn witchcraft from an older and more experienced witch. A witch is always an old, often ugly woman with physical defects – the concept of the young, beautiful witch is a relatively recent cultural adaptation. Witches can fly, turn into other creatures (most often butterflies) and make themselves invisible. A witch can float or perch on a single leaf, so there might be hundreds of witches on a single tree, especially a pear or a walnut: one per leaf. Eggshells and walnut shells in the household should be crushed so that witches do not use them for transportation. Witches also travel on horses, but their mounts are really men they have transformed into horses to serve them. A horse without any mark, especially a black horse, is said to be connected with vampires and witches. Whichever transport they use, or when they simply fly, witches are very fast and leave trails of light across the night sky: comets, meteors and meteor showers are thus interpreted as evidence of witches. Witches like gold, and they use golden cups when drinking with devils at orgies.

Those who become witches after death are the most dangerous type. At night, like vampires, they rise from their graves and attack children, devouring their hearts and livers. They can be destroyed like vampires, with a hawthorn stake through the heart. If you come upon a sleeping witch, you can render her unable to wake again by turning her around so that her feet lie where her head once was. A witch who is awake can be calmed by offering her a piece of bread dotted with three grains of salt. In order to prevent a witch from entering your house at night, the passage from the fireplace to the chimney should be closed and a broom must always be set near the hearth in order to sweep the dust, which contains souls. One of the most powerful defences against witches is garlic (as with vampires), because they cannot bear its odour. Similarly, witches cannot stand the smell of burned animal horn.

Witches cannot sink, but they can be destroyed by fire. Their inability to sink is a characteristic that led to some of the barbaric practices in Early Modern Europe and North America, in which alleged witches were thrown into water. If they floated, they were witches and would be burned. If they sank to the bottom, they were not witches but, having been proved innocent, they drowned. Witches are lustful, but they engage in orgies only with devils – unlike fairies, who prefer young men.

Beginning in the 14th century, superstitions relating to witches led to a wave of misogynistic European genocide: the trial and killing of (mostly) women suspected of being witches. In most places this practice had died out by the 18th century, although in Serbia there were trials of suspected witches as late as the early 19th century. Psychoanalytic interpretations of this situation are convincing: it is thought to have reflected a fear of older women who, having crossed the line from fertility into menopause, lived alone, as widows or without children. Often such women lived a little way from the centre of social events – in a 'lonely' house – which also placed them outside of the patriarchal hierarchy, doing their own thing, no longer easy for the male leaders of a community to supervise and no longer 'useful' for procreation or as sexual partners. Owing to their life experience and the knowledge they had gained from other women, they sometimes had important roles in the community: healing and the treatment of women in particular, assistance with childbirth or early forms of contraception, childcare, divination, magic. Older women were also the primary guardians and transmitters of oral culture, local customs, collective memory, techniques of crafting and making, recipes and rituals. The ambiguity of the term 'witch' still persists today.

PLANTS AND ANIMALS

Shamanic communication with animals involves three main categories: totem animals and hunting prey, animals as transmitters of souls, and imaginary hybrid animals.

The first group consists of large, powerful animals – the bear, horse, lynx, deer, bull, ram, reindeer and eagle. The second category, carriers of souls, includes smaller, fast animals: otters, foxes, birds, fish, insects. Imaginary hybrid animals include firebirds and golden animals. In shamanism, *all* animals are magical and can participate in understanding and interpreting the world and in the transmission of souls.

Competence in the use of plants is crucial to the shaman's skill set.[69] Knowledge of plants is important not only because of their healing properties but also because they can be used to induce ecstatic states, 'separating' the soul from the shaman's body. Eating and drinking herbal ingredients, inhaling smoke and breathing in odours are the most common methods of reaching a lethargic, narcotic or hypnotic state. Trees, mushrooms, flowers, leaves and fruits can all be home to invisible beings and they offer the shaman a rich choice of different procedures, calendar-based and ritualistic, that can be used to interpret all worlds – our own world, the divine world and the underworld – for the benefit of the shaman's collective.

In myth and in shamanic magic, trees, particularly oak, birch, pine, linden, fir, hawthorn and willow, represent connection with the higher world where deities reside. Trees that have been struck by lightning acquire a special ritual power. Beneath the tree canopy is an important social space, well suited to purposes such as collective meetings or decision-making. Walnut and pear trees are specifically associated with souls, demons and the underworld; witches gather on them at night, as well as on elm or ivy. Sleeping under a walnut or pear tree is said to cause infertility, madness or death itself, while sleeping under other types of tree can lead to ritual dreams that convey healing or medical knowledge upon the sleeper. Birch trees have apotropaic or protective powers: their sap is healthy, so witches fear birches.

Willow trees attract fairies. The willow is one of the most important trees for Slavs and is used in many fertility rituals, most of which include bathing and wearing wreaths made of willow branches and leaves. Willow branches replace palm leaves in rituals on Palm Sunday.

Linden trees are sacred among Slavs; even the deities appreciate their perfumed leaves and flowers, which are both medicinal and magical. A linden tree has the magic ability to travel, so it appears and disappears. Peace is made under the linden tree among family members, clan members or warring sides in a dispute. Kings are crowned there, too. In Slovenia, where the linden is the national tree, every village is meant to have a linden under which decisions are made and meetings held.

Elderberry flowers and branches are important in healing domestic animals. The tree itself is magical, and houses both fairies and devils. Elder is also the best wood to use for making a flute.

Twigs from various bushes, as well as the twigs and leaves of trees, are used in ritualistic whipping; for instance, hazel branches are traditionally used in schools to punish naughty pupils.

EDIBLE PLANTS AND SEEDS

Vegetables and fruits have various magical functions in Slavic lore. Many are heavily weighted with symbolism and can be used in ritual dietary practices as well as folk medicine, in the form of teas, tinctures and other concoctions. Their value is often confirmed in modern scientific or pharmaceutical contexts too, and some are also used as poisons.

One of the more unexpected plants to be regarded as magical by Slavs is the humble cabbage: Slavic oral tradition features various jokes, riddles and well-known expressions that turn on the supposed sexual connotations of this indigenous European plant. It's worth bearing in mind that early cabbage varieties typically had a long stalk with a small head – quite phallic, in fact. (Modern breeding gradually brought the head nearer the ground, leading to the development of popular French lore about newborn babies being found in rich, leafy cabbage heads.) In medieval jokes, the cabbage is sometimes compared to a much-used book; in Serbian, *kupusara* (*kupus*, cabbage) refers to a book used by many – a school textbook, for instance.[70]

Symbolically, the most powerful fruit is the apple. Apples in myths are often golden, as in the ancient Greek story of the Judgment of Paris, in which Paris gave a golden apple to Aphrodite, precipitating the Trojan War. The apple has a role in marriage rituals and is also generally used as a symbol of power. All red fruits have a similar ritual power, especially in the context of seduction and love.

Nuts were distributed during ancient Roman weddings, but in Slavic rituals, especially in the Balkans, nuts are the food of the dead. On Christmas Eve, the head of the household throws nuts into all four corners of the home. The aim is to feed the souls of the dead, who dwell in corners, on the hearth and close to it, in the attic or close to the threshold. Witches gather on nut trees (like the aforementioned walnut) during the full moon, and they can travel in nutshells. In the historical region of Pannonia, there were some famous nut trees known as witches' gathering places. Shamans used to distribute medicinal mixtures and concoctions beneath the canopy of a nut tree.[71]

Herbs provide the basic ingredients of shamanic magic, especially in healing. One of the most important is basil, used in death rituals for cleansing and the protection of the living. It has other apotropaic functions, healing many diseases and supporting fertility rituals. Girls and women wear basil leaves and flowers in their hair, as do young men. Children and women bathe in basil-scented water to remain healthy.

Clover, especially four-leafed clover, is a powerful opener of doors, hidden treasures and secret passages. It can also 'open' male and female hearts if the desired person is touched (in secret) by a leaf. This is the origin of the idea that finding a four-leafed clover brings good luck. According to Serbian tradition, tobacco has been blessed by Saint Sava, which means that the Devil supposedly cannot bear its smell and therefore leaves smokers unharmed. Hemp is a magic plant, used especially in death cults. Nettles can be a powerful remedy for inflammatory disease, and they also protect against thunder. Laurel protects against witches – a baby should always have a branch of laurel close to its bed. Shepherds use laurel branches to drive sheep on the first day of their journey to pasture.

Basic grains that were staple elements of the early Slavic diet, such as millet and wheat, are frequently used in rituals of death, birth and fertility. At funerals in the Balkans, a meal of cooked wheat, nuts and honey is served before the Christian ritual; these are foods that were offered to the dead in pre-Christian times.

We can gain insight into mythurgy, the process of making myths, when we analyse some of the newer Slavic myths constructed around plants that were introduced to Europe after the colonial occupations of the Americas, Africa and Asia: potato, peppers, coffee, chocolate and corn. These 'younger' myths are characterized by formulaic narratives and references to rituals previously associated with plants indigenous to Europe, only the details are structured in a slightly different way. Both peppers and coffee have been used as medicinal plants, especially useful in curing infections and healing wounds.

Primary crops and commodities such as milk, eggs, honey, hair, horn, nails and wool are often used in shamanism.[72] Natural materials such as stones, tree bark and pine cones can represent the souls of the dead. Round stones found near water can symbolize dead ancestors in various rituals; crystals and semi-precious stones function as 'antennae' in communicating with other worlds, especially in the context of divination. Metals have a similar role, whether in their natural form or in the form of manufactured tools and weapons: they are apotropaic, they banish and scare away demons.

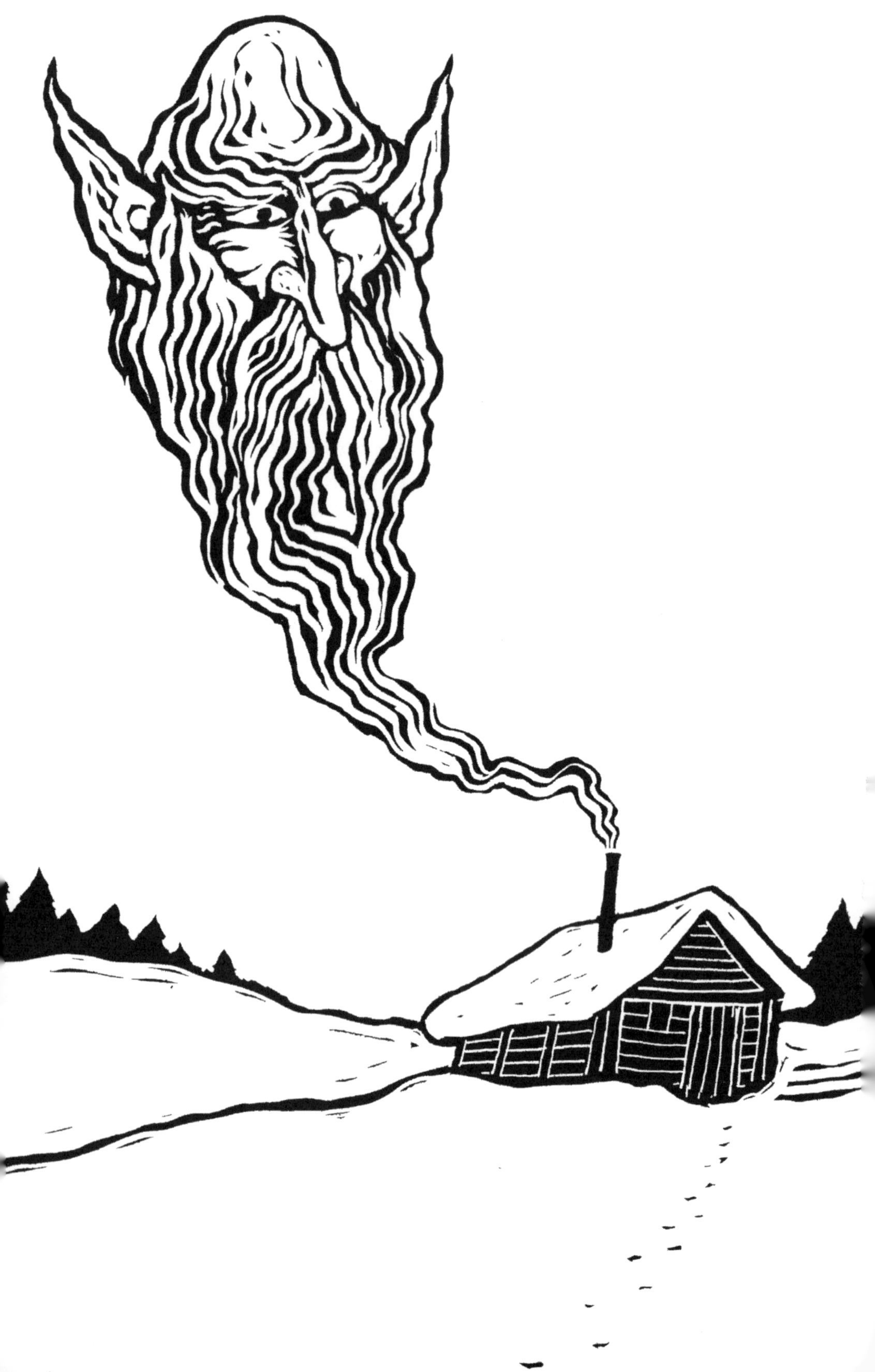

LAST WORDS

This book has, we hope, offered readers an accessible entry point into the complicated world of Slavic myths and their protagonists – a sprawling, unwieldy subject about which only isolated pockets of knowledge survive. And much of that knowledge has been so comprehensively reworked and adapted over the years, changing unavoidably along with broader shifts in culture and ideology, that it would now be barely recognizable to, say, a 9th-century Slav.

We decided from the start that the book should not consist purely of academic analysis. That is part of it, of course, but we have also opted to present new versions of some of the great Slavic myths in what we believe is a fresh, engaging form. The idea was for every reader to make use of the book in their own way, whether by reading from beginning to end, focusing only on the stories, or dipping in and out according to whim.

The corpus of myths associated with Slavic languages is rich and widespread, and its individual elements are not always easy to link in a logical, orderly manner to specific Eurasian or Mediterranean cultures. A further barrier to understanding for anglophone readers is that much work on Slavic mythology from the 20th century onwards has been published only in Slavic languages. Our hope is that the effort we have made here to clarify some of the most important concepts, drawing upon a representative range of international sources, will play a small part in expanding anglophone understanding of the Slavic mythos.

With so many possible stories to choose from, we also hope that you were not disappointed to find a personal favourite – perhaps one told to you before bedtime by your grandmother of Slavic descent – had been left out. Our selection was partly influenced by the global presence and interpretive completeness of certain myths; hence the decision to lead off with the vampire, preeminent among mythical beings of Slavic origin, surpassing all gods and even the werewolf in ubiquity and popular interest.

The Slavic pantheon is, as discussed in these pages, less familiar and a little more challenging to understand, scattered as it is like buckshot across different locations, languages, cultures and traditions. This was another factor in our decision to focus on some lesser-known local myths that at certain specific moments, sometimes not until relatively modern times, have acquired new depth and significance. We chose these in order to illustrate how, even today, myths can generate new layers of meaning in our world, and what a profound loss it would be if they were forgotten.

This volume is therefore not a comprehensive handbook but a personal selection of Slavic myths, bearing witness to their narrative and performative power and to the variety of interpretations they provoke.

Most of all, we hope that the book was a delight to read. The myths can be read aloud during candlelit winter evenings, as frost breathes onto snowbound windowpanes. The analytical material is there for anyone who might be interested in delving deeper, whether your interest is in connecting to your own Slavic roots or exploring the world of myth and legend more generally. But as you read, remember to keep a sharpened hawthorn stake close by your side, just in case you hear the distant howl of a *vukodlak* echoing through the darkling forest.

Svetlana and Noah

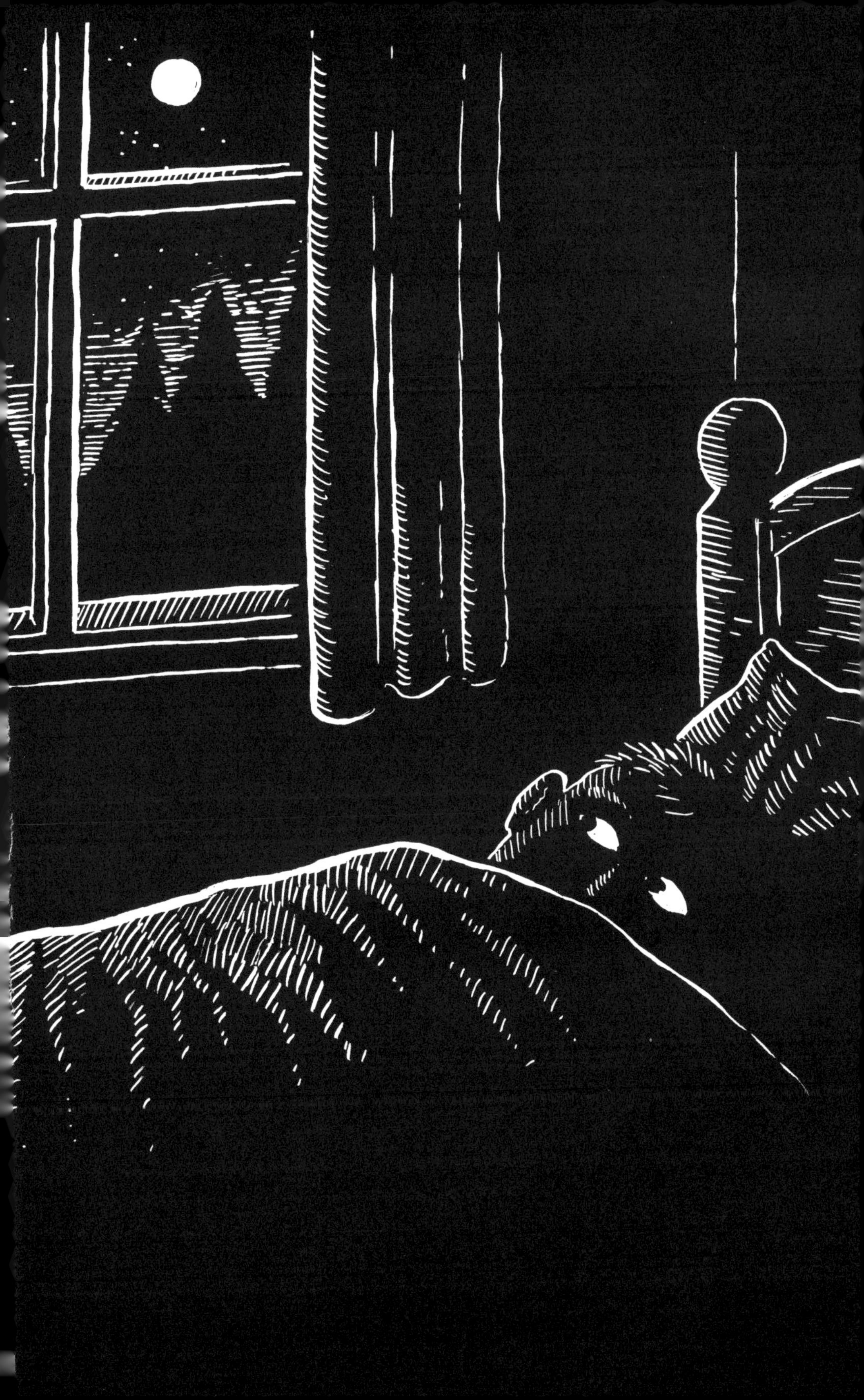

ESTONIA
SWEDEN
LATVIA
LITHUANIA
GERMANY
POLAND
CZECH REPUBLIC
SLOVAKIA
AUSTRIA
HUNGARY
SLOVENIA
ROMANIA
CROATIA
BOSNIA AND HERZEGOVINA
SERBIA
MONTE-NEGRO
KOSOVO
ITALY
MACEDONIA
ALBANIA
GREECE

RUSSIAN FEDERATION

BELARUS

UKRAINE

MOLDOVA

BULGARIA

TURKEY

ACKNOWLEDGMENTS

The authors are grateful to the Thames & Hudson team, beginning with Roger Thorp, who expressed interest in doing a book together years ago, the only question being which book. Ben Hayes led the project, ably assisted by India Jackson and Jen Moore. Camilla Rockwood was wonderfully helpful in the close edit and Joe McLaren's woodcut-style illustrations were perfect accompaniments to the text.

Svetlana would also like to thank her husband, archaeologist Božidar Slapšak, who kept her on track with both his sense of logic and method and their common deep experience in Greece, and her friend for more than forty years Dubravka Ugrešić, who died on 17 March, before writing a blurb for this book. Dubravka was a goddess of irony and a lonely torch of anti-nationalism, subversion and audacity, characteristics that also have rich Slavic roots.

Noah would like to thank his adopted homeland, Slovenia, for opening a new world to him. He has gone on the record as calling it 'the world's best country' and he still feels the same way, more than a decade into his time there. Finally, he thanks Slavic princesses Eleonora and Izabella and his very own Slavic goddess Urška for their support and endless love.

NOTES

Introduction
1. Procopius, *History of the Wars*, vol. 4, p. 273.
2. Ibid., pp. 269–71.
3. Jordanes, *The Origins and the Deeds of Goths*.
4. Procopius, *History of the Wars*, vol. 4, p. 273.

The Slav Epic
5. The earliest sources on Slavic mythology are Byzantine. Enlightenment intellectuals approached it from the point of view of curiosity; in the 19th century it became a topic for serious academic work. The 20th century saw the development of various theories on mythology, typology, systematic research, semasiology and linguistics.
6. Warner's idea responds to the work of German literary historian and theoretician Elisabeth Frenzel in the 1970s, but the most significant theoretician of the fairy tale is the 20th-century Soviet folklorist Vladimir Propp.
7. S. Georgoudi and J.-P. Vernant (eds), *Mythes grecs au figuré*.
8. We tried to resolve this by introducing the term *mythurgy*, which encompasses work and process, constant change and the collective making of myths by the vast number of people who use them. If *mythology* evokes the discourse on myths, *mythurgy* suggests working on the story, performing, changing, adapting. See S. Slapšak, 'A Cat on the Head'.

Vampires
9. J. W. von Valvasor, *Die Ehre deß Hertzogthums Crain*, vol. 6, pp. 329–41.
10. Ibid.
11. M. Ranft, *De masticatione mortuorum in tumulis*, vol. 2, paragraphs 56–9.
12. C. Frayling, *Vampyres* (2016), n.p.
13. Quoted in Á. Mézes, 'Vampire Contagion as a Forensic Fact', pp. 159–60, 161, 162.
14. Quoted in Frayling, *Vampyres* (2016), n.p.
15. Mézes, 'Vampire Contagion as a Forensic Fact', p. 171.
16. H. Walpole, *The Letters*, vol. 1, p. 3.
17. Quoted in Frayling, *Vampyres* (2016), p. 51.
18. 'Voltaire on Vampires', from *The Works of Voltaire*.
19. *Gazette des gazettes* ou *Journal politique pour l'année...1765*.
20. V. Karadžić, *Srpski rječnik*.
21. C. Frayling, *Vampyres* (1992), p. 108.
22. K. Marx, *Capital*, vol. 1, p. 163.
23. Ibid.
24. Singing, laughing, drums: singing alone in a lonely place is a kind of natural reaction we still have. Lada Stevanović's *Laughing at the Funeral* argues for the continuation of this ritual in the Balkans.

Werewolves
25. P. Skok, *Etimologijski rjecnik hrvatskoga ili srpskoga jezika*, s.v.
26. N. Groom, *The Vampire: A New History*.
27. S. Baring-Gould, *The Book of Were-Wolves*, p. 98.
28. I. Crawford-Mowday, 'Caul: A Sailor's Charm'.
29. James VI and I, *Daemonologie*.
30. R. Scot, *The Discoverie of Witchcraft*.
31. Anonymous, *A True Discourse*.

Libuše and Women
32. The actual Přemyslid dynasty ruled the Lands of the Bohemian Crown from 873 CE until the murder of King Wenceslaus III in 1306. The earliest known work that mentions a story about Přemysl and Libuše is found in the late 10th-century *Vita et passio sancti Vencaslai et sanctae Ludmilae aviae eius*, though some scholars believe this to be a forgery meant to give earlier credence to the tale. More assuredly, the legend in roughly the form we retell it appears in the *Chronica Boemorum*, written sometime between 1119 and 1125.
33. J. Jelínek, 'O konstruktivistce a esencialistovi'.
34. Čajkanović denies a historical origin for Jerina, but mentions the mythical location of her grave. He connects her story with those of various female ghosts who dwell in abandoned buildings and ruins, cursed to stay there for eternity. V. Čajkanović, *O vrhovnom bogu u srpskoj religiji*, p. 276.
35. M. Mateja, 'Elements of Folklore in Andrić's na Drini Ćuprija'.
36. R. Beaton, 'The Bridge of Arta as Myth', p. 63. The bridge was built in one day and then collapsed: a prophecy said that the builder's wife must be 'built into' the structure to keep it standing.

37. K. Bostrom, *A Female Ideal?*
38. B. Slapšak and S. Kojić, 'Šembilja – hudič na gorečem vozu', 27.
39. S. Zochios, 'Interprétation ethnolinguistique de termes mythologiques néohelléniques d'origine slave désignant des morts malfaisants'.
40. O. Sedakova and F. Gréciet, 'Le thème de la dolja dans le rite funéraire slave'.
41. V. Čajkanović, *Studije iz srpske religije i folklora 1925-1942*, pp. 150-63.

Three Versions of the Great Goddess

42. M. Gimbutas, *The Slavs*; M. Gimbutas, *The Goddesses and Gods of Old Europe*.
43. K. H. Meyer, *Fontes historiae religionis Slavicae*; V. V. Ivanov and V. N. Toporov, *Slavianskie iazykovye modeliruiushchie semioticheskie sistemy*.
44. P. Lajoye, 'Celto-slavica. Essais de mythologie comparée'.
45. G. Kabakova, 'Baba Yaga dans les louboks'; C. Rousselet, 'Sorcière ou nourricière'; S. Zochios, 'Baba Yaga, les sorcières et les démons ambigus de l'Europe orientale'.
46. D. Ugrešić, *Baba Yaga Laid an Egg*.
47. S. Slapšak, 'Petka i Nedeljka, dve antroponimičke prevedenice'.
48. Karadžić, *Srpski rječnik*.
49. The trip was duly recorded and described by a Bulgarian writer, Grigorij Tsamblak (about 1365–1420).

Perun, Supreme God

50. E. Gasparini, *Matriarcato slavo*.
51. Čajkanović, *Studije iz srpske religije i folklora 1925-42*, pp. 103-4.
52. V. V. Ivanov and V. N. Toporov, 'Slavjanskaja mifologija', in *Mify narodov mira*, 2, pp. 450-6.
53. Ibid.
54. King James Bible, 2 Kings 2:11.
55. From the Primary or Nestor's Chronicle.
56. V. Čajkanović, *Rečnik srpskih narodnih verovanja o biljkama*, pp. 30-1.
57. V. V. Ivanov and V. N. Toporov, 'Slavjanskaja mifologija', in *Mify narodov mira*, 2, pp. 450-6.

Creatures of the Deep

58. Čajkanović, 'Hidromantija kod Filipa Višnjića'.
59. J. Binotto, 'Glanz/Glance/Glas: On the Invisibility of Mirrors'.
60. D. Sinani, 'Le structuralisme dans l'étude de la religion populaire en Serbie'. The ritual is known among Romanians ('Peperuda'), Bulgarians and Russians.
61. G. Kabakova, 'Le projet du Dictionnaire de motifs et de contes-types étiologiques chez les slaves orientaux'; S. Skuza, 'La mer et sa couleur dans le mythe cosmogonique slave'.
62. A. N. Afanasyev, *Poeticheskiye vozzrenija slavyan na prirodu*.
63. L. N. Vinogradova and C. Pernette, 'Le corps dans la démonologie populaire des Slaves'.
64. A. Yudin, 'Les roussalkas dans la croyance populaire slave'.
65. T. Dordević, 'Veštica i vila u našem narodnom verovanju i predanju'; V. Čajkanović, 'Vile', in *Stara srpska religija i mitologija*, pp. 228-47.
66. J.-F. Gossiaux, 'Le groupe domestique dans la Yougoslavie rurale'.
67. É. Gessat-Anstett, 'Histoires de mutation. Les terminologies de parenté russe'.

Firebird

68. From the French version quoted in N. Felz, 'Igor Stravinsky: L'oiseau de feu deuxième suite (1919)'; author's own translation.

Slavic Magic

69. The richest source is Čajkanović in his posthumously published dictionary of plants, *Rečnik srpskih narodnih verovanja o biljkama*.
70. S. Slapšak, *Kupus in seksualnost* [Cabbage and Sexuality].
71. V. Čajkanović, *Studije iz srpske religije i folklora 1925-1942*, pp. 213-16. Čajkanović also notes that Karyatides, women who supported a temple on the Athenian Acropolis, were turned into nuts when punished by Artemis, who was also a goddess of death. Their name means 'nut-women' in Greek.
72. S. Slapšak, *Volna in telo* [Wool and the Body].

BIBLIOGRAPHY

Afanasyev, A. N. (ed.), *Poeticheskie vozzreniia slavian na prirodu*, 3 vols (The Hague, [1865–9] 1969–70).

— (ed.), *Poeticheskiye vozzrenija slavyan na prirodu*, vols 1–3 (Moscow, 1995).

Anonymous, *A True Discourse: Declaring the Damnable Life and Death of One Stubbe Peeter, a Most Wicked Sorcerer* (London, 1590).

Baring-Gould, S., *The Book of Were-Wolves* (Denver, [1865] 2007), https://archive.org/details/TheBookOfWere-wolves/mode/2up.

Beaton, R., 'The Bridge of Arta as Myth', in Alan Dundes (ed.), *The Walled-up Wife: A Casebook* (Madison, WI, 1996).

Belyakova, G. S., *Slavyanskaja mifologija* (Moscow, 1995).

Binotto, J., 'Glanz/Glance/Glas: On the Invisibility of Mirrors', in *Haus am Gern: AIRE DE BELLELAY* (Biel, 2015), pp. 5–17.

Bostrom, K., *A Female Ideal? Gender Roles in Smetana's Libuse* (Calgary, 2001).

Brückner, A., *Mitologia slowianska i polska* (Warsaw, [1918] 1980).

Budimir, M., *Memoria Slavorum antiquissima*, Acta II Congressus philol. class. Slav. (Prague) 450 (1931), Argumenta lectionum, 3–4.

—, *Sa balkanskih istočnika* (Belgrade, 1969).

—, *Sa slovenskog Olimpa*, Book 1 (Belgrade, 1992).

Čajkanović, V., *O vrhovnom bogu u srpskoj religiji* (Belgrade, 1994).

—, *Rečnik srpskih narodnih verovanja o biljkama* (Belgrade, 1994).

—, *Studije iz srpske religije i folklora, 1925–1942* (Belgrade, 1994).

Crawford-Mowday, I., 'Caul: A Sailor's Charm', *England: The Other Within – Analysing the English Collections at the Pitt Rivers Museum*, https://england.prm.ox.ac.uk/englishness-sailors-charm.html.

Đorđević, T., 'Veštica i vila u našem narodnom verovanju i predanju', *Srpski etnografski zbornik* 66 (1953).

Felz, N., 'Igor Stravinsky: *L'oiseau de feu* deuxième suite (1919)', *Musurgia* 6.3–4 (1999): 89–107.

Frayling, C., *Vampyres: Lord Byron to Count Dracula* (London, 1992).

—, *Vampyres: Genesis and Resurrection from Count Dracula to Vampirella* (London, 2016).

Freidenberg, O., *Image and Concept: Mythopoetic Roots of Literature* (Abingdon, 2006).

Frenzel, E., *Stoff-und Motivgeschichte* (Berlin, 1957).

—, *Stoffe der Weltliteratur* (Stuttgart, 2005).

—, *Motive der Weltliteratur* (Stuttgart, 2008).

Gasparini, E., *Matriarcato slavo* (Florence, 1973).

Gazette des gazettes ou Journal politique pour l'année…1765, 7/12, https://books.google.co.uk/books?id=CsZFAAAAcAAJ&pg=RA8-PA14#v=onepage&q&f=false.

Georgoudi, S., and J.-P. Vernant (eds), *Mythes grecs au figuré: de l'antiquité au baroque* (Paris, 1996).

Gessat-Anstett, É., 'Histoires de mutation. Les terminologies de parenté russe', *L'Homme* 154–5 (2000): 613–34.

Gimbutas, M., 'Ancient Slavic Religion: A Synopsis', in *To Honor Roman Jakobson: Essays on the Occasion of His Seventieth Birthday*, vol. 1 (The Hague, 1967), pp. 738–59.

—, *The Slavs* (London, 1971).

—, *The Goddesses and Gods of Old Europe, 7000 to 3500 BC: Myths, Legends and Cult Images* (London, 1974).

Gossiaux, J.-F., 'Le groupe domestique dans la Yougoslavie rurale', PhD thesis, L'École des hautes études en sciences sociales (EHESS), Paris, 1982.

Groom, N., *The Vampire: A New History* (New Haven, CT, 2020).

Haney, J. V., *Russian Legends* (Armonk, NY, 2003).

Ivanits, L., *Russian Folk Belief* (Armonk, NY, 1992).

Ivanov, V., and V. Toporov, *Slavianskie iazykovye modeliruiushchie semioticheskie sistemy: Drevnii period* (Moscow, 1965).

—, 'Slavjanskaja mifologija', in *Mify narodov mira*, 2 (Moscow, 1992).

James VI and I, *Daemonologie* (Edinburgh, 1597), https://archive.org/details/kingjamesfirstdm00jame/page/68/mode/2up.

Jelínek, J., 'O konstruktivistce a esencialistovi: Ke stylu a motivům dvou reinterpretací mýtu o Libuši', *Ceska Literatura* 3 (2021): 312–41.

Johnson, K., *Slavic Sorcery: Shamanic Journey of Initiation* (St Paul, MN, 1998).

Jordanes, *The Origins and the Deeds of Goths*, trans. C. Mierow, http://people.ucalgary.ca/~vandersp/Courses/texts/jordgeti.html#Top.

Kabakova, G., 'Baba Yaga dans les louboks', *Revue Sciences/Lettres* 4 (2016).

—, 'Le projet du Dictionnaire de motifs et de contes-types étiologiques chez les slaves

BIBLIOGRAPHY

orientaux', *Revue des études slaves* 89.1–2 (2018): 155–68.

Kapica, F. S., *Slavyanskije tradicionnije verovanija, prazdniki i rituali* (Moscow, 2001).

Karadžić, V., *Srpski rječnik* (Vienna, 1818).

Krauss, F. S., *Volksglaube und religiöser Brauch der Südslaven* (Münster, 1890).

Kulikowski, M., *A Bibliography of Slavic Mythology* (Columbus, OH, 1989).

Kulišić, Š., *Srpski mitološki rečnik* (Belgrade, 1970).

Lajoye, P., 'Celto-slavica. Essais de mythologie comparée', *Études celtiques* 38.1 (2012): 197–227.

Léger, L, *La mythologie slave* (Paris, 1901).

Levkievskaja, E. E., 'La mythologie slave: problèmes de répartition dialectale (une étude de cas: le vampire)', *Cahiers slaves n 1: Aspects de la vie traditionnelle en Russie et alentour* (1997).

Lofstedt, T. M., *Russian Legends about Forest Spirits in the Context of Northern European Mythology* (Berkeley, 1993).

Loving, M., 'Charles Nodier: The Romantic Librarian', *Libraries & Culture* (2003): 166–81.

Machek, V., 'Essai comparatif sur la mythologie slave', *Revue des études slaves* 23 (1947).

Mansikka, V. J., *Die Religion der Ostslaven* (Helsinki, 1922).

Marx, K., *Capital: A Critique of Political Economy*, https://www.marxists.org/archive/marx/works/1867-c1/index.htm.

Mateja, M., 'Elements of Folklore in Andrić's na Drini Ćuprija', *Canadian Slavonic Papers* 20.3 (1978): 348–57.

Meyer, K. H., *Fontes historiae religionis Slavicae* (Berlin, 1931).

Mézes, Á., 'Vampire Contagion as a Forensic Fact: The Vampires of Medveđa in 1732', *Historical Studies on Central Europe* 1.1 (2021): 149–76.

Mihajlov, N., *Mythologia Slovenica: poskus rekonstrukcije slovenskega poganskega izročila* (Trieste, 2002).

—, *Zgodovina slovanske mitologije v XX. stoletju* (Ljubljana, 2021).

Moszyński, K., *Kultura ludowa słowian*, vol. 2, *Kultura duchowa* (Krakow, 1939).

Niederle, L., *Manuel de l'antiquité slave*, vol. 2, *La civilisation* (Paris, 1926).

Nodilo, N., *Historija srednjega vijeka za narod hrvatski i srpski*, vols 1–3 (Zagreb, 1898–1905).

—, *Stara vjera Srba i Hrvata* (Split, 1981).

Orešković, L., 'Le thème des lycanthropes et des vampires, de Dom Calmet à l'abbé de Fortis: une approche des pays de confins', *Dix-huitieme siècle* 1 (2010): 265–84.

Palm, T., *Wendische Kultstatten: Quellenkritische Untersuchungen zu den letzten Jahrhunderten slavischen Heidentums* (Lund, 1937).

Perkowski, J. L., (ed), *Vampires of the Slavs* (Cambridge, MA, 1976).

—, *The Darkling: A Treatise on Slavic Vampirism* (Columbus, OH, 1989).

Peronneaud, Jean, 'Du dieu slave Volos à saint Blaise en Russie: dieux païens et saints chrétiens', PhD thesis, Paris-Sorbonne University, 1988.

Petruhin, A. Y., T. A. Arapkina, L. N. Vinogradova, and S. M. Tolstaya (eds), *Slavyanskaja mifologija* (Moscow, 1995).

Poppe, A., 'Review of *Naissance de la chrétienté russe: La conversion du Prince Vladimir de Kiev (988) et ses conséquences (XIe–XIIIe siècles)*', *The Slavonic and East European Review*, 68.1 (1990): 140–4.

Procopius, *History of the Wars*, 7 vols (vol. 4), trans. H. B. Dewing (Cambridge, MA, 1924).

Propp, V., *Istoricheskie korni volshebnoi skazki* (Leningrad, 1946).

—, 'The Historical Roots of Some Russian Religious Festivals', in Stephen P. Dunn and Ethel Dunn (eds), *Introduction to Soviet Ethnography*, vol. 2 (Berkeley, 1974), pp. 367–410.

—, *The Russian Folktale* (Detroit, 2012).

Ranft, M., *De masticatione mortuorum in tumulis (Oder von dem Kauen und Schmatzen der Todten in Gräbern), liber singularis: exhibens duas exercitationes, quarum prior historico-critica posterior philosophica est*, vol. 2 (Leipzig, 1728).

Reiter, N., 'Mythologie der alten Slaven', in Hans W. Haussig (ed.), *Wörterbuch der Mythologie*, vol. 2 (Stuttgart, 1973), pp. 165–208.

Rousselet, C., 'Sorcière ou nourricière: la Baba Yaga à l'épreuve de la pensée psychanalytique', *Revue Sciences/Lettres* 4 (2016).

Ryan, W. F., *The Bathhouse at Midnight: A Historical Survey of Magic and Divination in Russia* (University Park, PA, 1999).

Rybakov, B. A., 'Drevnie elementy v russkom narodnom tvorchestve (Zhenskoe bozhestvo i vsadniki)', *Sovetskaia etnografiia* 1 (1948): 90–106.

Schuldt, E., *Der altslawische Tempel von Gross Raden* (Schwerin, 1976).

Scot, R., *The Discoverie of Witchcraft* (London, 1584), https://www.gutenberg.org/files/60766/60766-h/60766-h.htm.

Sedakova, O., and F. Gréciet, 'Le thème de la dolja dans le rite funéraire slave', *Cahiers slaves* 3.1 (2001): 23-39.

Senn, A., 'Les Slaves et leur civilisation', *Études Slaves et Est-Européennes/Slavic and East-European Studies* 6.3/4 (1961): 177-87.

Shaparova, N. S., *Kratkaya enciklopedija slavyanskoj mifologii* (Moscow, 2001).

Shapiro, M., 'Baba-Jaga: A Search for Mythopoeic Origins and Affinities', *International Journal of Slavic Linguistics and Poetics* 27 (1983): 109-35.

Siminov, P., *Essential Russian Mythology: Stories that Change the World* (London, 1997).

Sinani, D., 'Le structuralisme dans l'étude de la religion populaire en Serbie', *Etnoantropološki problemi* 4.2 (2009): 199-217.

Skok, P., *Etimologijski rječnik hrvatskoga ili srpskoga jezika* (Zagreb, 1971-3).

Skuza, S., 'La mer et sa couleur dans le mythe cosmogonique slave: analyse ethnolinguistique', *Acta Philologica* 50 (2017): 103-15.

Slapšak, B., and S. Kojić, 'Šembilja - hudič na gorečem vozu', *Glasnik Slovenskega etnološkega društva* 16 (1976).

Slapšak, S., 'Petka i Nedeljka, dve antroponimičke prevedenice', *Onomastički zbornik* 1 (1979): 81-5.

—, 'A Cat on the Head: In Search of a New Word to Better Read Ancient Mythology', *I Quaderni del ramo d'oro* 3 (2010): 122-8.

—, *Kupus in seksualnost* (Ljubljana, 2016).

—, *Volna in telo* (Ljubljana, 2017).

Šmitek, Z., *Mitološko izročilo Slovencev: Svetinje preteklosti* (Ljubljana, 2004).

—, 'The Southern Slavic Folk Hero: National Liberation Struggle (1941-45) and Mythological Projections', *Ethnologie française* 42.2 (2012): 221-30.

Soloviova-Horville, D., *Les vampires: du folklore slave à la littérature occidentale* (Paris, 2011).

Stevanović, L., *Laughing at the Funeral* (Belgrade, 2009).

Studia Mythologica Slavica (Ljubljana, since 1998).

Tokarev, S. A., *Religioznye verovaniia vostochnoslavianskikh narodov XIX – nachala XX veka* (Moscow, 1957).

— (ed.), 'Mifi narodov mira', *Bolshaya Rossiyskaya Enciklopedija*, vols 1-2 (Moscow, 1998).

Tolstoy, N. I. (ed.), *Slavyanskije drevnosti* (Moscow, 1995).

Ugrešić, D., *Baba Yaga Laid an Egg* (Edinburgh and London, 2009).

Unbegaun, B. O., *La religion des anciens Slaves* (Paris, 1948).

Valvasor, J. W., *Die Ehre deß Hertzogthums Crain*, vol. 6 (Nuremberg, 1689).

Vinogradova, L. N., and C. Pernette, 'Le corps dans la démonologie populaire des Slaves', *Cahiers slaves* 9.1 (2008): 203-25.

'Voltaire on Vampires', from *The Works of Voltaire, A Contemporary Version*, vol. 7, trans. W. F. Fleming (New York, 1901), *Jason Colavito.com*, https://www.jasoncolavito.com/voltaire-on-vampires.html.

Vyncke, F., *De godsdienst der Slaven* (Roermond, 1969).

Walpole, H., *The Letters*, https://www.fulltextarchive.com/book/The-Letters-of-Horace-Walpole.

Warner, E., *Russian Myths* (Austin, TX, 2002).

Warner, M., *Fairy Tale: A Very Short Introduction* (Oxford, 2018).

Yankovitch, N., 'Le soleil dans l'antiquité serbe', *Antiquités nationales et internationales* 4.14-16 (April-December 1963): 70-80.

Yovino-Young, M., *Pagan Ritual and Myth in Russian Magic Tales: A Study in Pattern* (Lewiston, NY, 1993).

Yudin, A., 'Les roussalkas dans la croyance populaire slave', in *Rusalka. Lyrická pohádka o třech dějstvích* (Brussels, 2008), pp. 83-90.

Zelenin, D., *Ocherki slavianskoi mifologii* (St Petersburg, 1916).

—, *Russische (ostslavische) Volkskunde* (Berlin and Leipzig, 1927).

Znayenko, M., *The Gods of the Ancient Slavs: Tatishchev and the Beginnings of Slavic Mythology* (Columbus, OH, 1980).

Zochios, S., 'Baba Yaga, les sorcières et les démons ambigus de l'Europe orientale', *Revue Sciences/Lettres* 4 (2016).

—, 'Interprétation ethnolinguistique de termes mythologiques néohelléniques d'origine slave désignant des morts malfaisants', *Revue des études slaves* 89.3 (2018): 303-17.

INDEX

Abraham Lincoln: Vampire Hunter 81
Adam and Eve 17
Aesop 8
Africa 62, 155, 223
Ala 215
Alexander the Great 129
Alexandreida 117
Alexandria 111
Alibeg 86, 88–90
Alps 116
Amazonian tribes 12
Americas 223
Antae 9
Aphrodite 7, 222
apple 203, 222
Apollo 23
Aquileia 9
Arcadia 111
Ares (Mars) 7
Arta Bridge 131
Asclepios 164
Asia 155, 213, 223
Athena (Minerva) 7
Athens 7, 130
Athos, Mount 24
Austria 12, 25, 61, 64–9, 72–3, 80, 116
Austro-Hungarian Monarchy 24
Avars 12

baba 159, 160
Baba Yaga 8, 132, 142–5, 149, 150–2, 155, 158–60, 218
Bajazit, Sultan 163
Bajina Bašta 33, 77
Balaton 12
Balkans 8, 74, 79, 105, 111, 116, 131, 161, 163, 175–6, 180, 194, 198, 216, 222–3
Baltic 8, 14, 17, 175, 183
bannki 195
barbarians 10
Baring-Gould, Sabine 105
Barszczewski, Jan 117
basil 222
Báthory, Elizabeth 77
Bavaria 116
Belgrade, Beograd 35, 65, 81, 163, 183, 190–1, 195
Belobog 183
Bernes, Mark 195
Bilina 124

birch 33, 36–7, 51, 55, 169, 196, 220–1
Black Sea 191
Blade 81
Boeotia 193–4
Bohanec, Franček 117
Bohemia 25, 69, 127
Bojan (Baianus) 107
Bojana River 131
Bosnia-Herzegovina 24
Branković, Đurađ 131
Branković, Vuk Grgurević (*Zmaj Ognjeni Vuk*) 108
British Isles 77
Brjačislavič, Vseslav 107, 108
Buda 194, 215
Budimir, Milan 62
Buffy the Vampire Slayer 81
Bulgakov, Mikhail 116
Bulgaria 163, 215, 13–14, 19, 107
Burton, Richard 29
butterflies 33, 36, 44–9, 58, 105
bylina 176, 179
Byron, George Noel Gordon 78, 79
Byzantine authors 9, 10, 12, 21, 111, 184
Byzantine Empire 9, 13, 80, 111, 131, 179

cabbage 151–2, 221–2
Čajkanović, Veselin 176
Calmet, Antoine Augustin 69
Carantania 12
Carniola 62
Carpathian Mountains 8, 15, 61
Catholicism 8
Celtic peoples, gods 14
Central Europe 8, 12, 26, 194
Cerknica 63
Chaney, Lon 107
Charles IV, King 127
Charles VI, King 64
Chernigov 171
Chicago 24
China 8
Christ 64, 73, 160, 167
Christ Child 48
Christianity 8, 13–17, 21–8, 54, 75, 104, 113, 155–6, 160, 163, 175–7, 179, 181, 184, 196–7, 200, 213–14, 223
Christmas 24, 73
Christmas Eve 116, 222
Christophor, Saint 104
Church Slavonic (language) 12–13
Cinderella 22

clover 222–3
coffee 188, 223
Colburn, Henry 78
Corvinus, King Matthias 108
Crane, Charles Richard 24–5
cranes 195
Crete 8
Črnobog 183
Croatia 21, 27–8, 62–3, 72, 117, 132, 179, 215, 218
Cyril, Saint 13, 104
Cyrillic (script) 13, 104
Czech Republic 8, 129, 213

Dagestan 195
Dalmatia 105, 132, 215
Danube River 131, 190, 193
Daphne 23
Dažbog 15, 177, 181
Demeter 17, 161
Devil 15, 103–4, 117, 181, 189, 216, 223
Diodati, Villa 78
Disney, Walt 81
Dnieper River 193
Dobšinský, Pavol 109
Dodola 194
dolls (magic) 135–52
Domovoy 132
Đorđe 85–100
Dracula 61, 77, 79–80, 110, 117
dragon men 108, 199, 215–18
dragons 79, 108, 130, 180, 191, 199
Dubrovnik 179
D'Urfe, Marquis 85
Dušman, Matija 44, 46
Dušman, Živan 35, 38, 40–1, 52–3, 55, 58–9
Dvořák, Antonín Leopold 197

Easter 73, 197
Eastern Europe 24, 61
egg, eggshells 24, 160, 194, 203–4, 208–11, 218, 223
elderberry 221
Eliade, Mircea 129
Elias, Saint 177
Elijah, Saint 161, 177
elm 46, 54–7, 220
Emona (ancient Ljubljana) 130
Enlightenment 63, 66, 71, 103, 109
Epidaurus 163
Epivates 163
Eurasia 8, 225
Eyriès, Jean-Baptiste Benoît 78
Expressionism 81

236

INDEX

fairies 8, 22–3, 29, 117, 130, 194–5
fairy ring, dance 198
Finnish mythology 17
Firebird 203–11, 220
fish 191–5, 200
Flückinger, Johannes 68
folk tales 21, 22, 23, 29, 130
France 22, 96, 199
Frankenstein 78
Frayling, Christopher 67, 78, 81
French Revolution 27
Friday 160–1
frogs 194, 208
Frombald, Kameralprovisor 64–5

Gaia 23, 155
Galen 111
Gamzatov, Rasul 195
Gazette Française 70
Geneva, Lake 78
genocide of women (witch hunts) 219
Gentleman's Magazine 69
George, Saint 199
George II, King 69
Georgia 191
German peoples, gods 13–14, 22, 27, 69, 75, 78, 111, 114, 160–1
Gestapo 26
Gimbutas, Marija 156, 160, 183
Glagolitic (script) 13
Glaser (medical specialist) 67
Glenarvon 79
Glišić, Milovan 75–7
Glory of the Duchy of Carniola 62
Goethe, Johann Wolfgang von 72
Gogol, Nikolai Vasilevič 77, 116, 197
golem 8
Gojkovica, 131–2
golden fleece 7, 130
Goltzius, Hendrick 111
Gorča 85, 88–100
Grando, Giure 63–4, 74
Great Moravia 12–13
Great Mother 17
Greco-Roman gods *see individual gods*
Greece 8, 24, 82, 104, 107, 111, 131, 163–4, 193
Gret of Parnau 115
Grimm, brothers Jacob and Wilhelm 8, 21–2, 72
Groom, Nick 105
Grunwald, battle of 25

Habsburgs 19
Hades 15
hajduk 66
Hans, Kanti 115
Harry Potter 62, 117
hawthorn 33, 44–6, 52, 55, 58, 64, 66, 73–7, 80, 82, 86–7, 89, 96, 144, 218, 220, 226
hazel 125, 127, 221
Heaven 176–7, 213–14
Helicon, Mount 193
Helios 177
Hell 115, 213–14
Hellenism, Hellenistic period 29, 129
Helsing, Abraham van 80
Hephaestus 15
Heracles 29
Hermes 157
Hesiod 110
Hestia 132
Hollywood 29, 107
Holy Land 163
honey 151, 188–9, 223
horses 15, 53, 55–6, 73, 86, 97, 104, 113, 123–4, 138, 141, 145–8, 153, 169, 177, 180, 183, 187, 193–4, 204–6, 218, 220
Hotel Transylvania 118
Humboldt, Alexander von 72
Hungary 12, 25, 69–70, 108
hydromancy 194
Hygiea 164

ibn Fadlan, Ahmad 12
Idavere 115
Ilios (Troy) 129
'Illyrian movement' 28
Ilos 129
impaling 74, 80
Interview with a Vampire 81
iris 179
Irving, Henry 79
Isis 7
Isontio 9
Istanbul 163
Istria 63, 71, 74, 104
Italy 9, 215
Ivanov, Vyacheslav Vsevolodovich 181, 183

James VI, King 113
Jarovit 177, 183
Jason 7, 130
Jefimija 163
Jirásek, Alois 23
Jordan River 163

Jordanes 9–10
Jung, Karl Gustav 81
Justinian I, Emperor 9

Kantakouzine, Irene (Jerina) 131
Karadžić, Vuk 22, 71–7, 80–1, 161
Karloff, Boris 103
Karlova Street, Prague 130
Kazi, Princess 122–3
Kazin Castle 122
Kikimora 132
Kisilova 64
kmet 34–5, 39, 41–2, 44, 59
Kopitar, Jernej 73
Koschei the Deathless 205
Kosovo, Battle of 163
Kraljević, Marko 29, 180
Kresnik 176
Krinck 63
Krok, King 121–2
Krumlow Castle 26
ktitor 131
Kunstmärchen 22
Kuprin, Alexander 116
Kyiv 108, 171–3, 179

Lado and Lada 17
Lamb, Caroline 79
Lari 132
Latin (language and script) 9–10, 13, 61, 110, 114, 161, 184
Latvia 19, 115
laurel 223
Lazar (Serbian ruler) 163
Lazarević, Stefan 163
lecanomancy 194
Lenin, Vladimir Ilych Ulyanov 118
Leptirica 75
Libuše, Queen 14, 23, 28–9, 121–32
Libušin Castle 122
Lidomir 127
linden 122, 125, 188, 220–1
Little Ice Age 116
Little Red Riding Hood 22
Livonia (currently Latvia and Estonia) 115
Ljubljana 130, 187, 189, 199
Ljubljanica River 187
Loki 7
Lord, Albert 29
Lord Ruthven 79
Lupin, Professor 118
Lycaon 110–11, 117
lycanthropy 107, 110–15

237

INDEX

magic 8, 15, 62–3, 105, 107–10, 113–14, 121–2, 129, 142, 170, 172, 195, 203, 209, 213–14, 219–23
Märchen 22
Maria-Theresa, Empress 66
Marvel (comics and films) 7
Marx, Karl 81
Masaryk, Tomaž 26
Matz, Libbe 115
Mediterranean cultures, gods 14, 225
Medveđa 66–8
mermen 8
Methodius, Saint 13, 104
Mézes, Ádám 67–8
Mičanová, Daniela 117
Michael III, Emperor 13
Mickey Mouse 183
Mickievitz, Adam 117
Miklošič, Franz 197
Milasič (marshall) 64
Milica (Serbian ruler) 163
Miliza 67
mill 33–4, 37–43, 46–52, 55–6, 59, 74, 77
milk 35, 92, 132, 140, 223
Minotaur 7
Mira 43–6
mirrors 194
Mokoš 17, 132, 155–8, 176
Moldova (Moldavia) 8, 61, 70–1, 80, 86, 94, 163
Montenegro 72, 104, 131, 215
Moscow 28
Mratinci (festival) 105
Mucha, Alphonse 24–7
Munch, Edvard 80
Murnau, Friedrich Wilhelm 81
Muromets, Ilya 167–73, 179–80
mythology 7–8, 17, 19, 21–2, 27–9, 61, 63, 69, 104, 116, 155, 175–6, 195, 213, 225
mythurgy 30, 223

Nazis 130, 180, 198
Neruda, Jan 117
nettles 223
New Testament 72, 114
Nezamysl 127
Nicholas, Saint 200, 216
Nightingale the Robber 172
Nitra 12
Njegoš, Petar Petrović 72, 179
Nodilo, Natko 21
Norse peoples, gods 7–8, 176, 179
Nosferatu 81

Novgorod 179
Nović Otočanin, Joksim 117
Nowak, Jenny (Jana Moravcová) 117
nuts 34, 127, 188–9, 218, 220, 222–3
Nyctimus 111
nymphs 10, 29, 196–7

oak 15, 17, 86, 97, 167, 179, 206, 216, 220
Obrenović, Miloš 72
Odin 7, 15, 179, 204
Odyssey 158
Old Church Slavonic (language) 12–13
Olizarowski, Tomasz 117
Orthodox 8, 68, 72, 86, 99
Osiris 7
Ottoman (Osman) Empire 26, 61, 65
Ovid 23, 110

Pan-Slavic Congress 27–8
Pan-Slavism 26–7
Paole, Arnold 66, 70, 80
Paris 24, 117, 143, 222
Parry, Milman 22
Paulus Aegineta 111
Pechersky, Ilya 29
Peg Leg Pete 183
Pegasus 194
Penelope 158
Peperuda 194
peppers 223
Pergamon 111
Perrault, Charles 22
Persephone 161
Persia 208
Perun 123, 157, 175–83, 194
Petar 62, 65, 72, 86–9, 92–6, 100, 105, 176, 179
Peter, Saint 75, 177
Peter Bogišar, Saint 179
Petka, Saint 155, 160–3, 175
Plato 110
Plečnik, Jože 26
Plogojowitz, Peter (Blagojević, Petar) 64
pobratim, posestrima 198
Poland 19, 25, 103, 117, 160
Polidori, John 78–9, 116
Polonsky, Yakov 203
Polovtsi 171
polycephaly 183
Porovit 177
Poseidon (Neptune) 7
Potocki, Jan 103, 107, 110, 117

Prague (Praha) 14, 23–4, 26–8, 129–30, 132
Preacher 81
Přemysl, King 121, 125–7
Prešeren, France 199
Pribojević, Vinko 27
Primic, Julija 199
Pripegala 183
Procopius 9–10
Propp, Vladimir 160
Psoglav 104
Pushkin, Alexander 116, 197
Puss in Boots 22

Radetič, Miho 63
Radgost 183
Radobyl 127
Radojka 35–6, 38, 42, 51–2, 58
Ranft, Michael 65–6
Ranke, Leopold von 8, 72, 78
Rapunzel 22
Red Army 26
Rey, Mikolaj 117
Rod and Rožanica 17
Roma people 161
Roman 7–8, 14, 17, 21, 68, 75, 104, 127, 130, 132, 197, 222
Romania 79, 109, 129, 131
Romulus and Remus 129
Rosalia 197
Rujevit 183
Russia 8, 13–14, 24, 28, 61, 77, 107–9, 116, 118, 132, 159, 175–6, 179–80, 183–4, 195, 197, 213

Samo, King 20
Sapkowski, Andrzej 126
Satan 15, 115
Sava River 35, 187
Sava, Saint 223
Savanović, Sava 33–59, 75, 77
Savanović, Stanko 53
Sclaveni 9
Scot, Reginald 113
Scythians 107
Semargl, Sim and R'gl 183
Šembilja 132
Serbia 13–14, 22, 29, 33, 42, 58, 61–2, 65–8, 70–6, 80–1, 85, 104, 108–9, 116–17, 131–2, 163, 194, 200, 214–16, 219, 222–3
Serbian Despotate 108
Serbo-Croatian (language) 72, 179, 215, 218
shamanism 164, 213–14, 220, 223
Shelley, Percy Bysshe 78
Sheridan Le Fanu, Joseph Thomas 80

238

INDEX

Shevchenko, Taras Hryhorovych 197
Siberia 19, 118, 213
Simeon, Tsar 107
Sklaboi 9
Skodra (Skadar) 131
Skok, Petar 62, 105
Slav Epic 21–30
Slavic pantheon 7, 14, 107, 156, 161, 179, 226
Slovakia 12, 14, 19, 26, 77, 109, 129
Slovenia 12–13, 15, 19, 26, 62–3, 71, 73, 117, 130, 132, 176, 183, 197, 199, 221
Smederevo Castle 131
snakes 108, 132, 193
Snow White 22
Sokol organization 28
Southey, Robert 80
Spasovdan 73
Sporoi 9
Spring of Nations 19, 27
Stadice 124
Stalinism 130
Stephen V, Pope 13
Stoker, Bram 23, 61, 79–80, 110
Stribog 181
Stumpp, Peter 114–15
Styx, River 195
Sudeta, Đura 117
suicide 54, 197, 214
Summers, Montague 118
Svarog 12, 15, 177, 181, 183
Svarožič 12, 177, 183
Svetovid 15, 177, 183
Svjatoslavič, Volga 108
Svyatogor (*bogatyr*) 169–71
swans 195
Switzerland 78, 103

taboos 158, 161, 164
Tacitus, Publius Cornelius 75
Tales of Mother Goose 22
Tatars 108, 173, 176
Tepes, Vlad 79–81
Teta, Princess 122–3
Teutonic Knights 25
Theseus 7
Thessaloniki 13, 104
Thietmar of Merseburg 12
Thiess of Kaltenbrun 115
Thomas, Titza and Greta 115
Thor 176
Thursday 161, 197
Tito, Josip Broz 29, 131, 180
Tmutarakan 108
tobacco 37, 49, 223

Tolstoi, Alexei 23, 103, 116
Tom Thumb 22
Toporov, Vladimir Nikolayevich 176, 181, 183
totems 15, 75, 104, 157, 214, 220
Trdina, Janez 117
Tree of the World 17
Triglav 15, 183
Trnovo 163
True Blood 81
Tsarevitch, Ivan 203
Tsarevna 206, 208–11
Tuesday 161
Tyche 129
Twilight 81, 107

Ugrešić, Dubravka 160
Underworld 17, 115, 181, 200, 220
United States 24–5
Urška 187–91
USSR 26

Valjevo 33, 77
Valvasor, Janez Vajkard 51, 62–4
vampir (vampire) 7–8, 14, 23, 34, 49, 51–2, 54, 56–8, 61–82, 103–7, 116–18, 161, 216, 218–19, 226
Vasilissa the Beautiful 135–53, 159, 196
Vastermoisa 115
Veles 7, 15, 176, 181
Veneti 9
Vernant, Jean-Paul 29–30
Versailles 86
veštica (witch) 218
Vienna 72–3, 116, 189
vila (fairy) 197–9
Virgin Mary 156
Vladimir, Prince and Saint 168–72, 179
Vodyanoy 208–9
Voldemort, Lord 62
Volga River 12
Voltaire 70
Všeslavevna, Marfa 108
Vuk 7, 14–15, 17, 75, 87, 104–5, 107–9
vukodlak (werewolf) 17, 62, 75, 85–7, 103–5, 116, 226
Vysehrad (High Castle) 122, 124, 127

Wallachia 67, 80–1
walnut 34, 218, 220, 222
Walpole, Horace 69
waltz 189–91

Warner, Marina 22–3
water 40, 52, 55, 57–8, 62, 109–10, 122, 144–5, 156–8, 167–9, 188, 190–1, 193–200, 204, 208–9, 222–3
Waterman 187–99
Wednesday 159, 161
werewolf syndrome 111
werewolves 14, 17, 23, 62, 73–5, 81, 103–18, 226
Weyer, Johann 113
Wienerisches Diarium 65
Wiesthaler, Fran 117
willow 34, 220–1
wine 144, 151–2, 172, 183, 189
Wolfssegen 116
wolves 14–15, 33, 49, 62, 75, 81, 87, 103–18, 140, 181, 203, 206, 208–9, 226
Wollstonecraft, Mary Shelley 78
wool 157–8, 223
World War, First 28, 81
World War, Second 26, 198

yatagan (dagger) 90
Yugo-nostalgia 180
Yugoslavia 15, 27, 29, 72, 75, 180

Zeus (Jupiter) 7, 14, 15, 111, 175, 177
Zbiroh Castle 25
zduhać 105, 215–16, 218
Zuarasici 12

Noah Charney is an American art historian and internationally best-selling author of fiction (*The Art Thief*, published in fourteen languages) and non-fiction (*The Art of Forgery, The Collector of Lives, The Museum of Lost Art*). He teaches at the University of Ljubljana and presents for television and radio, including for the BBC.

Svetlana Slapšak is a leading specialist in Balkan studies and award-winning essayist who has published more than a hundred books. She won the American PEN Freedom of Expression Award in 1993 and was nominated for the Nobel Peace Prize in 2005. She has served as a professor, researcher and dean at various universities, including the Ljubljana Graduate School of Humanities and Rutgers University in New Jersey. Both Charney and Slapšak live in Slovenia.

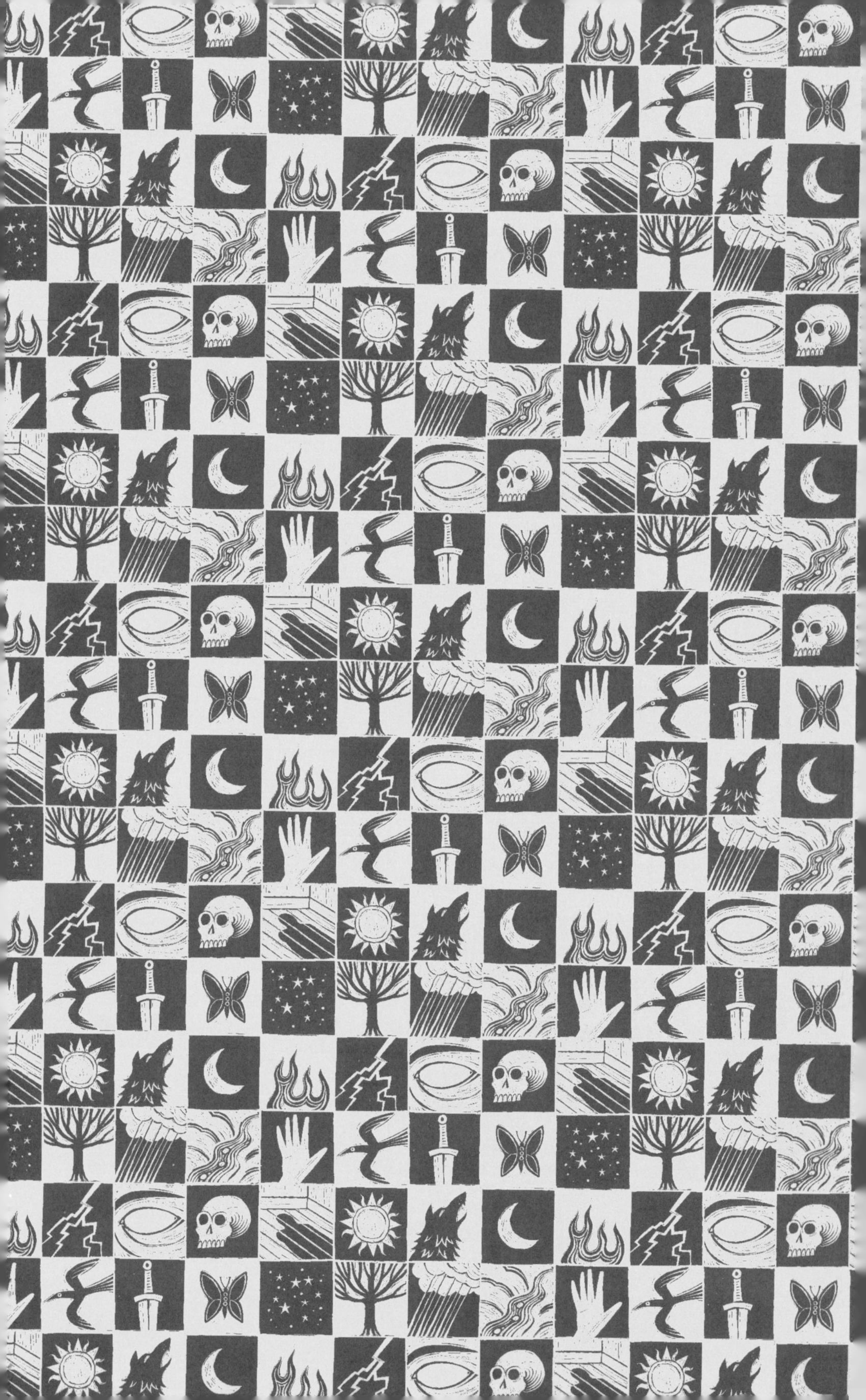